ALEXANDER LITVINENKO
YURI FELSHTINSKY

BLOWING UP RUSSIA

The Secret Plot to Bring Back KGB Terror

Acts of Terror, Abductions, and Contract Killings
organized by the Federal Security Service
of the Russian Federation

Translated from Russian by Geoffrey Andrews and Co.

GIBSON SQUARE
LONDON

First edition published in 2007 by Gibson Square.

Gibson Square website address www.gibsonsquare.com

Manufactured in the United Kingdom by Clays Ltd

First Paperback Edition

9781903933978

CONTENTS

Foreword

THE LAST TIME I talked to Alexander was by phone on November 8, 2006. Around 5 A.M. Boston time, I received a call from the Moscow newspaper *Novaya Gazeta* with the request to comment on the incoming information that Alexander had been poisoned. I asked them to call me back later, and dialed Alexander's mobile. At that time he was already in a London hospital. He told me that he had lost around 15 kilograms of weight, that his body was rejecting all food and liquids. But his voice was very strong, and we talked for at least 15–20 minutes, maybe longer.

That day, Alexander believed that he had survived the assassination attempt. He understood that he had been poisoned; he knew that this was done by Russia's Federal Security Service (FSB), and he was sure that the order had come from the President of Russia, Vladimir Putin. But he was also sure that he had survived, and that the worst was over. I did not ask him many questions, thinking that he was too weak to analyze the situation and to answer my inquiries. "In a few days," he told me, "I will be home. We will have time to talk later."

On the 23rd of November, Alexander Litvinenko died. He was a former Lieutenant Colonel of the Federal Security Service's special anti-organized crime unit. This was his profession. This was his life.

I had known him since 1998. That was a very difficult time for him. He had received an order from his superiors, and for the first time in his life, he did not know what to do. The order was to kill a very rich Jewish Russian who had accumulated a lot of money during the Yeltsin era in Russia. The name of that Russian Jew was Boris

Berezovsky, who at the time was a government official—the Executive Secretary of the Commonwealth of Independent States.

Alexander made his choice. He came to Berezovsky and told him about the order. He went public with his story at a press conference, declaring that some top generals of the FSB were definitely breaking the law and giving their junior officers illegal orders.

This was the end of Alexander's career with the FSB. He was fired.

I met him for the first time the day he was getting ready for that historic press conference.

Alexander was a very energetic person. An athlete, he neither smoked nor drank—a very rare case for a man in Russia. We talked a lot. I had just come to Moscow, where I had not lived since 1978, when I had immigrated to the United States. Everything was new to me, and I was ready to listen. He told me stories of his life for hours. Many of his stories were terrifying, since he worked for the powerful FSB and lived a very difficult life. Some of the stories I did not like at all: stories about the atrocities of the Russian army in Chechnya, about Chechens who were burned or buried alive, graphic descriptions of tortures.

Alexander knew that, sooner or later, he would be punished for his "betrayal" at that press conference, and that even the rich and influential Boris Berezovsky would not be able to help him. He was right. In March of 1999, Alexander was arrested and imprisoned for a fictitious "crime" that the government claimed he had committed some years earlier.

By the time he was released from prison in December of 1999, I had already left Russia and Mr. Putin soon became President. I did not like what Putin was doing with Russia from the very beginning of his term, when he dissolved the high chamber of the Russian Parliament, reintroduced the old Soviet Hymn, and promoted into top government positions his old friends and colleagues from the FSB. Many times, I remembered one of my earlier conversations with Alexander, in the office of Boris Berezovsky in Moscow. Alexander said that if Putin came to power, he would start purges. People would be killed or arrested. "I can feel this. He will kill all of us as well. Trust me. I know what I am saying." This was in the beginning of 2000, shortly before Putin became President. How could Alexander have known that he would be arrested? How could he have understood Putin so well so early, when others still considered him to be a modern democratic leader?

At that time I was involved in my new study, investigating the apartment building explosions of September 1999 that had taken place in several cities across Russia and claimed the lives of more than 300 people. This was the largest terrorist act ever committed in Russia.

I came to the conclusion that those terrorist acts had been conducted by the Russian security services and blamed on the Chechens in order to start the Second Chechen War (which indeed began shortly following the attacks, on September 23, 1999). But there were many things that I could not know or understand. I needed Alexander. So I flew to Moscow to see him and ask for his help. We talked through the night. He told me that something very similar to the explosions of 1999 had taken place in Moscow in 1994, prior to the First Chechen War and the previous presidential election. "Find everything you can about Max Lazovsky. He was an FSB operative and he was in charge of the terrorist campaign of 1994. If you understand Lazovsky, how he operated, how his organization was built, you will understand everything. But, Yuri, be careful. If anyone else finds out that you are investigating Lazovsky, they will kill you, since they will figure out very quickly that you are interested in 1999, not in 1994. But the key to everything is Lazovsky and his system."

I left Moscow the next morning, on September 24, 2000. With me, I brought the notes that became the skeleton of our book *Blowing Up Russia: The Secret Plot to Bring Back KGB Terror.* This was my last trip to Russia.

That same night in Moscow, we also discussed Alexander's escape. He had been released from prison, but was under 24-hour surveillance by the FSB. Two cars with three persons in each followed him during the day. One car was always on duty during the night. I saw this with my own eyes when I came to see him. He had no future in Russia, and his next arrest was only a question of time.

In May 2000, I made my first and last attempt to negotiate with the FSB—to see if I could make some kind of deal with them and to obtain a guarantee of immunity for Alexander. It seemed to me that the nine months which Litvinenko had illegally spent in prison were more than enough "punishment" for the press conference of November 1998. Through a middleman, who had no relation to the FSB, I arranged to meet with Litvinenko's old boss, FSB General Evgeny Khokholkov.

"Only it won't be easy for you to talk to him," Alexander warned me. "He is a very serious person, a fighting general. So be careful with him. And one more thing... He was shell-shocked in action. When he gets mad, he doesn't show it, but he starts to stutter a bit. All of us knew that if Khokholkov starts stuttering, that's it—it's the end for everybody."

The meeting took place on May 22, in a private restaurant on Kutuzovsky Prospect, in an affluent neighborhood well known to Muscovites. The person who had organized our meeting had informed me that it would most likely be possible to buy Litvinenko's life and freedom for several million dollars. And to be honest, my expectation was that, in the end, everything would come down to an ordinary bribe, as often happens in Russia.

I arrived at the little restaurant at 7:30 in the evening. The sign on the door said "closed." I opened the door and went in. It was a cozy place, and in the middle of the room a table was already set. The cook, who was arranging the table, was receiving instructions from the owner, a tall, broad-shouldered man.

"I'm probably early?" I asked the owner. "I'm here to meet with General Khokholkov."

"No, no. You're right on time," the gracious owner replied. "Come in, welcome. I am General Khokholkov."

"So this restaurant is yours?" I asked, surprised, not having planned on beginning our conversation by talking about restaurants.

"Yes, it's mine. And the cook is mine. I brought him with me from Tashkent. He worked for me in Tashkent. I used to be stationed in Tashkent, you know."

Thoughts flashed through my mind. Tashkent. The capital of Uzbekistan. The Uzbeki political mafia. Khokholkov had been stationed there when Uzbekistan was part of the Soviet Union.

"You know," Khokholkov went on, "I don't have this restaurant to make money. I have it for my friends. It's very convenient. It's a place where you can go, sit down, have a conversation—like you and I now. Where would we meet if this restaurant wasn't here? On the street? My cook, by the way, is very good. Do you drink vodka?"

"I do."

"Wonderful."

The general poured each of us our first glass and the conversation took off.

I tried to determine whether the FSB was prepared to leave Litvinenko in peace, and if so, on what conditions. I had only one argument. Litvinenko had already served a nine-month sentence. This was enough of a punishment for his "crime," and if the FSB could guarantee that Litvinenko would not be harmed, then I was ready to make a deal and guarantee that Litvinenko, as a former agent of the FSB, would not make public the compromising information that he had in his possession.

In response, the general explained to me that there would be no forgiveness for Alexander; that he had gone against the system and this was something not permitted to anyone; and that the nine months which he had already spent in prison were only the beginning of his problems. And that if he, General Khokholkov, were to run into Litvinenko tomorrow by accident, then he would strangle him with his own two hands.

As he said this, the general showed exactly how his hands would grip Alexander's throat. And Khokholkov's face, which up to that moment had been quite kind and calm, suddenly changed and become frightening.

A pause followed, which seemed to me very long. The silence was broken by the general.

"I meant that f-f-figuratively, of course, f-f-figuratively," he said, stuttering heavily.

"Actually," he continued, having calmed down a bit, "of course there is a way out of the situation. The FSB used to have an economic department. It employed 300–400 of our agents, who specialized in economic issues. You know, today, with the growth of the market economy, there's been a sharp rise in economic crime. People steal money from the government, open casinos, stores, restaurants, don't pay their taxes, and conduct all business in cash. It is completely impossible to keep track of them. In order to deal with these crimes, the FSB created a new economic department. Well, our common acquaintance, Berezovsky, convinced the president to shut this department down. He told the president that it had been created to help the FSB extort money from businesses. And 300–400 of our best experts were fired. They have families, children. And they have nothing to eat. So if Berezovsky restores this department, then probably Alexander Litvinenko can be forgiven."

"So this restaurant is a place where the hungry children of out-of-work FSB agents can get a free meal?"

"That's exactly right, as a matter of fact," Khokholkov replied, quick on his feet. "Because we ourselves, as law enforcement agents, have very low salaries. We can't even afford to go to normal restaurants. No money."

"But Berezovsky told me that once, when he was staying at one of the most expensive hotels in Switzerland, he came down to the pool and saw in that pool General Alexander Korzhakov—the retired head of President Yeltsin's security apparatus."

"That was just a present to him from all of us. He himself does not have a ruble in his pocket. So each of us contributed a ruble or two, all the agents who knew him, and bought him a trip to an expensive resort as a present."

"I see. But Litvinenko has told me that there is a videotape of you losing tens of thousands of dollars at a casino in the course of a single evening."

"That was in the line of duty. I was on a case. We were conducting an operation in a casino. I was given official funds to gamble with, and I lost them, so to speak. Naturally, afterward, the casino reimbursed me the money I had lost. I mean, reimbursed us, the treasury, the government. So maybe there is a videotape, but there was no crime, just work for the government."

"Isn't there another way to leave Litvinenko in peace without restoring the economic department? You understand, we're not just going to abandon him and we're not going to let him be eaten by you. You were his boss, you have a better idea of how much Litvinenko knows and what he is capable of doing. If you don't leave him alone, we're going to fight you. You shouldn't underestimate us. We don't have any guns or official FSB IDs, but Berezovsky has money and influence, Alexander has information, and I have knowledge. You shouldn't underestimate us. If you don't leave Litvinenko alone, we will fight. Believe me, it won't seem like a minor matter."

"It's already 12:30 A.M.," Khokholkov said. "I have to get up early for work tomorrow morning. You probably have to go home, too. Do you have a car?"

"No, I'll catch a taxi."

"Don't worry. My cook will drive you home. You know, Moscow isn't so safe at night nowadays. You and I have had a frank and honest talk. You shouldn't underestimate us either. And above all, don't overestimate Berezovsky's influence. As for what you've said, I have no doubt that you have a lot of knowledge. I've been to a lot of places myself. I speak several European languages. So—you shouldn't underestimate us."

Khokholkov had not brought up the subject of money. I did not say a word about money either.

"Here's the story," I told Alexander when I saw him. "It's bad. You and Marina have to get out of here. You won't survive until the end of year. In the best case, they'll put you in prison. In the worst case, you understand for yourself."

We did not finish that conversation on that day. I came back to Alexander's apartment on the night of September 24, 2000, when I flew in to discuss our future book with him.

The plan was extremely simple. In the next two weeks, Alexander was to cross the border, and he would choose the place for the border-crossing by himself, without letting anyone know about it in advance, myself included. As soon as he crosses the border, I fly out to meet him, wherever he is, to make sure that everything is really in order, that he is really outside the country and not in the office of an FSB prosecutor. I then let Marina Litvinenko know that Alexander is free, and Marina goes to a travel agency and buys a vacation travel package for herself and her son Anatoly to any European country-wherever it is easiest to get a visa. She pays whatever it takes to get out of the country as soon as possible. As soon as Marina and Anatoly have left Russia, I make contact with the embassy of some Western European country or the United States, quickly arrange for asylum for Litvinenko's family, and the operation can be considered complete.

"You just cross the border. That's the main thing. The rest you can leave to me."

"I'll cross the border," Alexander told me. "Don't you worry about that."

Less than two weeks later, he did indeed cross the border. In the Russian city of Sochi, Alexander boarded a steamboat that, since the times of the Soviet Union, had been traveling between the ports along the coast of the Black Sea. In the old days, all of these ports had belonged to the great empire of the USSR. The empire fell apart, the ports become parts of different countries, but the little steamboat still followed its old route. Alexander arrived in Sochi and boarded the Black Sea steamboat with his Russian passport. He bribed the border guard $10 not to check for the name in his passport on the list of persons who were not permitted to leave Russia, and those $10 secured him passage to the nearest Georgian port. From there he traveled to the capital of Georgia, Tbilisi, and then he called me. I immediately flew out to Georgia. In the meantime, Marina Litvinenko was already in the process of obtaining a two-week travel package to Marbella, Spain, in order to enjoy a vacation in the south of Spain with her son Anatoly and a group of Russian tourists.

For Alexander, the next few days were the most difficult. Our only hope was that the FSB would not realize what was going on quickly enough—that they would not notice that had already lost track not only of Alexander, but of his family as well. It was a race for time, and every hour counted. Everything was going according to plan, but Alexander was nervous. And he could not call Marina. Any phone call could be intercepted and ruin everything. Our schedule was all worked out. By a certain date and time, I was supposed to arrive at the airport in Malaga and meet Marina and Anatoly there. I left Alexander in Tbilisi and flew to Spain as planned. And while I was on the plane, as Alexander later told me, he broke down and called Marina from our Georgian mobile phone, at the risk of ruining the whole operation.

"Marina, where are you?"

"We're taking off. I'm going to lose the connection. . ." was all that Marina had time to shout.

And the connection was lost.

I was standing at the bottom of the escalator in the Malaga airport, waiting for the group of Russian tourists. Marina and Anatoly had almost no luggage. According to her instructions, she was not supposed to take with her anything that could in any way suggest to Russian customs officials and border guards that she and Anatoly were going to Spain not for two weeks, but forever.

As soon as I spotted their faces, I called up Alexander: "Your family is in Spain." I drove Marina to the hotel in Marbella, following the group of Russian tourists, and explained to her the plan of action. I spent several days in Marbella, until Marina and Anatoly got used to the situation a little bit, and then flew back to Georgia. Meanwhile, Alexander was rushing around Tbilisi like a caged tiger.

After losing sight of Alexander and Marina, the FSB immediately deduced that the Litvinenkos had run away. Correctly concluding that their escape had in all likelihood been organized by me, the Federal Security Service of the Russian Federation decided to try catching us through my mobile phone, which the FSB knew. Every half hour, I kept receiving phone calls on my mobile phone from two people who wanted to find out how I was doing and what the weather was like in Boston—my old acquaintance who had organized my meeting with General Khokholkov in May, and FSB Major Andrei

Ponkin, who had been assigned to Litvinenko's family by the FSB in the role of "family friend." I told them in detail about my own life and the weather in Massachusetts, and I could not turn off my phone, since it was my only connection to Alexander and Marina. Our only hope was that we would be faster and more mobile than the flying squad of hired killers that the FSB had dispatched to Georgia. And we were.

By this time, the American embassy in Georgia had already been alerted to the situation. The US security services began discussions with me regarding the fate of the Litvinenko family. But the US embassy in Tbilisi could not meet our time constraints. And when, in our opinion, the situation became critical, and Alexander calculated that the FSB's hired assassins had already arrived in Tbilisi, we flew to Turkey-without letting the American embassy know about it, since we had no reason to believe that that the FSB was not listening in on our negotiations with the US embassy. Turkey was a country that required no entry visa either for Alexander or for his family. After bringing Alexander to the Turkish city of Antalya and leaving him at a hotel, I immediately flew to Spain, where Marina and Anatoly were waiting for me, in the already familiar Malaga airport. On October 27, I brought Marina and Anatoly to Alexander in Antalya, to a five-star hotel where we registered under a false name (under my own name, I rented several rooms at a hotel in a different part of town, but naturally we never even set foot there).

The US embassy in Georgia handed over the Litvinenko case to the US embassy in Turkey. But even here, we had no sense that the embassy would make a quick decision about granting the Litvinenkos political asylum. Naturally, all of this was very upsetting to me, and I flew back home to Boston in order to continue my negotiations with the CIA on the spot. So that Alexander and his family should not remain in Turkey alone, Alexander Goldfarb took the next flight from New York to Antalya. Both he and I were flying through London. But in Heathrow Airport our paths crossed only by telephone. I briefly described the situation to him and flew to the States, where the CIA definitively confirmed their decision not to accept the Litvinenkos.

On November 1, Goldfarb flew them out to London, where Alexander and his wife and son asked for asylum. In August 2001, several chapters from our future book were published in Russian in Moscow's *Novaya Gazeta*.

Since then, several people who had been assisting us were killed. Vladimir Golovlyov and Sergei Yushenkov, members of the Russian Parliament (the State Duma), were helping us to transport the forbidden tapes of the banned documentary *Assassination of Russia*, based on the book. They were both gunned down. Golovlyov was killed on August 21, 2002, and Yushenkov on April 17, 2003. Yuri Schekochikhin, a member of the Russian Parliament and the deputy editor-in-chief of *Novaya Gazeta*, where the recently murdered Anna Politkovskaya worked, was poisoned. He was in a coma for some time and died on July 3, 2003. I had met Schekochikhin in Zagreb, Croatia in June 2001 and had given him the manuscript of *Blowing Up Russia* for publication in his newspaper.

At the end of 2003 we printed 5000 copies of the Russian edition of *Blowing Up Russia* in Riga, Latvia. This edition was shipped to Moscow for sale, legally and openly. But the shipment was confiscated by the FSB on its way to Moscow. The government stated that the book revealed the state secrets. The greatest, of course, was the fact that the Russian security services had been behind the terrorist acts of 1999. Thus, for the first time since the 1970s, when Alexander Solzhenitsyn's books were prohibited in the USSR, a book was officially banned in Russia.

Despite those killings, we continued our work and collected new materials. We did as much as we could. We tried to be safe and to stay alive. We failed. I lost my co-author, six years after he landed in London. On November 1, 2006, he was poisoned, and this edition of *Blowing Up Russia* will have a foreword signed only by me.

YURI FELSHTINSKY
February 4, 2007

Introduction

*We did not reject our past. We said honestly: "The history of
the Lubyanka in the twentieth century is our history. . . ."*
N. P. PATRUSHEV, Director of the FSB
From an interview in *Komsomolskaya Pravda* on December 20,
2000, on the Day of the FSB

THE PEDIGREE of the Federal Security Service of the Russian Federation (FSB) scarcely requires any comment. From the very earliest years of Soviet power, the punitive agencies established by the Communist Party were alien to the qualities of pity and mercy. The actions of individuals working in these departments have never been governed by the values and principles of common humanity. Beginning with the revolution of 1917, the political police of Soviet Russia (later the USSR) functioned faultlessly as a mechanism for the annihilation of millions of people; in fact, these structures have never taken any other business in hand, since the government has never set any other political or practical agenda for them, even during its most liberal periods. No other civilized country has ever possessed anything to compare with the state security agencies of the USSR. Never, except in the case of Nazi Germany's Gestapo, has any other political police ever possessed its own operational and investigative divisions or detention centers, such as the FSB's prison for detainees at Lefortovo.

The events of August 1991—when a rising tide of public anger literally swept away the communist system—demonstrated very clearly that the liberalization of Russia's political structures must inevitably result in the weakening, perhaps even the prohibition, of the Committee of State Security (KGB). The panic which reigned among the leaders of the coercive agencies of the state during that period found expression in numerous, often incomprehensible, instances of old special service agencies being disbanded and new ones set up. As early as May 6, 1991, the Russian Republic Committee of State Security was set up with V. V. Ivanenko as its chairman in parallel to the All-Union KGB under the terms of a protocol signed by Russian president, Boris Yeltsin, and chairman of the USSR KGB, V. A. Kriuchkov. On November 26, the KGB of Russia was transformed into the Federal Security Agency (AFB). Only one week later, on December 3, the president of the USSR, Mikhail Gorbachev, signed a decree "On the Reorganization of the Agencies of State Security." Under the terms of this law, a new Interdepartmental Security Service (MSB) of the USSR was set up on the basis of the old KGB, which was abolished.

At the same time, the old KGB, like some multi-headed hydra, split into four new structures. The First (Central) Department (which dealt with external intelligence) was separated out as the new Central Intelligence Service, later renamed the External Intelligence Service (SVR). The KGB's Eighth and Sixteenth Departments (for governmental communications, coding, and electronic reconnaissance) were transformed into the Committee for Governmental Communications (the future Federal Agency for Governmental Communications and Information, or FAPSI). The border guard service became the Federal Border Service. The old KGB Ninth Department became the Bodyguard Department of the Office of the President of Russia. The old Fifteenth Department became the Governmental Security and Bodyguard Service. These last two structures later became the President's Security Service (SBP) and the Federal Bodyguard Service (FSO). One other super-secret special service was also separated out from the old Fifteenth Department of the KGB: the President's Central Department for Special Programs.

On January 24, 1992, Yeltsin signed a decree authorizing the creation of a new Ministry of Security (MB) on the basis of the AFB and MSB. A Ministry of Security and Internal Affairs appeared at the same time, but only existed for a short while before being dissolved. In

December 1993, the MB was, in turn, renamed the Federal Counter-intelligence Service (FSK), and on April 3, 1995, Yeltsin signed the decree "On the Formation of a Federal Security Service in the Russian Federation," by which the FSK was transformed into the FSB.

This long sequence of restructuring and renaming was intended to shield the organizational structure of the state security agencies, albeit in decentralized form, against attack by the democrats, and along with the structure to preserve the personnel, the archives, and the secret agents.

A largely important role in saving the KGB from destruction was played by Yevgeny Savostianov (in Moscow) and Sergei Stepashin (in Leningrad), both of whom had the reputation of being democrats, appointed in order to reform and control the KGB. In fact, however, both Savostianov and Stepashin were first infiltrated into the democratic movement by the state security agencies, and only later appointed to management positions in the new secret services, in order to prevent the destruction of the KGB by the democrats. Although, as the years went by, many full-time and free-lance officers of the KGB-MB-FSK-FSB left to go into business or politics, Savostianov and Stepashin did succeed in preserving the overall structure. Furthermore, the KGB had formerly been under the political control of the Communist Party, which served to some extent as a brake on the activities of the special agencies, since no significant operations were possible without the sanction of the Politburo. After 1991, the MB-FSK-FSB began operating in Russia absolutely independently and totally unchecked, apart from the control exercised by the FSB over its own operatives. This all-pervading predatory structure was now unrestrained by either ideology or law.

Following the period of evident confusion, resulting from the events of August 1991, and the mistaken expectation that operatives of the former KGB would be subjected to the same ostracism as the Communist Party, the secret services realized that this new era, free of communist ideology and party control, offered them certain advantages. The former KGB was able to exploit its vast personnel resources (both official and unofficial) to position its operatives in virtually every sphere of activity throughout the vast state of Russia.

Somehow, former prominent KGB men began turning up at the very highest echelons of power, frequently unnoticed by the uninitiated: the first of them were secret agents, but later, they were former or serving officers. Standing at Yeltsin's back, from the very first days of the events of August 1991, was KGB man Alexander Korzhakov, former bodyguard to the chairman of the KGB and general secretary of the Communist Party, Yuri Andropov. Retired GRU colonel Bogomazov headed the security service of the MIKOM GROUP, and the vice president of the Financial and Industrial Group was N. Nikolaev, a KGB man of twenty years' standing, who had once worked under Korzhakov.

Filipp Bobkov, four-star general and first deputy chairman of the KGB of the USSR, who in Soviet times had been the long-serving head of the so-called "fifth line" of the KGB (political investigation), found employment with business tycoon Vladimir Gusinsky. The "fifth line" numbered among its greatest successes the expulsion from the country of Alexander Solzhenitsyn and Vladimir Bukovsky, as well as the arrest and detainment in camps for many years of those who thought and said what they believed was right and not what the party ordered them to think and say. Standing at the back of Anatoly Sobchak, mayor of Leningrad (St. Petersburg) and a prominent leader of the reform movement in Russia, was KGB man Vladimir Putin. In Sobchak's own words, this meant that "the KGB controls St. Petersburg."

How this all came about has been described in detail by the head of the Italian Institute of International politics and Economics, Marco Giaconi, who teaches in Zurich. "The attempts made by the KGB to establish control over the financial activities of various companies always follow the same pattern. The first stage begins when gangsters attempt to collect protection money or usurp rights which are not their own. After that, special agency operatives arrive at the company to offer their help in resolving its problems. From that moment on, the firm loses its independence forever. Initially, a company snared in the KGB's nets has difficulty obtaining credit or may even suffer major financial setbacks. Subsequently, it may be granted licenses for trading in such distinctive sectors as aluminum, zinc, foodstuffs, cellulose, and timber. These provide a powerful stimulus for the firm's development. This is the stage at which it is infiltrated by former KGB operatives and also becomes a new source of revenue for the KGB."

However, the years from 1991 to 1996 demonstrated that despite being plundered rapaciously by the coercive state structures (who acted both openly, and through organized criminal groups under the total control of the secret services), Russian business had managed, in a short period, to develop into an independent political force which was by no means always under the full control of the FSB. Following Yeltsin's destruction in 1993 of the pro-communist parliament, which sought to halt liberal reform in Russia, the leaders of the former KGB, who had gone on to head Yeltsin's MB and FSK, decided to destabilize and compromise Yeltsin's regime and his reforms by deliberately exacerbating the criminal situation in Russia and fomenting national conflicts, first and foremost in the North Caucasus, the weakest link in the multinational Russian state.

At the same time, an energetic campaign was launched in the mass media to promote the message that impoverishment of the general public and an increase in criminal and nationalist activity were the results of political democratization, and the only way to avoid such excesses was for Russia to reject democratic reforms and Western models, and follow its own Russian path of development, which should be based on public order and general prosperity. What this propaganda really promoted was a dictatorship similar to the standard Nazi model. Of all the dictators, great and small, enlightened and bloodthirsty, the one chosen as a model was the most personable and least obvious, the Chilean general, Augusto Pinochet. For some reason, it was believed that if a dictatorship did emerge in Russia, it would be no worse than Pinochet's Chile. Historical experience, however, demonstrates that Russia always chooses the worst of all possible options.

Until 1996, the state security services fought against the democratic reformers, since they saw the most serious threat in a democratic ideology, which demanded the immediate implementation of radical, pro-Western economic and political reforms, based on the principles of a free-market economy, and the political and economic integration of Russia into the community of civilized nations. Following Yeltsin's victory in the 1996 presidential election, when Russian big business showed its political muscle for the first time by refusing to permit the cancellation of the democratic elections and the introduction of a state of emergency (the demands being made by the pro-dictatorship faction in the persons of Korzhakov, FSO head M. I. Barsukov, and their like) and, most importantly, was able to ensure the victory of its own candidate, the state security services redefined the major target of their offensive as the Russian business elite. Yeltsin's victory at the polls in 1996 was followed by the appearance, at first glance inexplicable, of propaganda campaigns dedicated to blackening the reputations of Russia's leading businessmen. Heading up the vanguard in these campaigns were some familiar faces from the agencies of coercion.

Russian language acquired a new term, "oligarch," although it was quite obvious that even the very richest man in Russia was no oligarch in the literal meaning of the word, since he lacked the basic component of oligarchy, power. Real power remained, as before, in the hands of the secret services.

Gradually, with the help of journalists, who were operatives or agents of the FSB and SBP, and an entire army of unscrupulous writers eager for easy, sensational material, the small number of "oligarchs" in Russian business came to be declared thieves, swindlers, and even murderers. Meanwhile, the really serious criminals, who had acquired genuine oligarchic power and pocketed billions in money that had never been listed in any accounts, were sitting behind their managers' desks at the Russian state's agencies of coercion: the FSB, the SBP, the FSO, the SVR, the Central Intelligence Department (GRU), the General Public Prosecutor's Office, the Ministry of Defense (MO), the Ministry of the Interior (MVD), the customs service, the tax police, and so on.

It was these people who were the true oligarchs, the gray cardinals and shadowy managers of Russian business and the country's political life. They possessed real power, unlimited and uncontrolled. Behind the secure protection of their identity cards from the agencies of coercion, they were genuinely untouchable. They abused their official positions on a regular basis, taking bribes and stealing, building up their ill-gotten capital, and involving their subordinates in criminal activity.

This book attempts to demonstrate that modern Russia's most fundamental problems do not result from the radical reforms of the liberal period of Yeltsin's terms as president, but from the open or clandestine resistance offered to these reforms by the Russian secret services. It was they who unleashed the first and second Chechen wars, in order to divert Russia away from the path of democracy and towards dictatorship, militarism, and chauvinism. It was they who organized a series of vicious terrorist attacks in Moscow and other Russian cities as part of their operations intended to create the conditions for the first and second Chechen wars.

The explosions of September 1999, in particular the terrorist attack that was thwarted in Ryazan on September 23, are the central theme of this book. These explosions provide the clearest thread for following the tactics and strategy of the Russian agencies of state security, whose ultimate aim is absolute power.

The reader may find the genre of this work somewhat surprising, something between an analytical memoir and a historical monograph. The abundance of names and facts and the laconic style of presentation will come as a disappointment to anyone hoping for an easy-reading detective story. As conceived by the authors, this book should be distinguished from superficial journalism and belletristic memoirs by its intrinsic faithfulness to historical fact. It is a book about a tragedy which has overtaken us all, about wasted opportunities, lost lives, and a country that is dying. It is a book for those who are capable of recognizing the reality of the past and are not afraid to influence the future.

Abbreviations and Terms

AFB Federal Security Agency.

CIA Central Intelligence Agency (USA).

CIS Commonwealth of Independent States.

FAPSI Federal Agency for Government
Communications & Information.

FBI Federal Bureau of Investigation (USA).

FSB The Federal Security Service of the Russian Federation.

FSK The Federal Counterintelligence Service; then FSB.

FSO Federal Bodyguard Service.

GRU Central Intelligence Department.

KGB Committee of State Security.

KRAZ Krasnoyarsk Aluminum Plant.

MB Ministry of Security.

MCHS Ministry of Emergencies.

MO Ministry of Defense.

MSB Interdepartmental Security Service.

MUR Moscow Criminal Investigation Department.

MVD Ministry of the Internal Affairs.

NTV TV channel.

ORT TV channel.

OSCE Organization for Security and Co-operation
in Europe.

REU District housing management office

RTR TV channel.

RUOP Regional Department for Combating
Organized Crime.

SVR External Intelligence Service.

SWAT Special Weapons Assault Team (MVD).

TNT Trinitrotoluene, a chemical explosive.

UPP Long-Term Programs Office.

URPO FSB's Office for the Analysis of Criminal Organizations.

USSR Union of Soviet Socialist Republics, the Soviet Union, 1922–1991.

VDV Airborne Assault Troops.

Cast of Characters

Basaev, Shamil-Chechen — warlord who, according to FSB, has ordered the 9/99 attacks. Leader of the fundamentalist wing among the Chechen rebels. Basayev ran for the Chechen presidency in 1997, but lost to Aslan Maskhadov. Served as Prime Minister in Maskhadov government between the two wars. On August 8, 1999 his forces entered western Dagestan from Chechnya, an incursion that was one of the causes for the 2nd Chechen war.

Dekkushev, Adam — a Russian Muslim accused by the FSB of complicity in the Moscow and Volgodonsk blasts. In July 2002, he was detained in Georgia and extradited to Russia, where he is currently under investigation at the Lefortovo prison in Moscow. A tape with his alleged confession was released by the FSB to Russian television in July 2002.

Galkin, Alexei — a senior lieutenant of the special forces of GRU (Russian military intelligence), captured by the Chechen rebels in 1999. His testimony implicating Russian special services in the 9/99 bombings, taped by a Turkish journalist was provided to the London Observer. Believed to be dead until he resurfaced in Moscow in 2002. In an inteview with 'Novaya Gazeta' he said that his 1999 testimony was obtained under turture.

Gochiyayev, Achimez — a Moscow businessman of North Caucasus origin who is the FSB's principal suspect in the Moscow bombings. He is alleged to be hiding in Georgia. Alexander Litvinenko and Yuri

Felshtinsky obtained Gochiyayev's testimony asserting his innocence. According to Gochiyaev, he had been lured by an FSB agent posed as a business partner into unwittingly renting basements in the apartment houses. After the second explosion, he said he called the police about two other buildings where he had rented space. Authorities found explosives and timers in those locations.

Kartofelnikov, Alexei — a bus driver, resident of 14/16 Novosyelov Street in Ryazan, who alerted authorities about strangers in front of his house on Sep 22, 1999, thus preventing a bombing and starting the 'FSB trail' in the 9/99 terror investigation.

Khattab — an Islamic militant who, according to FSB, masterminded and financed the 9/99 bombings. Killed in Chechnya by Russian forces in 2002. After his death, FSB released Khattab's photographs with Gochiyayev, which independent experts say may be faked.

Kovalev, Sergei — prominent human rights activist who chairs the public commission investigating 9/99 terror attacks. Elected State Duma deputy in 1993 and 1995; member of the Russian delegation to the Parliamentary Assembly of the European Council; chairman of the Presidential Human Rights Commission 1993-1996. Kovalev complained about the lack of official cooperation in his investigation.

Krymshamkhalov, Yusuf and Batchayev, Timur — Russian Muslims of the so-called 'Karachaev Group' accused by FSB of complicity in 1999 terror attack. Krymshamhalov was captured in Georgia and extradited to Russia in December 2002. He is presently held in the FSB Lefortovo prison. Batchayev was reportedly killed in the same raid. Prior to that raid, Krymshamhalov and Batchayev made statements admitting that they had been duped by an FSB agent-provocateur posing as a militant into transporting explosives to Moscow in 1999, which they believed would be used in strikes against Russian military targets.

Luzhkov, Yuri — mayor of Moscow since 1992, who was quick to blame the Chechens for explosions of apartment buildings in Moscow.

Maskhadov, Aslan — President of the Chechen Republic. Signed a peace treaty with Boris Yeltsin in 1997. Currently Moscow brands him a terrorist and no longer recognizes his government.

Morozova, Tatyana — a former resident of Moscow, currently living in the US, whose mother died in the explosion at Guryanov Street. Tatyana is the principal protagonist of Disbelief, the 2004 documentary by Russian director Andrei Nekrasov.

Morozova, Alyona (Elena) — a survivor of the blast at Guryanov Street, who lost her mother in the attack. A student at an American University, she is seeking political asylum in the U.S.

Patrushev, Nikolai — Director of the FSB. On September 24, 1999, announced that the incident in Ryazan was a readiness training exercise and that the sacks found in the apartment block basement contained sugar, not explosives, creating an national uproar. In response to the documentary 'Assassination of Russia', accused Berezovsky of providing financial support to Chechen terrorists.

Putin, Vladimir — President of Russia. A career K.G.B. officer, Putin was President Yeltsin's the Director of the Federal Security Service (FSB). He was named Prime Minister in 1999. His popularity rose sharply after the terror attacks of 9/99, when the majority of the population applauded his decision to launch the 2nd Chechen War. He was elected Russian President on March 26, 2000.

Romanovich, Vladimir — an undercover FSB agent specializing in infiltrating Chechen groups, who allegedly rented the space used for the bombing at Guryanov St. He was killed by a hit-and-run car in Cyprus a few months after the bombings.

Rushailo, Vladimir — Interior Minister in 1997-2000, Putin's national security adviser since March 2001. On September 24th, half an hour before Patrushev's statement about the 'training exercises' in Ryazan, announced that events in Ryazan were a failed terrorist act.

Rybakov, Yuly — Chairman of the Human Rights Subcommittee of the State Duma in 1999-2003. Took an active role in the Public Commission investigating the bombings.

Seleznev, Gennady — Speaker of the Duma who was informed by an aide about the attack in Volgodonsk three days before fact. The incident was never explained.

Shchekochikhin, Yuri — State Duma Deputy who advocated parliamentary investigation of the bombings and a member of the Public Commission on Terror-99. Died of apparent poisoning in Moscow in July 2003.

Tkachenko, Yuri — the police sapper who defused the FSB 'exercise' bomb in an apartment building in Ryazan.

Trepashkin, Mikhail — Moscow attorney of Tatyana Morozova, and consultant of the Public Commission investigating the bombings, who discovered the identity of Vladimir Romanovich, the FSB agent involved in the Moscow bombings. Trepashkin was arrested in Moscow on October 22, 2003, on fabricated evidence.

Yushenkov, Sergei — State Duma Deputy, and co-chair of the Liberal Russia Party, who tabled the unsuccessful motion to start a parliamentary investigation of the 9/99 bombings. A co-chairman of the Public Commission investigating the bombings, he was killed by an assassin in front of his home in Moscow on April 17, 2003.

Zdanovich, Alexander — spokesman for the FSB who led the PR campaign to explain the incident in Ryazan.

BLOWING UP RUSSIA

CHAPTER ONE

The FSB Foments War in Chechnya

NO ONE BUT a total madman could have wished to drag Russia into any kind of war, let alone a war in the North Caucasus. As if Afghanistan had never happened. As if it weren't clear in advance what course such a war would follow, or just what would be the outcome and the consequences of a war declared within the confines of a multinational state against a proud, vengeful, and warlike people. How could Russia possibly have become embroiled in one of its most shameful wars during the very period of its development, which was most democratic in form and most liberal in spirit? This war required the mobilization of resources and increased budgets for agencies of coercion, government departments, and ministries. It enhanced the importance and increased the influence of men in uniform and sidelined or rendered irrelevant the efforts made by supporters of peace, democracy, and liberal values to maintain the impetus of pro-Western economic reforms. This war resulted in the isolation of the Russian state from the community of civilized nations, since the rest of the world did not support it and could not understand it. A previously popular, well-loved president, therefore, sacrificed the support of both his own public and the international community. Once he had fallen into the trap, he was left with no option but to resign before the end of his term, and hand over power to the FSB in return for a guarantee of immunity for himself and his family. We know who it was that benefited from all of this—the people to whom Yeltsin handed over power. We know how the result was achieved—by means of the war in Chechnya.

All that remains to be discovered is who set the process in motion.

Chechnya had become the weakest link in Russia's multinational mosaic, but the KGB raised no objections when Djokhar Dudaev came to power there, because they regarded him as one of their own. General Dudaev, a member of the Communist Party of the Soviet Union since 1968, might as well have been transferred from Estonia to his hometown of Grozny, especially so that in 1990 he could retire, stand for election in opposition to the local communists, become president of the Chechen Republic, and in November 1991, proclaim the independence of Chechnya, thereby seeming to demonstrate to the Russian political elite the inevitability of Russia breaking apart under Yeltsin's liberal regime. It was probably no accident that another Chechen who was close to Yeltsin, Ruslan Khasbulatov, would also be responsible for inflicting fatal damage on his regime. Khasbulatov, a former Communist Youth Organization Central Committee functionary and a Communist Party member since 1966, had become chairman of the parliament of the Russian Federation in September 1991.

The history of escalation in the complex and confused relations between Russia and Chechnya is a theme for a different book. In any case, by 1994, the political leadership of Russia was already aware that it could not afford to grant Chechnya independence like Belarus and Ukraine. To grant Chechnya sovereign status could pose a genuine threat for the disintegration of Russia. But could they afford to start a civil war in the Northern Caucasus? The "party of war," based on the military and law enforcement ministries, believed that they could afford it, as long as the public was prepared for it, and it would be easy enough to influence public opinion, if the Chechens were seen to resort to terrorist tactics in their struggle for independence. All that was needed was to arrange terrorist attacks in Moscow and leave a trail leading back to Chechnya.

Knowing that Russian troops and the forces of the anti-Dudaev opposition might begin their storm of Grozny at any moment, on November 18, 1994, the FSK made its first recorded attempt to stir up anti-Chechen feeling by committing an act of terrorism and laying the blame on Chechen separatists: if the chauvinist sentiments of Muscovites could be inflamed, it would be easy to continue the repression of the independence movement in Chechnya.

It should be noted that on November 18 and in later instances, the supposed "Chechen terrorists" set off their explosions at the most inopportune times, and then never actually claimed responsibility (rendering the terrorist attack itself meaningless). In any case, in November 1994, public opinion in Russia and around the world was on the side of the Chechen people, so why would the Chechens have committed an act of terrorism in Moscow? It would have made far more sense to attempt to sabotage the stationing of Russian troops on Chechen territory. Russian supporters of war with Chechnya were, however, only too willing to see the hand of Chechnya in any terrorist attack, and their response on every occasion was to strike a rapid and quite disproportionately massive blow against Chechen sovereignty. The impression was naturally created that the Russian military and law enforcement agencies, while quite unprepared for the terrorist attacks, were incredibly well prepared to launch counter-measures.

The explosion of November 18, 1994, took place on a railroad track crossing the river Yauza in Moscow. According to experts, it was caused by two powerful charges of approximately 1.5 kilograms of TNT. About twenty meters of the railroad bed were ripped up, and the bridge almost collapsed. It was quite clear, however, that the explosion had occurred prematurely, before the next train was due to cross the bridge. The shattered fragments of the bomber's body were discovered about one hundred meters from the site of the explosion. He was Captain Andrei Schelenkov, an employee of the oil company Lanako. His own bomb had blown him up as he was planting it on the bridge.

It was only thanks to this blunder by the operative carrying out the bombing that the immediate organizers of the terrorist attack became known. Lanako's boss, who had given his firm a name beginning with the first two letters of his own last name, was thirty-five-year-old Maxim Lazovsky, a highly valued agent of the Moscow and Moscow Region Department of the FSB, who was known in criminal

circles by the nicknames of "Max" and "Cripple." At the risk of anticipating events, we can also point out the significant fact that every single
one of Lanako's employees was a full-time or free-lance agent of the
Russian counterespionage agencies.

On the day of the explosion on the river Yauza, November 18,
1994, an anonymous phone call to the police claimed that a truck
full of explosives was standing outside the Lanako offices. As a result,
the FSB department actually discovered a truck close to the firm's
offices containing three MON-50 mines, fifty charges for grenade
launchers, fourteen RGD-5 grenades, ten F-1 grenades, and four
packs of plastic explosives, with a total weight of six kilograms. The
FSB claimed, however, that it had been unable to determine who
owned the truck, even though a Lanako identity card was found on
Schelenkov's remains, and the explosives used in the Yauza bombing
were of the same kind as that on the truck.

War in Chechnya offered a very easy way to finish off Yeltsin polit-
ically, a fact understood only too well by those who provoked the war
and organized terrorist attacks in Russia. There was, in addition, a
primitive financial aspect to relations between the Russian leadership
and the president of the Chechen Republic: the Russians were con-
tinuously extorting money from Dudaev. It began in 1992, when
bribes were accepted from the Chechens in payment for the Soviet
armaments left behind in Chechnya that year. The bribes for these
weapons were extorted by head of the SBP Korzhakov, head of the
FSO Barsukov, and First Deputy Prime Minister of the Russian Federation Oleg Soskovets. Of course, the Ministry of Defense was in on
the deal. Some years later the naive citizens of Russia began to wonder how all those weapons the Chechens were using to kill Russian
soldiers could have been left behind in Chechnya. The answer was
nothing if not mundane: they were paid for by Dudaev in multi-million dollar bribes to Korzhakov, Barsukov, and Soskovets.

After 1992, the Moscow bureaucrats continued their successful
bribe-based collaboration with Dudaev, and the Chechen leadership
continued sending money to Moscow on a regular basis, because
there was no other way Dudaev could resolve a single political ques-

tion. However, in 1994, the system began to falter, as Moscow extorted larger and larger sums of money in exchange for political favors relating to Chechen independence. Dudaev started refusing to pay. The financial conflict gradually developed into a political standoff, and then a contest of strength between the Russian and Chechen leaderships. The threat of war hung heavily in the air. Dudaev requested a personal meeting with Yeltsin, perhaps even intending to tell him what had been going on. But the threesome, who controlled access to Yeltsin, demanded a bribe of several million dollars for organizing a meeting between the two presidents. Dudaev refused to pay and demanded that the meeting with Yeltsin take place without any money changing hands in advance. Furthermore, for the first time, he threatened the people who had been helping him strictly for payment with the disclosure of documents in his possession, which contained compromising information about the functionaries' self-serving dealings with the Chechens. Dudaev believed that possession of these documents was his insurance against arrest. He could not be arrested; he could only be killed, since he was an eyewitness to crimes committed by members of Yeltsin's entourage. Dudaev had miscalculated. His blackmail failed, and the meeting he wanted never took place. The president of Chechnya was now a dangerous witness who had to be removed. So a cruel and senseless war was deliberately provoked. Let us trace the sequence of events.

On November 22, 1994, the State Defense Committee of the Chechen Republic, which Dudaev had founded by decree the previous day, accused Russia of launching a war against Chechnya. As far as the journalists could see, there was no war, but Dudaev knew that the "party of war" had already made its decision to commence military action. The Chechen State Defense Committee which, in addition to Dudaev, included the leaders of the military and other agencies of coercion, as well as a number of key governmental departments and ministries, held an emergency session in response to "the threat of military incursion" into Chechnya. A statement by the State Defense Committee which was distributed in Grozny, claimed that "Russian regular units are occupying the Nadterechny district, part of the territory of the Chechen Republic," adding that in the days immediately ahead, it was planned "to occupy the territory of the Naursk and Shelkovsk districts. For this purpose, use is being made of regular units of the North Caucasus Military District, special sub-units of the Russian Ministry of the Interior, and army aircraft from the North Caucasus Military District. According to information received by the State Defense Council, special subunits of the Russian FSK are also taking part in the operation."

The Central Armed Forces HQ of Chechnya confirmed that military units were being concentrated on the border with Chechnya's Naursk district, in the village of Veselaia, in the Stavropol Region: there were heavy tanks, artillery and as many as six battalions of infantry. It later became known that the backbone of the forces, drawn up for the storming of Grozny, consisted of a column of Russian armored vehicles assembled on the initiative of the FSK, which paid for it and also hired soldiers and officers on contract, including members of the elite armed forces from the armored Taman and Kantemirov divisions.

On November 23, nine Russian army helicopters, presumably MI-8s, from the North Caucasus Military District, launched a rocket attack on the town of Shali, located approximately forty kilometers from Grozny, in an attempt to destroy the armored vehicles of a tank regiment located there, and were met with anti-aircraft artillery fire. There were wounded on the Chechen side, which announced that it had a video recording showing helicopters bearing Russian identification markings.

On November 25, seven Russian helicopters from a military base in the Stavropol Region fired several rocket salvoes at the airport in Grozny and at nearby apartment buildings, damaging the landing strip and the civilian aircraft standing on it. Six people were killed and about twenty-five were injured. In response to this raid, the Ministry of Foreign Affairs of Chechnya forwarded a statement to the authorities of the Stavropol Region pointing out, among other things, that the region's leaders "bear responsibility for such acts, and in the case of appropriate measures being taken by the Chechen side," all complaints "should be directed to Moscow."

On November 26, the forces of the "Provisional Council of Chechnya" (the Chechen opposition) supported by Russian helicopters and armored vehicles, attacked Grozny from all four sides. More than 1,200 men, fifty tanks, eighty armored personnel carriers, and six SU-27 planes from the opposition took part in the operation. An announcement, made by the Moscow center of the puppet "Provisional Council of Chechnya," claimed that "the demoralized forces of Dudaev's supporters are offering virtually no resistance, and everything will probably be over by the morning."

In fact, the operation was a total failure. The attackers lost about 500 men and more than twenty tanks, and another twenty tanks were captured by Dudaev's forces. About 200 members of the armed forces were taken prisoner. On November 28, a column of prisoners was marched through the streets of Grozny "to mark the victory over the forces of opposition." At the same time, the Chechen leadership disclosed a list of fourteen captured soldiers and officers who were members of the Russian armed forces. The prisoners confessed in front of television cameras that most of them served in military units 43162 and 01451 based outside Moscow. The Ministry of Defense of the Russian Federation replied that the individuals concerned were not serving members of the Russian armed forces. In response to an inquiry concerning prisoners Captain Andrei Kriukov and Senior Lieutenant Yevgeny Zhukov, the Ministry of Defense stated that these officers had indeed been serving in army unit 01451, but they had not reported to the unit since October 20, 1994, and an order for their discharge from the armed forces was being drawn up. In other words, the Russian Ministry of Defense declared the captured soldiers to be deserters. The following day, Yevgeny Zhukov's father refuted the ministry's statement. In an interview with the Russian Information Agency Novosti, he said that his son had left his unit on November 9, telling his parents that he had been assigned for ten days to Nizhny Tagil. The next time Yevgeny's parents had seen him was in a group of captured Russian soldiers in Grozny on the weekly television news program Itogi on November 27. When he was asked how their son came to be in Chechnya, Unit Commander Zhukov refused to answer.

Following this came the colorful account of the events of November 26, given by Major Valery Ivanov, following his release in a group of seven members of the Russian armed forces on December 8:

> By unit order of the day, all those who had been recruited were granted compassionate leave due to family circumstances. For the most part, they took officers without any settled domestic arrangements. Half of them had no apartments—you were supposed to be able to refuse, but if you did refuse, when they started handing out apartments you'd find yourself left out. On November 10, we arrived in Mozdok in Northern Ossetia. In two weeks we made ready fourteen tanks with Chechen crews and twenty-six tanks for Russian servicemen. On November 25, we advanced on Grozny. . . . I personally was in a group of three tanks that took control of the Grozny television center at mid-day on the 26th. There was no resistance from the Interior Ministry forces defending the tower. But three hours later, in the absence of communications with our command, we came under attack by the famous Abkhazian battalion. We were surrounded by tanks and infantry and decided it was pointless to return fire, since the [anti-Dudaev] opposition forces had immediately run off and abandoned us, and two of our three tanks were burnt out. The crews managed to bail out and surrender to the guards of the television center, who handed us over to President Dudaev's personal bodyguard. They treated us well, in the last few days they hardly guarded us at all, but then there was nowhere we could run off to.

The impression given by all this was that the armored column had been deliberately introduced into Grozny on November 26, so that it would be destroyed. The column was not capable of disarming Dudaev and his army, or of taking the city and holding it. Dudaev's army was at full strength and well armed. The column could not possibly have been anything more than a moving target.

Russian Minister of Defense Pavel Grachyov hinted that he had not been involved in the irresponsible attempt to take Grozny. From a military point of view, Grachyov declared at a press conference on November 28, 1996, it would be entirely possible to take Grozny "in two hours with a single regiment of paratroopers. However, all military conflicts are ultimately settled at the negotiating table by political methods. Introducing tanks into the city without infantry cover was really quite pointless." But why then were they sent in?

General Gennady Troshev would later tell us about Grachyov's doubts concerning the Chechen campaign: "He tried to do something about it. He tried to extract a clear assessment of the situation from Stepashin and his special service, he tried to delay the initial introduction of troops until the spring, he even tried to reach a personal agreement with Dudaev. We know now that such a meeting did take place. They didn't come to any agreement." General Troshev, who at this stage was in control of the second war in Chechnya, could not understand how Grachyov had failed to reach an understanding with Dudaev. The reason, of course, was that Dudaev insisted on a personal meeting with Yeltsin, and Korzhakov refused to set up the meeting unless he was paid.

The brilliant military operation in which a Russian armored column was burnt out was, indeed, not organized by Grachyov, but by director of the FSK Stepashin and head of the Moscow FSB Savostianov, who was responsible for handling questions relating to the overthrow of Dudaev's regime and the introduction of troops into Chechnya. Those who expatiated at great length on the crude miscalculations of the Russian military leaders, who had sent the armored column into the city only for it to be destroyed, failed to understand the subtle political calculations of the provocateurs who organized the war in Chechnya. The people who planned the introduction of troops into Grozny wanted the column to be wiped out in spectacular fashion by the Chechens. It was the only way they could provoke Yeltsin into launching a full-scale war against Dudaev.

Immediately after the rout of the armored column in Grozny, President Yeltsin made a public appeal to Russian participants in the conflict in the Chechen Republic, and the Kremlin began preparing public opinion for imminent full-scale war. In an interview for the Russian Information Agency *Novosti*, Arkady Popov, a consultant with the president's analytical center, announced that Russia could take on the role of a "compulsory peacemaker" in Chechnya, and that all the indications were that the Russian president intended to take decisive action. If the president were to declare a state of emergency in Chechnya, the Russian authorities could employ "a form of limited intervention, which would take the form of disarming both sides to the conflict by introducing a limited contingent of Russian troops into Grozny"—exactly what had been tried in Afghanistan. So, having provoked a conflict in Chechnya by providing political and military support to the Chechen opposition, the FSK now intended to launch a war against Dudaev under cover of peacemaking operations.

The Chechen side took Yeltsin's statement to be an "ultimatum" and a "declaration of war." A statement issued by the Chechen government confirmed that this statement, and any attempt to put it into effect, were "in contravention of the norms of international law," and gave the government of Chechnya "the right to respond by taking adequate measures for the protection of its independence and the territorial integrity of its state." In the opinion of the government of the Chechen Republic, the threat of a Russian declaration of a state of emergency on Chechen territory expressed "an undisguised desire to continue military operations and interfere in the internal affairs of another state."

On November 30, Grozny was subjected to air strikes by the Russian air force. On December 1, the Russian military command refused to allow into Grozny an aircraft carrying a delegation of members of the Russian State Duma. The delegation landed in the Ingushetian capital of Nazran and set out overland to Grozny for a meeting with Dudaev. While they were traveling to the Chechen capital, on December 1, at about 14.00 hours, eight SU-27 planes carried out a second raid on the Chechen capital, encountering dense anti-aircraft fire in the process. The planes specifically shelled the district of the city where Dudaev lived. According to the Chechen side, anti-aircraft defense forces shot down one plane.

On December 2, the chairman of the Duma Defense Committee and head of the delegation that had arrived in Grozny, Sergei Yushenkov, declared that reliance on force in Russian-Chechen relations was doomed to failure. Yushenkov also stated that familiarization with the situation on the ground had convinced him that negotiation was the only possible way to resolve the situation that had arisen, and claimed that the Chechen side had not set any preconditions for negotiations.

Public opinion was still on the side of the Chechens, but the leadership of the FSB had become absolutely convinced that it could be manipulated by the use of acts of terrorism blamed on the Chechens. On December 5, the FSK informed journalists that foreign mercenaries had surged across the state border into Chechnya and, therefore, "activity by the terrorist groups being infiltrated into Russia today cannot be ruled out in other regions of the country as well." This was the first undisguised announcement by the FSK that acts of terrorism with "a trail leading back to Chechnya" would soon begin in Russia. At this point, however, they still spoke of Russia being infiltrated by foreign agents, a ploy drawn, no doubt, from the pages of the old Soviet KGB handbooks.

On December 6, Dudaev declared in an interview that Russia's policy was creating a rising tide of Islamic sentiment in Chechnya: "Playing the 'Chechen card' may bring into play the global interests of foreign Islamic states, who could make it impossible to control the development of events. A third force has now emerged in Chechnya, the Islamists, and the initiative is gradually shifting over to them." Dudaev characterized the mood of the new arrivals in Grozny with the words: "We are no longer your soldiers, Mr. President, we are the soldiers of Allah," and summed up: "the situation in Chechnya is beginning to get out of control, and this concerns me."

As though in reply to Dudaev, Russian Minister of Defense Grachyov held a public relations exercise that took the external form of a peacemaking gesture, but in reality, provoked a further escalation of the conflict. Grachyov proposed that the Chechen opposition headed by Avturkhanov, which was financed, armed, and staffed by the FSK, should disarm, on condition that Dudaev's supporters would agree to give up their weapons at the same time. In other words, he suggested to Dudaev that the Chechens should disarm uni-laterally (since there was no suggestion of the Russian side dis-arming). Naturally the government of the Chechen Republic did not accept this proposal. On December 7, Grachyov had a meeting with Dudaev, but the discussions proved fruitless.

On the same day in Moscow, the Security Council held a session devoted to events in Chechnya, and the State Duma held a closed ses-sion, to which the leaders of the government departments responsible for the armed forces and other agencies of law enforcement were invited. However, they failed to show up at the Duma, because they did not wish to answer the parliamentarians' questions about who had given the orders to recruit members of the Russian armed forces and bomb Grozny. We now know that the Russian military personnel were recruited by the FSK on Stepashin's instructions, and that the direc-tives to bombard Grozny were issued by the Ministry of Defense.

On December 8, the Chechen side announced it was in possession of information that Russia was preparing to advance its forces on to Chechen territory and launch an all-out land war against the republic. At a press conference, held at the State Duma in Moscow on Decem-ber 9, the chairman of the Duma Federal Affairs and Regional Policy Committee and chairman of the Republican Party of Russia, Vladimir Lysenko, announced that in that case, he would table a motion in the Duma for the Russian government to be dismissed. On December 8, the Working Commission on Negotiations for the Settlement of the Conflict in the Chechen Republic managed to broker an agreement between the representatives of President Dudaev and the opposition, under which negotiations were due to start in Vladikavkaz at 15.00 hours on December 12. The Russian federal authorities' delegation to the negotiations was to have consisted of twelve members led by the deputy minister for nationalities and regional policy, Vyacheslav Mikhailov. The delegation from Grozny was to have numbered nine members, headed by the Chechen minister of the economy and finance, Taimaz Abubakarov. From the opposition there was to have been a three-man delegation led by Bek Baskhanov, the public prosecutor general of Chechnya. It was provisionally agreed that the main problems to be discussed at the negotiations between Moscow and Grozny were halting the bloodshed and establishing normal relations. Negotiations with the supporters of the Chechen opposition were only supposed to deal with questions of disarmament.

All this increased the chances of peace being preserved, and left the "party of war" with very little time until December 12. In effect, the announcement by the Working Commission for the Settlement of the Chechen Conflict determined the date on which military land operations began. If the peace negotiations were due to start on December 12, the war had to be launched on December 11. The Russian leadership acted accordingly: on December 11, land forces crossed the demarcation line into the Chechen Republic, and for the first few days, Russian military reports spoke of the absence of any real resistance or any losses.

By December 13, Soskovets had already determined his main lines of action, and he informed journalists that the total cost of implementing measures to normalize the situation in Chechnya could amount to about a trillion rubles. (This was the sum that would first have to be allocated from the budget, so that it could be systematically embezzled.) He said that the government's first priority was to get the aid delivered to the population of Chechnya, and special attention would be paid to ensuring that it was not wasted or stolen (we now know for certain that no aid ever reached Chechnya, and all of it was wasted and stolen).

Soskovets emphasized that members of the Chechen diaspora, living in Moscow and other Russian cities, should not be considered potential terrorists. Note this phrase. So far, nobody had even dreamed of regarding the members of the Chechen diaspora as potential terrorists, and there had not actually been any terrorist attacks. The war with Chechnya was still not even regarded as a war, but something more in the nature of a police operation, and there had not yet been any serious casualties. Yet, for some reason the First Deputy Prime Minister seemed to think it possible that the Chechens might organize acts of terrorism on Russian soil. Soskovets' remark that no discriminatory measures would be applied to the general mass of Chechen citizens, and that the federal authorities were not even considering the enforced deportation of Chechens, was clearly a suggestion from the "party of war" that war should be waged against the entire Chechen people throughout the whole of Russia, including by both discriminatory measures and enforced deportation.

Lieutenant-General Alexander Lebed, commander of the 14th Russian Army in Pridniestrovie (the region along the Dniester River in Moldova), fiercely opposed the "party of war," because he understood perfectly well what Soskovets was hinting at and the price Russia would have to pay. In a telephone interview from his headquarters in Tiraspol, he declared that "the Chechen conflict can only be resolved by diplomatic negotiations. Chechnya is repeating the Afghanistan scenario point for point. We are risking unleashing war with the entire Islamic world. Solitary fighters can go on forever burning our tanks and picking off our soldiers with individual shots. In Chechnya, we have shot ourselves in the foot exactly as we did in Afghanistan, and that is very sad. A well-reinforced and well-stocked Grozny is capable of offering long and stubborn resistance." Lebed reminded everyone that in Soviet times Dudaev had commanded an airborne division of strategic bombers capable of waging war on a continental scale, and that "fools were not appointed" to such posts.

Beginning on December 14, Moscow was transferred to a state of semi-military alert, and Muscovites were deliberately frightened with the prospect of inevitable Chechen terrorism. The agencies of the Ministry of the Interior stepped up their protection of the city's vital installations, and FSK personnel worked to improve their security. Police patrols armed with automatic weapons guarded a large number of state institutions. The Ministry of the Interior announced that this was all a response to the threat of terrorist groups being sent to Moscow from Grozny. The first suspected Chechen terrorists began to be sought out. On the evening of December 13, the Chechen Israil Getiev, a native and resident of Grozny, had been arrested for setting off New Year firecrackers outside the Prague restaurant on the Novyi Arbat Street and detained at the station of the Fifth Moscow Police Precinct. At this stage, announcements like this could still raise a smile, but on December 14, it was suddenly announced that after less than three full days of military operations, "casualties on both sides are already in the hundreds." It was all getting beyond a laughing matter.

On December 15, the true scale of the operation being launched was revealed. Advancing on Grozny, alongside subunits of the Ministry of the Interior, were two general army divisions from the North Caucasus Military District and two assault brigades at full strength. Composite regiments also entered Chechen territory from the Pskov, Vitebsk, and Tula divisions of the airborne assault forces (VDV), with 600 to 800 men in each. In the region of Mozdok, disembarkation had begun of composite regiments from the Ulyanovsk and Kostroma divisions of the VDV. Grozny was being approached along four main lines of advance: one from Ingushetia, two from Mozdok, and one from Dagestan. The Russian forces were preparing to storm the city. On the Chechen side, according to information from the Russian Ministry of the Interior and the FSK, more than 13,000 armed men had been assembled in and around Grozny.

Yeltsin was moving towards the edge of an abyss. A session of the Security Council, held under his chairmanship on December 17, reviewed a plan for "the implementation of measures to restore constitutional legality, the rule of law and peace in the Chechen Republic." The Security Council made the Ministry of Defense (Grachyov), the Ministry of the Interior (Viktor Yerin), the FSK (Stepashin), and the Federal Border Service (Nikolaev) responsible for using every possible means to disarm and destroy illegal armed formations in Chechnya and to secure the state and administrative borders of the Chechen Republic. The work was to be coordinated by Grachyov.

This was the day that marked the end of Russia's liberal-democratic period. President Yeltsin had committed political suicide.

On December 17, the Russian Ministry of Foreign Affairs announced that from 00.00 hours on December 18, units of Interior Ministry and Defense Ministry forces would be obliged to take decisive action, and make use of all means at their disposal to re-establish constitutional legality and the rule of law on the territory of Chechnya. Groups of bandits would be disarmed and, if they offered resistance, destroyed. The Ministry of the Interior statement claimed that the civilian population of Chechnya had been informed of the urgent need to leave Grozny and other centers of population in which rebel groups were located. The Interior Ministry strongly recommended foreign citizens and journalists in the zone of hostilities to leave Grozny and make their way to safe areas. (Despite the warnings from the Russian leadership, most of the foreign journalists remained in Grozny, and at The French Courtyard Hotel where they stayed, rooms were in as short supply as ever.)

On the same day, Soskovets announced to the world that President Dudaev had been summoned to Mozdok to meet a Russian government delegation headed by Deputy Prime Minister Nikolai Yegorov and FSK director Stepashin. Soskovets stated that if Dudaev did not come to Mozdok, the Russian forces would take action in accordance with the regulations for the elimination of illegal armed formations, and he also announced that expenditure on the operations over the preceding week amounted to sixty billion rubles by the Ministry of the Interior and 200 billion rubles by the Ministry of Defense.

Four hours before the deadline expired, at eight in the evening on December 17, Dudaev made his final attempt to avert war and wired the Russian leadership that he would agree "to start negotiations at the appropriate level without any preconditions and to lead the governmental delegation of the Chechen Republic in person." In other words, Dudaev was again demanding a personal meeting with Yeltsin, but since Dudaev persisted in his refusal to pay any money for such a meeting to be arranged, his cable went unanswered.

At nine in the morning on December 18, the Russian forces blockading Grozny began storming the city. Front-line air units and army helicopters delivered "precision blows against Dudaev's command post at Khankala near Grozny, the bridges over the Terek River to the north and also against maneuverable groups of armored vehicles." An announcement from the Temporary Information Center of the Russian High Command stated that following the destruction of the armored vehicles, the plan was for the forces blockading Grozny to advance and proceed with the disarmament of illegal armed groups on the territory of Chechnya. President Yeltsin's plenipotentiary representative in Chechnya announced that Dudaev now had no choice but to surrender.

On December 18, Soskovets, having been appointed to yet another post as head of the Russian government's operational headquarters for the coordination of action taken by agencies of the executive authorities, informed the press that in Grozny "they are studying the possibility" of carrying out terrorist attacks aimed at military and civilian targets in Central Russia and the Urals, and also of hijacking a civilian passenger plane. The First Deputy Prime Minister's astonishingly detailed information was, in fact, an indication that terrorist acts could be expected within a few days.

On December 22, the press office of the Government of the Russian Federation announced that Chechens were blowing themselves up in order to throw the blame for the explosions on to the Russian army. The statement issued read as follows:

Today at 10 in the morning a meeting was held under the chairmanship of first deputy chairman of the government Oleg Soskovets which was attended by members of the government, members of the Security Council, and representatives of the President's Office. The meeting discussed the situation which has arisen in the Chechen Republic and the measures being taken by the president and the government to restore constitutional legality and provide economic assistance to the population of areas which have been liberated from the armed formations of the Dudaev regime. Reports made by those present at the meeting indicate that last night operations to disarm the armed bandit formations continued, and bombing raids were carried out against their strongholds. The city of Grozny was not subjected to bombardment. However, the guerrillas made attempts to imitate the bombardment of housing districts. At about one in the morning, an office building and an apartment block were blown up. The residents, both Chechen and Russian, were not given any warning of the planned attack. The imitation of bombardment was undertaken in order to demonstrate the thesis of 'a war being waged by the Russian leadership against the Chechen people.' This thesis was proclaimed yesterday in Dudaev's 'appeal to the international community.'

In other words, the Russian government's press office attempted to blame the Chechens for the destruction by Russian forces of an office building and apartment block containing civilians.

Initiated by Soskovets, this announcement couched in Stalinist prose was made public one day before the explosion between the stations of Kozhukhovo and Kanatchikovo on the Moscow circular railroad (there were no casualties and no terrorists were found).

December 23 is the date which can be regarded as the beginning of the FSB's terrorist campaign against Russia. From then on, terrorist attacks became a commonplace occurrence.

CHAPTER TWO

The Secret Services Run Riot

IT IS WORTH NOTING the way in which the press office of the Russian government described the terrorist attack carried out on December 23: "Information has been received concerning the dispatch to Moscow [from Chechnya] of three experienced guerrilla fighters, including one woman, who have instructions to assume the leadership of groups of terrorists sent here previously. A group of foreigners who were seeking contact with guerrillas from Grozny has been detained, and a number of radio-controlled explosive devices they were carrying have been confiscated, together with twenty kilograms of TNT and sixteen radio-controlled anti-personnel and anti-tank mines. On the night of December 23, the rails were blown up on one section of the Moscow circular railroad. Another bomb was rendered harmless. Measures are being taken to identify sabotage groups active in Moscow and the Moscow Region."

No investigation of any acts of terrorism was carried out. The picture was clear enough anyway: first the Chechens sent "sabotage groups" to Moscow and the Moscow Region; then they sent three experienced guerrilla leaders to help them; and finally, a "group of foreigners" was brought in to help them from abroad with TNT and bombs (apparently they were carrying the bombs on their persons as they entered the country). The result of all these complicated preparations was a terrorist attack on one section of the Moscow circular railroad, which indicated that the groups of saboteurs already sent to

Moscow and the Moscow Region had not yet been neutralized (one could assume that the terrorist attacks would continue).

Everything in the press office statement was absolutely untrue, except for the announcement that there had been an explosion on a section of the Moscow circular railroad on December 23. The *modus operandi* suggests that Lazovsky's people also carried out this attack. In any case, it is impossible to regard as mere coincidence the fact that only four days later yet another terrorist attack was carried out in Moscow. At nine in the evening on December 27, 1994, Vladimir Vorobyov, a free-lance FSB agent and employee of Lazovsky's company Lanako, who came from a long line of military men (in 1920, his grandfather had been in charge of the Arsenal arms plant in Tula), and had a Candidate degree (i.e., Ph.D.) in Technical Sciences and was employed at the Zhukovsky Academy (on the development of a new anti-missile defense system), planted a remote-controlled bomb in a bus at a bus stop on Route 33. There were no passengers on board the bus when the bomb exploded, and the only casualty was the driver, Dmitry Trapezov, who suffered severe bruising and concussion. Trolley buses standing close by were lacerated by shrapnel.

Vorobyov's boss, Lazovsky, worked not only for the FSK, but also for the SVR, where his controller was the experienced officer, Pyotr Suslov, who was born in 1951. Lazovsky was one of his secret agents. Suslov officially quit the intelligence service and went into business in 1995, after which he made repeated journeys to war-torn Grozny, Baghdad, Teheran, the Arab Emirates, and other countries in the Middle East. In fact, Suslov was organizing extra-legal reprisals. In order to carry out missions involving acts of coercion and killings, he hired qualified former operatives from special units, in particular from the special missions unit of the First (Central) Department of the KGB of the USSR, known as *Vympel*, who possessed advanced sniper's skills. *Vympel*'s officers were involved both as instructors and front line operatives, and a special *Vympel* Fund was even established to finance this work. The chairman of the fund was a criminal "boss" well known in Russia, Sergei Kublitsky (his underworld nickname was "Vorkuta"). Suslov was the vice-chairman. At the same time,

Suslov was also chairman of the board of directors of the "Law and Order" regional social fund (Moscow, Voronkovskaya Street, 2 1).

Suslov maintained extensive contacts in the state's departments of law enforcement and agencies of coercion, including the leadership of the FSB. In particular, Suslov maintained close contact with Major-General Yevgeny Khokholkov, head of the Long-Term Programs Office (UPP) established in summer 1996, which provided the basis for the establishment in 1997 of the FSB's Office for the Analysis of Criminal Organizations (URPO). Alexei Antropov, a graduate of the intelligence school of the External Intelligence Service, was a sector head in the Third Section of the URPO, specializing in the struggle against internal terrorism. Both Lazovsky and Suslov were on good terms with Antropov.

It is worthwhile examining in greater detail this secret department of the FSB with its long, incomprehensible title that is impossible to remember and was frequently changed to prevent the public penetrating its veil of secrecy. The Office for the Analysis of Criminal Groups was established in order to identify and then neutralize (liquidate) sources of information representing a threat to state security. In other words, to carry out extra-judiciary killings, acts of provocation and terrorism, and abductions. One of Khokholkov's deputies was major-general N. Stepanov and another was the former minister of state security for the Republic of Kabardino-Balkaria, A. K. Makarychev. The UPP possessed its own external surveillance section; its own security consultant, Colonel Vladimir Simaev; its own technical measures section, and two private detective and bodyguard agencies called Stealth and Cosmic Alternative. The latter specialized in bugging pagers and mobile phones and other technical operational measures, while Stealth had a legendary reputation.

A private bodyguard and detective agency which changed its name periodically, Stealth was registered as a business in 1989, at the very dawn of perestroika by a Moscow resident called Ivanov, who was an agent of the Fifth Department of the KGB of the USSR (which subsequently became Department Z). Ivanov was used in the struggle against internal terrorism, and his line of contact was with a member of Colonel V. V. Lutsenko's department, which had provided operational support for the establishment and activities of Stealth. With the assistance of Lutsenko, who used the private bodyguard firm to resolve personal rather than operational matters (the free provision of various types of protection, or "roofs," for commercial organizations), during the period from 1989 to 1992, Stealth developed extensive contacts in the criminal underworld and the sphere of law enforcement, becoming one of the most well-known security agencies in Russia.

Following his discharge from the special agencies in 1992, Lutsenko took control of the detective and bodyguard firm, which he re-registered with himself as one of the partners. Lutsenko's solid connections in various departments of the former KGB, in combination with the exodus from the Russian security services of large numbers of experienced operatives who also maintained their own well-tested contacts and networks of agents, meant that Lutsenko was able to hire highly qualified professionals to work in Stealth.

From his old area of operations (the struggle against terrorism) Lutsenko had retained reliable contacts with representatives of the former Ninth Department of the KGB (protection of high-level national leaders). This made it possible for him to contact Korzhakov, Barsukov, and their entourages and offer them the services of Stealth, under his management, to assist the SBP and FSK in the less traditional forms of struggle against organized criminal activity.

His suggestion met with approval, and a general plan of action was rapidly developed with input from Korzhakov's first deputy, General G. G. Ragozin. The program envisaged the use of criminal and extremist organizations, individual criminals, and retrained military personnel from the special missions department of the GRU of the Ministry of Defense, the Ministry of the Interior, and the FSB to undermine and break up criminal groupings and physically eliminate underworld "bosses" and leaders of criminal organizations.

In practice, everything turned out according to that eternal Russian principle: "we wanted to do better, but things turned out the same as always." Stealth provided a "roof" for a range of commercial organizations and carried out various kinds of operations to put pressure on criminal and commercial competitors, up to and including contract killings. In support of this activity, Korzhakov, Barsukov, and Trofimov arranged for possible criminal investigations of the bodyguard firm by the law enforcement agencies and the security forces (the FSB, Ministry of the Interior, the tax police, the Public Prosecutor's Office) to be neutralized. The heads of all of these state departments were informed of the contents of the initial program for which Stealth had been set up, and an understanding was reached that their agencies would not investigate Stealth's activities.

Stealth used the Izmailovo organized criminal group as its strike force, but gradually the financial influence of the group and the infiltration of its personnel transformed Stealth into the Izmailovo group's "roof," or cover, and Lutsenko became its puppet leader. Other private security companies, such as Kmeti and Cobalt, also found themselves in the same situation. All of them were exploited to implement the existing program for combating organized crime by non-traditional means. They became implicated in a series of well-known contract killings of criminal leaders, businessmen, and bankers. The operatives who carried out these murders were hired killers from free-lance special agency groups. As a rule, all of the operations were planned and carried out in a highly professional manner, with the subsequent elimination, if necessary, of the hired killers themselves and the individuals who provided their cover. There was no prospect of investigations into this kind of crime ever producing a trial. Any criminals involved in the crimes, who happened to be detained, simply didn't live long enough to get to court.

In time, Stealth developed into an efficient bodyguard and detection organization, equipped with a wide range of technology, including special items and weapons (some of them illegal), with a payroll of up to 600 individuals. Approximately seventy percent of its personnel consisted of former members of the FSB and SBP, and about thirty percent were former members of the police force. Stealth was transferred to the UPP when it was set up in 1996, although it did maintain a certain degree of autonomy.

The main principle on which the UPP operated was "problem-solving": if there's a problem, then a solution must be found. Clues to the existence of this operating principle can be found in Pavel Sudoplatov's memoirs, published in Moscow in 1996, which happen to be the favorite reference text of the UPP's leaders. The murder of the president of Chechnya, Djokhar Dudaev, provides a good example of the problem-solving approach to the achievement of a combat goal. The people who organized this killing were also involved in setting up the UPP.

In a certain sense Dudaev's murder was a contract killing, but in this case, the leadership of the state put out the contract. The oral, but nonetheless official, order to eliminate Dudaev was given by Russian President Yeltsin. The prehistory to this decision is vague and mysterious. Some time after May 20, 1995, informal negotiations began between the Russian and Chechen sides on a cessation of military operations and the signing of a peace agreement. On the Chechen side, the negotiations were organized by the former General Public Prosecutor of Chechnya, Usman Imaev, and on the Russian side by the well-known businessman, Arkady Volsky. The Russians tried to persuade the Chechens to capitulate. On behalf of the Russian leadership, Volsky offered Dudaev the chance to leave Chechnya for any other country on his own terms (as Yeltsin put it: "anywhere he wants, and the farther from Russia the better").

The meeting with Dudaev was far from pleasant for Volsky. Dudaev felt he had been insulted, and he was in a fury. Volsky was probably only saved from immediate measures of reprisal by his parliamentary status. Imaev was not spared Dudaev's wrath either; soon afterwards he was accused of collaborating with the Russian secret services. Having been withdrawn from the negotiation process and demoted, Imaev returned to his native village of Kulary, where he turned pious and began preaching the norms of Muslim Shariah law. The Russian authorities made no attempt to prevent Imaev from traveling to Istanbul and Krakow, where the Chechens felt secure enough to engage in open anti-Russian propaganda. Dudaev expressed concern about Imaev's journey. Imaev returned to Chechnya shortly

before the Chechen president was assassinated and was last seen at a
Russian fortified position near the village of Kulary, where he had
gone for a meeting with representatives of the federal authorities.
Imaev told the men who accompanied him on the way to Kulary that
he would be back in a week. He and the people who had been waiting
for him flew off in a helicopter to an unknown destination, and he
was never seen again.

However, the negotiations begun by Volsky and Imaev did have a
sequel: Dudaev was able to reach an agreement with Moscow on
halting military operations. For the appropriate decree, Dudaev was
asked to pay another multi-million dollar bribe. He paid the money
so that no more people would be killed for nothing, but no decree
calling a halt to military operations emerged. The people in Yeltsin's
entourage had "dumped" the Chechens.

Then Dudaev ordered his lieutenant, Shamil Basaev, either to get
the money back or arrange for the beginning of peace talks and the
halt to military action, for which money had already been paid over.
Basaev came up with a novel idea. On June 14, 1995, he attempted
to coerce Korzhakov, Barsukov, and Soskovets into honoring their
debt by seizing a hospital in Budyonnovsk with more than a thousand
hostages. After all, this was a serious business deal he was trying to
close!

Responding to Basaev's occupation of the hospital, the Russian
special operations squad Alpha had already taken the first floor of the
building and was on the point of freeing the hostages and disposing
of the terrorists, when Russian Prime Minister Viktor Chernomyrdin,
who had undertaken to mediate, judged correctly that the Chechens
had been "dumped out of order." He promised to start peace talks
immediately, insisted on a halt to the operation to free the hostages,
and guaranteed Basaev's men an unhindered withdrawal to Chechnya. There was another chance to liberate the hostages and eliminate
Basaev's men on their way home, with the interior forces special sub-
unit Vityaz standing by, simply waiting for the order. However, the
order was not given: Chernomyrdin had given Basaev certain guarantees, and he had to keep his word.

On July 3, 1995, President Yeltsin signed the decree that Dudaev had paid for, No. 663: "On the stationing of agencies for the military management of communications, military units, institutions, and organizations of the armed forces of the Russian Federation on the territory of the Chechen Republic." On July 7, Yeltsin signed a second decree detailing the procedure for implementing the first.

After the seizure of the hostages at Budyonnovsk the Kremlin bureaucrats added Shamil Basaev's name to Dudaev's in their list of undesirable witnesses. They decided to eliminate him with the assistance of a specially established combat operations unit, commanded by the head of the Third Section (Intelligence) of the Military Counter-intelligence Department of the FSB of the Russian Federation, Major-General Yuri Yarovenko.

At the same time, a combat operations group was set up under the command of Khokholkov (in Chechnya, he worked under the pseudonym Denisov) in order to eliminate Dudaev. The group included a captain, first rank, Alexander Kamyshnikov (the future deputy head of the URPO), and a number of other officers. It was stationed at the military base in Khankala. Chechen nationals were also brought into the group, such as Umar Pasha, who had previously served in Dagestan, and following Dudaev's elimination was promoted and transferred to Moscow. Also used in the operation was the air arm of the GRU, which had two planes for targeting rockets on beacons in radiotelephones. Dudaev's ordinary phone was successfully switched for one with such a beacon.

On April 22, 1996, Dudaev, his wife Alla, and several companions set out from the settlement of Gekhi-Chu in the Urus-Martansk district of western Chechnya, where they had spent the night, and made their way into the woods. Dudaev always moved out of settled areas when he needed to make phone calls, because it was harder to get a fix on his position away from centers of population. There was no unbroken forest cover in that area, only scrub with occasional trees. Alla began preparing a meal, while the men stood off to one side. Dudaev didn't allow them to come close to him when he was talking on the phone, since there had already been one case of an air strike against him while he was making calls, but on that occasion the rocket had missed.

This time, however, Dudaev spoke on the phone for longer than usual (they say he was talking with the well-known Russian business-man and politician, Konstantin Borovoi, who stayed on the line to Dudaev until he was cut off). A guided missile from a Russian SU-24 assault plane, targeted on the signal from Dudaev's satellite phone, exploded close to Dudaev, and his face was burned a yellowish-orange color. The car was brought up, they put Dudaev in the back seat, and his wife sat beside him. Dudaev was unconscious, and he had a wound behind his right ear. He died without regaining con-sciousness. The State Defense Committee of Chechnya entrusted the arrangements for his funeral to Lecha Dudaev, the Chechen presi-dent's nephew. Dudaev's burial place can only have been known to a small circle of individuals, including Zelimkhan Yandarbiev, who suc-ceeded Dudaev as the chairman of the State Defense Committee and acting president of the Chechen Republic until the election of 1997, when Aslan Maskhadov was elected as president. According to Chechen sources, when Alla, the president's widow, and Musa Idigov, the president's personal bodyguard, were arrested at the airport in the town of Nalchik, Dudaev's remains were hurriedly reburied at a new site. Since Lecha Dudaev was killed during the second Chechen war, there have been no official sources stating where Djokhar Dudaev is buried.

The elimination of Dudaev was probably the most successful operation carried out by Khokholkov and his group. Khokholkov himself was nominated for the order of "Hero of Russia" for success-fully completing his mission, but he preferred the post of head of the newly founded URPO, with the rank of major general.

In the summer of 1996, after the Korzhakov-Barsukov-Soskovets group had fallen from power and General Lebed had been dismissed from his post as secretary of the Security Council, Stealth could no longer count on support from state structures and was left entirely under the control of the Izmailovo criminal group. Lutsenko's only remaining serious contacts at state level were now in the URPO, which was headed by General Khokholkov. The absorption of organized criminal groups into the state's agencies of coercion had seemed a natural and logical step to the leadership of the FSB. Unfortunately the logic of events tended more and more frequently to draw the secret services into purely criminal activity. In theory this tendency should have been countered by the Internal Security Department of the FSB, but in practice, the Internal Security Department was incapable of maintaining the fight against mass crime committed with the direct connivance or participation of the FSB and the SBP. The only hope left was the single remaining law enforcement agency, the Criminal Investigation Department. In January 1996, thirty-eight-year-old Vladimir Tskhai, "criminal investigation's last romantic," was transferred to the Moscow Criminal Investigation Department (the MUR).

CHAPTER THREE

Moscow Detectives Take on the FSB

TSKHAI WAS MADE head of the Twelfth Section, which specialized in solving contract killings, and only ten months later he was already the deputy chief of the MUR. He had previously worked in the Central Criminal Investigation Department of the Russian Ministry of the Interior. Tskhai was regarded as being an exceptionally hardworking and talented detective. "He was a born detective, and there'll never be another like him," was what his friends told us. "Tskhai was easy and interesting to work with," said Andrei Suprunenko, especially important cases investigator for the Moscow Public Prosecutor's Office. "A competent and decent man. One of the romantics. He provided the link between the operatives and the investigators, he believed that even the most complicated cases could be untangled. . ."

It was Tskhai who succeeded in exposing the group that produced fake identity cards from the departments of coercion. In that case, FAPSI contributed the efforts of its Internual Security Department headed by Colonel Sergei Barkovsky. In an article which was evidently commissioned by the FSB, the Moscow journalist, Alexander Khinshtein, wrote that Lazovsky himself oversaw the production of false documents, and that was why his people had cover documents from the FSB, FAPSI, GRU, and MO. However, this was not the case. Lazovsky had absolutely nothing to do with the business of forging official identity documents, which Tskhai uncovered. Naturally enough, Barkovsky doesn't even mention Lazovsky in his version of

events and names entirely different people as the organizers. Here are
Barkovsky's own words:

> Even the specialists found it rather difficult to distinguish the
> fakes from genuine documents. Sometimes the quality of the
> "dud" was actually better. Expert analysis showed that there
> was clearly just one workshop involved. Following a whole
> series of operational and investigative measures four, very far
> from ordinary, people were detained. One was the former
> deputy head of a section of the KGB of the USSR, who had
> become the head of a firm with the attractive name of Honor.
> Another was the head of one of the printing shops in Moscow
> and the former head of the printing shop of the administration
> of the Central Committee of the Communist Party. Detained
> together with them was a former FAPSI lieutenant who had
> been involved in processing passes during his period of serv-
> ice. It is assumed that the idea of producing counterfeit docu-
> ments must have been his. And there was one very talented
> engraver.

From Barkovsky's account, it follows that the forgeries were not
produced by bandits, but by a former member of the *nomenklatura*,
the Soviet professional elite (from the administrative apparatus of the
Central Committee of the Communist Party) and a member of the
secret services (FAPSI). If that is the case, the possibility cannot be
excluded that the laboratory for producing high-quality forgeries was
also set up with the permission of the FSB and FAPSI, and controlled
by them.

Let us get back to Lazovsky. The liquidation of his group during
the period from February to August of 1996 was the greatest success
achieved by the Twelfth Section of the MUR. The personnel of
Lazovsky's group were not organized on local territorial lines like
ordinary criminal groupings. Lazovsky's brigade was international,
which was a pointer to its distinctive nature. Working under Lazovsky
were Chechens, people from Kazakhstan, and gunmen from groups

based in towns close to Moscow. Marat Vasiliev was a Muscovite, Roman Polonsky was from Dubna, and Vladimir Abrosimov was from Tula, and Anzor Movsaev was from Grozny. . . . The brigade was very well equipped, too.

Lazovsky had been on the Russian federal wanted list from 1995, for offenses under article 209 ("banditry") of the Criminal Code of the Russian Federation. He was accused in connection with a number of different episodes. For instance, in December 1993, Lazovsky's group killed the guards who were transporting cash for the MMST Company, and 250 thousand dollars were stolen.

At the same time there were disputes between Lanako and the Viktor Corporation over deals involving deliveries of oil products. On January 10, 1994, persons unknown (obviously working for the Viktor Corporation) shelled the automobile of Vladimir Kozlovsky, a director and chairman of the management board at Lanako, with a grenade thrower. (The first syllable of Kozlovsky's surname had provided the third syllable of the name Lanako.) Barely two days later, on January 12, a bomb exploded outside an apartment belonging to one of Viktor's managers with such massive controlled force that the steel door was hurled into the apartment and clean through the next wall standing in its way. It was purely a matter of luck that no one in the apartment was hurt. The explosion, however, triggered off a fire in the apartment block, and neighbors were forced to jump from the windows. Two of them were killed, and several other people were injured.

On January 13, unknown persons turned up at Lanako's Moscow offices, at corpus 3 of 2 Perevedenovsky Lane, where insult swapping with Lanako's staff was followed by an exchange of gunfire. Ten minutes later, two busloads of SWAT officers arrived at the Lanako offices, where they overcame armed resistance and took the office by storm (it was only by good luck that there were no casualties). They then proceeded to ransack the offices, arrest about sixty people, and take them away to the station, where they were recorded on videotape. After that, almost everyone was allowed to go. The only persons still detained at the station the following day were four bodyguards who had firearms in their possession when they were arrested. They were later tried, but received surprisingly lenient treatment for a shoot-out with the police. The court released two, and two were given one year's penal servitude.

On March 4, 1994, a full-scale battle broke out in the Dagmos Restaurant on Kazakov Street between Lazovsky's gunmen and members of a Dagestani criminal organization, with about thirty men involved from each side. The final tally was seven dead and two wounded. All of the dead were members of the Dagestani group.

On June 16, 1994, three members of the Taganka criminal group were mowed down by machine-gun fire near the offices of the Credit-Consensus Bank. Lazovsky had demanded that the bank pay him two-and-a-half billion rubles in interest on a sum of money over which the bank was in dispute with the Rosmyasmoloko firm, and the bank had turned for help to the Taganka group, its "roof." The battle was sparked off by the Taganka bandits' refusal to pay Lazovsky.

Lazovsky committed one of his most brutal crimes on September 5, 1994. That year, arguments had flared up between Lazovsky and his partner, the joint owner of the Grozny Oil Refinery, Atlan Nataev (whose surname had provided the second syllable of Lanako's company title). Nataev was last seen at about ten o'clock in the evening on September 5, close to the Dinamo subway station, in a dark-blue BMW 740 that belonged to Lanako. He was with two bodyguards, Robert Rudenko and Vladimir Lipatov, who disappeared with him. Lazovsky did not bother to report the disappearance of his colleagues to the police.

By circumstantial coincidence, on September 7, the head of the Regional Department for Combating Organized Crime (RUOP), Vladimir Dontsov, escorted by ten men wielding automatic weapons, carried out an "operational inspection" at the Lanako offices. During the search, RUOP's personnel discovered a certain quantity of unlicensed arms, in particular TT pistols intended for resale on the illegal market. However, the find was not treated as seriously as it should have been, and no arrests were made.

It emerged later that Nataev, Rudenko, and Lipatov had been kidnapped by Polonsky and Schelenkov, and taken to a dacha in the Academy of Science's suburban settlement outside Moscow. Nataev was killed, and his corpse was beheaded. Then the corpse and the two bodyguards were driven to the peat bogs in the Yaroslavl district, where Rudenko and Lipatov were also beheaded. All three bodies were buried in the peat, from which members of the MUR recovered them in 1996. The identity pass of a General Staff officer was discovered on Nataev's corpse.

On September 18, Nataev's brother arrived in Moscow in a state of alarm. Lazovsky summoned him to talks at a parking lot on Burakov Street, which belonged to his uncle, Nikolai Lazovsky. The owner of the parking lot sent his bodyguards home so that there would be no witnesses, and when the second Nataev arrived, Schelenkov, Polonsky, and Grishin met him with a hail of bullets from automatic weapons, pistols and even a sawn-off shotgun. Nataev returned fire fourteen times, and before he was killed, he managed to gun down Polonsky and Grishin. The exchange of fire was so intensive that several cars in the parking lot caught fire. When the police arrived on the scene, all they found were pools of blood and spent cartridges. A few minutes later, news reached them from an emergency ambulance station where doctors had Polonsky's body (six unknown persons had blocked off Korolenko Street with their Volga automobile, stopped an emergency ambulance, and handed over Polonsky to the medics).

Lazovsky's group was also responsible for the killing of the general director of the Tuapsi Oil refinery, Anatoly Vasilenko, an old business associate of Lanako, who was shot in Tuapsi shortly before a meeting of the partners in the refinery. According to operational information, not long before the shooting, Lazovsky had taken a charter flight to Tuapsi for a meeting with Vasilenko (Lazovsky was met at the airport by members of the Tuapsi FSB), and had apparently failed to reach an understanding with him. Lazovsky was also suspected of the abduction in 1996 of State Duma deputy Yu. A. Polyakov, but this case remained a "loose end" that was never tied up.

It is obvious that no attempt was made to bring in Lazovsky before Tskhai was transferred to the MUR. No attention had been paid to Lanako after the Yauza bombing, primarily because it was an FSB outfit. According to the MUR, almost all the members of Lazovsky's group used "cover documents" which were not fakes, but the genuine item. This led the MUR operatives to draw the correct conclusion that Lanako had close links with the secret services, especially as Lazovsky himself took part in operations to free FSB personnel who had been taken prisoner in Chechnya.

The MUR, which at that time was headed by Savostianov, repeatedly observed and even detained senior Lanako personnel in the company of FSB officers. Lazovsky's personal bodyguard and his firm's security service were headed by a serving officer from the Moscow Department for Illegal Armed Formations of the FSB, Major Alexei Yumashkin, who employed FSB officers Karpychev and Mekhkov (on one of the occasions when Lazovsky was arrested, they produced their FSB passes and were released, together with Lazovsky). Lazovsky's close friend and comrade-in-arms, Roman Polonsky, used to carry in his pocket the identity card of a member of the GRU and General Staff officer. When Polonsky was shot down at the parking lot on Burakov Street on September 18, he had a GRU holster on his belt and a GRU identity card in his pocket.

In February 1996, MUR operatives traced Lazovsky to an apartment on Sadovo-Samotechnaya Street in Moscow, which belonged to an individual by the name of Trostanetsky. Lazovsky and his bodyguard Marcel Kharisov were arrested in the yard of the building as they got into a jeep, which was being driven by Yumashkin (who was also immediately detained). Tskhai arrested Lazovsky in person. He himself had obtained the sanction for his arrest and the search warrants, since no one else wanted to get involved in the case. When searched, Lazovsky was found to be carrying 1.03 grams of cocaine and a loaded PM pistol, while a revolver, a grenade, and a shotgun were removed from Trostanetsky's apartment. Kharisov was also discovered to be carrying an unlicensed TT pistol. He and Lazovsky were taken to the FSB's detention center at Lefortovo, where they refused to answer the investigator's questions. The FSB duty officer took Yumashkin away.

In addition to MUR, Lazovsky's case was also dealt with by the First Section of the Department for Combating Terrorism of the FSK of the Russian Federation, where it had been handled since 1994 by Major Yevgeny Makeiev, a senior operations officer for especially important cases. The head of the First Section at that time was Alexander Platonov. Even then, the operatives understood just who Lazovsky was and who stood behind him, which was why Platonov warned Makeiev that it was a difficult and complicated case, gave him a small separate office to share with just one colleague on the ninth floor of the newly refurbished old Lubyanka building, and asked him not to discuss the contents of the operational report with any one. The colleague who found himself in Makeiev's office was Alexander Litvinenko, one of the authors of this book, who first learned from Makeiev that the Moscow Department of the FSB had been transformed into a gang of criminals.

Makeiev worked in a highly conspiratorial manner. As a rule, he himself was the only member of his section who attended joint operations meetings with the MUR, carrying a MUR identity pass as a cover. In 1995, Platonov was removed from operational duties and Lieutenant Colonel Yevgeny Kolesnikov (who is now a major-general) became the new head of the section. Kolesnikov joined the FSB from the FSO after Barsukov was appointed head of the FSB in June 1995. Further work on the case of Lazovsky's group was blocked. The only person who would now sanction any measures concerning Lazovsky was the deputy section head, Anatoly Rodin, who was appointed in Platonov's time. Then Rodin and Makeiev were both dismissed.

In its investigations into Lazovsky and Lanako, MUR identified six Moscow Department FSB operatives as being involved in Lazovsky's gang. Journalists got wind of this and on November 11, 1996, *Novaya Gazeta* published the text of a letter of inquiry written by its deputy senior editor, Yuri Schekochikhin, a deputy of the State Duma:

To: Director of the FSB of the Russian Federation
N. D. Kovalyov

Copies: Minister of the Interior of the Russian Federation
A. S. Kulikov; Public Prosecutor General of the Russian Federation Yu. I. Skuratov; Head of the Office of the President of the Russian Federation A. B. Chubais.

The Security Committee of the State Duma of Russia has received a letter addressed to me from a high-ranking officer of the Ministry of the Interior of the Russian Federation. The letter claims, in particular, that "recent times have seen the emergence of a tendency for organized criminal groupings to merge with members of the agencies of law enforcement and the secret services." In order to be able to confirm or refute the conclusion drawn by the author of the letter, I request you to reply to the following series of questions.

1. Are the following people named in the letter listed among the personnel of the FSB for Moscow and the Moscow Region: S. N. Karpychev, A. A. Yumashkin, E. A. Abovian, L. A. Dmitriev, A. A. Dokukin?

2. Is it true that since last year Sergei Kublitsky, who has a criminal record and is now the president of the firm *Vityaz*, which specializes in oil operations, has been using as his personal bodyguards members of the FSB for Moscow and the Moscow Region, S. N. Karpychev and S. N. Mekhkov, and that on several occasions they have accompanied him to meetings with the management of the Tuapsi Oil Refinery and representatives of the firm Atlas, which holds a controlling interest in the refinery?

3. Is it true that investigators from the Public Prosecutor's Office of the city of Krasnodar have made several attempts to

interview as a witness to the murder of a director of the Tuapsi Oil Refinery one Major A. A. Yumashkin, an employee of the FSB for Moscow and the Moscow Region, who also provides personal security services to M. M. Lazovsky, the leader of an inter-regional criminal grouping, but that they have been unable to do so? How accurate is information that since 1994, Major A. A. Yumashkin has been Lazovsky's intimate business partner and that they have on several occasions traveled together to Tuapsi and Krasnodar, where they have jointly decided matters relating to the oil business?

4. Is it true that on February 17 of this year, employees of the FSB for Moscow and the Moscow Region, A. A. Yumashkin, S. N. Karpychev, and S. N. Mekhkov, were detained together with S. P. Kubitsky and M. M. Lazovsky by employees of the Ministry of the Interior of the Russian Federation? If so, then how true is it that after the FSB identity cards presented by Karpychev and Mekhkov had been checked, they were both released? Were the leadership of the FSB and First Deputy Minister of the Interior of the RF Lieutenant-General V. I. Kolesnikov informed that employees of the FSB for Moscow and the Moscow Region had been detained? It is true that the prisoner Lazovsky is suspected by agencies of law enforcement and the Office of the Public Prosecutor of the RF of involvement in a number of contract killings? Has the prisoner Kublitsky been questioned at the request of specialists from the law enforcement agencies of the Krasnodar Region who are investigating the murder of the director of the Tuapsi Oil Refinery?

5. Is it true that on October 16 of last year, employees of the Moscow RUOP detained A. N. Yanin, born 1958, a resident of Moscow, and that the documents confiscated from him included a check for luggage checked in at the left luggage office of the Central Airport Terminal? Is it true that members of the police discovered in Yanin's luggage five AKS-74U automatic

weapons not registered in the card index of the MVD of the
RF, five magazines for the AKSes, 30 5.45 caliber, and three
7.62 caliber cartridges? Is it accurate to assert that these arms
had been confiscated from criminal groups and, according to
official documents, were kept onsite at the FSB for Moscow
and the Moscow Region? Is the information correct, according to which after investigator Sholokhova initiated criminal
proceedings against A. N. Yanin at the 'Airport' Criminal
Police Service under the number 1646 in accordance with
article 218 4.1 of the Criminal Code of the Russian Federation, two employees of the Service for Combating Illegal
Armed Formations and Banditry of the FSB for Moscow and
the Moscow Region arrived at RUOP and that one of them,
Colonel Edward Abovian, obtained the release of the prisoner
Yanin from custody? If this is so, did Colonel Abovian, in
insisting on Yanin's release, have any basis for asserting, and
did he, in fact, assert that he was carrying out instructions
from his immediate superior, General Semeniuk, and that
First Deputy Director of the FSB of the RF and head of the
FSB for Moscow and the Moscow Region, General Trofimov,
was aware of this? Does Colonel Abovian have free access to
the special technology and armaments, which the FSB for
Moscow and the Moscow Region has at its disposal? What
connection, if any, exists between colonel Abovian and the
commercial activities of the Mosinraschyot Bank and the Tver
Beer Combine?

6. Is it true that on October 17 of this year, employees of the
RUOP of the Northern District of the City of Moscow detained
a BMW 525 automobile with detachable number plates 41-34
MOK, which had previously been used by S. P. Kubitsky, whom
I have already mentioned and who is better known in criminal
circles as "Vorkuta?" Did the automobile contain a driver who
was carrying no documents and three passengers who showed
the RUOP employees identity cards for employees of the FSB

for Moscow and the Moscow Region in the names of captain
L. A. Dmitriev and Warrant Officer A. A. Dokukin, following
which they were released?

> Yours sincerely,
> Yuri Schekochikhin,
> Member of the Security Committee of the
> State Duma of the Russian Federation

Abovian, the FSB colonel working in the section for combating illegal
bandit groups who is mentioned in Schekochikhin's inquiry, was
Lazovsky's controller at the FSB.

On November 23, 1996, First Deputy Minister of the Interior
Vladimir Kolesnikov, sent Schekochikhin a reply via the Duma committee in which he stated: "Indeed . . . in the course of operations
undertaken in Moscow to capture armed criminals in addition to
Lazovsky, the persons handed over to the agencies of the Ministry of
the Interior included individuals who presented identification from
the law enforcement agencies and other state services. . . . Under the
present state of measures taken, Lazovsky and the other accomplices
stand accused of more than ten premeditated murders in various
regions of Russia. . . ."

Kolesnikov avoided giving direct answers to the specific questions
raised by Schekochikhin in his inquiry. There was nothing to do but
wait for the criminals to be brought to trial.

FSB director Kovalyov had two meetings with Schekochikhin. At
the end of the year, Schekochikhin received two replies from him,
essentially identical in content. One was secret and has remained in
the archives of the State Duma. Schekochikhin made the other, open
reply public:

> The Federal Security Service has carried out an internal inves-
> tigation into facts and circumstances presented in the Duma
> deputy's letter of inquiry in *Novaya Gazeta*. . . . Investigations
> have determined that the actions of the [FSB employees]

involved certain deviations from the requirements of departmental regulations which, in combination with a lack of practical experience and professionalism, could well have served as
the cause of the incident which has attracted your attention. In
this regard, particular concern is occasioned by the fact that a
conflict occurred between the members of two departments
that engage in operational and investigative activity in the criminal environment. Nonetheless, despite this regrettable misun-
derstanding, the main goal was achieved, since Lazovsky's
gang was neutralized. . . .

Kovalyov's "particular concern" was not occasioned by the collaboration of the FSB for Moscow and the Moscow Region with organized
criminal groups, terrorists, and underworld "bosses," but by the
actions of MUR employees under Tskhai's leadership. As for the
actual employees of the FSB, Kovalyov discerned in their behavior no
more than "certain deviations from the requirements of departmental
regulations." From his own point of view Kovalyov was right. He saw
no difference in principle between members of the secret services and
Lazovsky's gunmen, and so he genuinely could not understand the
reasons for Schekochikhin's indignation. Schekochikhin believed that
the representatives of the people, in the persons of members of the
State Duma, and the agencies of state security, fight together against
bandits and terrorists. However, Kovalyov knew that the FSB and the
extra-departmental agencies of coercion, which the people call bandits and terrorists, actually wage their struggle against the very people
represented in the Duma by Schekochikhin and others like him.

Naturally, no internal FSB inquiry was ever held, and nobody was
dismissed. Abovian was apparently given a new name and retained in
service. No records of any investigations were submitted to any court
or military tribunal. A reply was received from the first deputy senior
military prosecutor, lieutenant-general of justice G. N. Nosin, to the
following effect: "On the basis of the results of an investigation concerning the officers of the FSB for Moscow and the Moscow Region
mentioned in the letter, the instigation of criminal proceedings has

been rejected." In reply to an inquiry from a correspondent of the Kommersant newspaper concerning Yumashkin, the Moscow FSB gave the honest answer that Yumashkin had been carrying out a special mission to monitor the activities of Lazovsky's group. In 1997, however, Major Yumashkin was finally exposed and became a key figure in criminal proceedings concerning contract killings, which were initiated by the Tagansky District Public Prosecutor's Office of the City of Moscow. Since even his involvement in organizing contract killings was apparently part of his special mission, Yumashkin continued to serve in the Moscow FSB, and in 1999, he was promoted on schedule to the military rank of lieutenant colonel.

The only person to suffer as a result of Schekochikhin's inquiry was the head of the Moscow FSB and deputy director of the FSB of Russia, Anatoly Trofimov, who was removed from his post in February 1997. Sergei Yastrzhembsky, press secretary to the president of Russia, declared that Trofimov had been removed "for gross irregularities exposed by an inquiry conducted by the Accounting Chamber of the Russian Federation and dereliction of duty." It is widely believed, however, that Trofimov was simply made a scapegoat.

According to another version of events, Trofimov was dismissed because he attempted to do something about the substance of Schekochikhin's inquiry. Supposedly, having read the letter of inquiry, Trofimov summoned one of his deputies and ordered him to draw up the paperwork for the dismissal of all the members of the FSB who were mentioned in it. His deputy refused. Trofimov then suggested that he should submit his resignation. In the end, the scandal surrounding the arrest of two of Trofimov's subordinates was exploited to have Trofimov himself dismissed. The two were arrested for dealing in cocaine by the MUR and the Central Department for the Illegal Circulation of Narcotics. Trofimov was fired two days after the media reported the arrest of drug dealers carrying the identity passes of officers in the Moscow FSB.

It should be emphasized that the question of the involvement of particular FSB officers or of the FSB, as a whole, in terrorist activity, which had been attributed to the Chechens, was not raised either in

Schekochikhin's inquiry or in the replies given by various officials. The court did not pass a guilty verdict on any of the members of the coercive departments who were suspected, according to Vladimir Kolesnikov, of a total of more than ten murders. On January 31, 1997, Lazovsky and Kharisov appeared before the Tver court in a trial which lasted only three days. They were accused of possessing weapons and drugs and of forging FAPSI and MO documents. Not a single prosecutor or judge so much as hinted at terrorist attacks and contract killings. The accused's lawyers demonstrated quite correctly that no forgery had been committed, since they had carried genuine identity documents for agents of the secret services and agencies of coercion, and so the charge of forging documents had to be dropped. The case materials contained no information at all about the use of forgeries by the accused (which was in itself weighty evidence of the interfusion of the structures headed by Barsukov, Kovalyov, and Lazovsky). The count of possessing and transporting dangerous drugs was also dropped—so that Lazovsky and Kharisov would not have to be charged under such a serious article of the Criminal Code.

Lazovsky's lawyer, Boris Kozhemyakin, also tried to have the charge of possessing weapons set aside. He claimed that when they were arrested, Lazovsky and Kharisov were with FSB employee Yumashkin, with whom they had spent a large part of the day, that both Lazovsky and Kharisov were engaged in carrying out certain tasks for the secret services, and that was why they had been given weapons and cover documents. (When he was arrested, FSB agent Yumashkin was also found to be in possession of a cover document, a police identity card.) However, for some reason, the question of collaboration between Lazovsky and Kharisov and the secret services failed to interest judge Elena Stashina, and representatives of the FSB refused to appear in court, with the result that the accused were in any case found guilty of the illegal possession of weapons, and sentenced by an impartial court to two years' imprisonment and a fine of forty million rubles each. When he heard the sentence, Boris Kozhemyakin said, he had been counting on a more lenient verdict.

Lazovsky served his time in one of the prison camps near Tula together with his co-defendant and bodyguard Kharisov (which is strictly forbidden by regulations). While in the camp, he recruited new members for his group from among the criminal inmates, studied the Bible, and even wrote a treatise on the improvement of Russia. He was released in February 1998, since the time he spent in custody, while under investigation, was counted against his sentence.

Meanwhile in 1996, Russia had lost the war in Chechnya. Military operations had to be halted and political negotiations conducted with the Chechen separatists. There was a real threat that the conflict between two nations, which had cost the secret services so much effort to provoke, might end in a peace agreement, and Yeltsin might be able to return to his program of liberal reforms. In order to undermine the peace negotiations, the FSB carried out a series of terrorist attacks in Moscow. Since terrorist attacks, which didn't kill or maim had failed to make any impression on the inhabitants of the capital, the FSB began carrying out attacks which did. Note, once again, how well the supporters of war timed their terrorist attacks, and how damaging they were to the interests of supporters of peace and the Chechens themselves.

Between nine and ten in the evening on June 11, 1996, there was an explosion in a half-empty carriage in a train at the Tulskaya station of the Serpukhovskaya line of the Moscow subway. Four people were killed and 12 were hospitalized. Exactly one month later, on July 11, a terrorist bomb exploded in a number twelve trolley in Pushkin Square: six people were injured. The following day, July 12, an explosion destroyed a number 48 trolley on Mir Prospect: twenty-eight people were injured. Information about the "Chechen connection" of the terrorist attacks was actively disseminated throughout Moscow (even though no terrorists were caught, and it was never actually determined whether they were Chechens or not). Before even a provisional investigation had been conducted, the mayor of Moscow, Yuri Luzhkov, declared at the site of the second trolley explosion that he would expel the entire Chechen diaspora from Moscow, even though he had no reason to suspect that the explosions were the work of the diaspora, or even of individual Chechen terrorists.

However, this second wave of terror failed, like the first, to produce any sharp swing in public opinion. In early August 1996, guerrilla fighters battled their way into Grozny, and in late August, the
Khasavyurt Accords were signed by Security Council Secretary
A. Lebed and the new president of Chechnya, Aslan Maskhadov. The
supporters of war in Chechnya had lost, and terrorist attacks in
Moscow came to a halt-until the FSB launched a new operation
designed to spark off another Chechen war.

It is hard to tell just which of the FSB's operatives organized the
explosions in Moscow in the summer of 1996. Lazovsky was under
arrest. It is clear, however, that the FSB had a choice of many similar
structures, and not just in Moscow. On June 26,1996, the newspaper *Segodnya* published a commentary on the FSB's criminal
organization in St. Petersburg, which consisted "primarily of former
members of the KGB." Having set up several firms, in addition to
what might be called "clean" business dealings, the ex-KGB men also
managed the trade in hand-guns, explosives and drugs, dealt in stolen
automobiles and imported stolen Mercedes and BMWs into Russia.

The explosions in Moscow could, however, have been set up by
members of Lazovsky's group who were still at large. In fact, there is
very good reason for believing this to be the case.

In February 1996, MUR agents arrested a certain Vladimir Akimov outside the pawnshop on Moscow's Bolshaya Spasskaya Street for
trying to sell a "Taurus" revolver. Akimov turned out to be Lazovsky's
former chauffeur. Under the influence of reports in the media about
the new wave of terrorist attacks on public transport in Moscow in
June and July 1996, Akimov began providing testimony about an
explosion in a bus on December 27, 1994. "Today, here in detention
center 48/1, and seeing the political situation on the television," Akimov wrote, "I consider it my duty to make a statement on the explosion of the bus. . . ." In his statement he claimed that on December
27, he and Vorobyov had set out to "reconnoiter" the bus stop in a
Zhiguli automobile. They noted possible lines of retreat. On the
evening of the same day, Akimov and Vorobyov left the Zhiguli not far

from the stop at the end of the bus route and went back to Mir Prospect, where they boarded the number 33 bus. When there were just a few passengers left in the bus, Akimov's testimony continued, they planted a bomb with forty grams of ammonite under a seat near the right rear wheel. When they got out at the last stop, Akimov went to warm up the engine of their car, and Vorobyov used a remote control unit to set the bomb.

On the morning of August 28, 1996, retired Lieutenant Colonel Vorobyov had been arrested by Tskhai, as he was on his way to a meeting with an FSB agent and taken to the MUR department at 38 Petrovka Street, where, if the judgment of the court is to be believed, he told the entire story to the Moscow detectives without attempting to conceal anything, including the fact that he was a free-lance FSB agent. Shortly thereafter, Akimov withdrew his testimony, even though it had been given in writing. Vorobyov then also withdrew his testimony. The Moscow City Court, under presiding Judge Irina Kulichkova, evidently acting under pressure from the FSB, dropped the charges against Akimov of complicity in a terrorist bombing and sentenced him to three years imprisonment for the illegal sale of a revolver. Since the guilty verdict was pronounced in late April 1999, and Akimov had spent three years in custody while under investigation, he left the court a free man.

Vorobyov was sentenced to five years in the prison camps. The case was held *in camera*, and not even Vorobyov's relatives were allowed into the courtroom. As his employer, the FSB gave Vorobyov a positive character reference that was included in the case materials. In his final address, Vorobyov declared that the case against him had been fabricated by parties who wished to blacken the name of the FSB and his name as a free-lance agent of the special service. Vorobyov described the sentence as "an insult to the special agencies." Later, the Supreme Court of the Russian Federation reduced Vorobyov's sentence to three years (most of which Vorobyov had already served by that time). In late August 1999, Vorobyov was released, despite the fact that Akimov and the investigators believed that he had been involved in the terrorist attacks of 1996. The FSB had demonstrated yet again that it would not abandon its own agents and would eventually obtain their release.

Tskhai also learned about the involvement of Lazovsky's group in the summer explosions from one other source, Sergei Pogosov. In the late summer and early fall of 1996, an operational source reported that a certain Sergei Pogosov was living in the center of Moscow on the Novyi Arbat Street, not far from the bookstore Dom Knigi and the Oktyabr cinema in a huge penthouse apartment totaling 100 or 150 square meters. His firm's office was located in the ground-floor apartment of the same block. According to information received, Pogosov was directly linked with Lazovsky and his gunmen and financed many of Lazovsky's undertakings. Pogosov's telephones were tapped and monitored for two weeks on the instructions of the First Section of the Antiterrorist Center of the FSB. From conversations overheard, it became clear that Pogosov was paying Lazovsky's legal fees and was preparing a large sum of money to pay bribes for his release.

This operational information was relayed to Tskhai, who personally obtained permission from the Public Prosecutor's Office for a search of Pogosov's flat and office as part of the criminal investigation into Lazovsky's case. A few days later, the search was carried out jointly by the Twelfth Section of the MUR and the First Section of the Antiterrorist Center of the FSB, which lasted almost all night. Under Pogosov's bed, a sack was found containing 700 thousand dollars. No one tried to count the rubles, which were lying everywhere, even in the kitchen in empty jars. Cocaine was also found in the apartment (Pogosov's girlfriend was a drug addict). The search at Pogosov's office on the ground floor turned up several mobile phones, one of which was registered to Lazovsky. Pogosov and his girlfriend were taken to the police station, but that very day a member of the Moscow FSB drove to the station and collected them. The police did not confiscate the money. The tax police said that it had nothing to do with them and didn't even bother to turn up. No criminal case was brought in connection with the discovery of the cocaine. Apparently nobody was interested in Pogosov or his money.

Knowing the way things were done in the Russian agencies of coercion, Pogosov expected that the people who had come to search his apartment would just take him away and kill him, so he attempted to save himself by giving a written undertaking to cooperate (under the pseudonym of Grigory). Pogosov told one of the operatives about Lazovsky's connections in the Moscow FSB and the kind of activity in which he was involved. Pogosov had heard from "Max" that his brigade was not a group of bandits, but more like a secret military unit, that Lazovsky handled tasks of state importance, and there were people like him in every country. Pogosov said Lazovsky was a state assassin who eliminated people according to instructions, and organized acts of sabotage and terrorism. Lazovsky himself only carried out the instructions, and he got those from the top.

Concerning the money, Pogosov said it was for Lazovsky, and he was only an intermediary. Pogosov's legal cover for his activities was importing "Parliament" cigarettes into Russia, which generates quite a good income in itself. Pogosov said that he expected Lazovsky to be freed soon, since he hadn't broken down under questioning, he hadn't given anyone away, and had behaved "with dignity." Pogosov sincerely recommended not interfering with the activities of Lazovsky's group and said Tskhai would have serious problems if he tried.

A few days after Pogosov was released, he had his second and final meeting with the operative who had recruited him. First of all, Pogosov offered money for the return of his note. He said that his controllers in the Moscow FSB were extremely displeased about his note and had told Pogosov to "ransom" it. His controllers had also made direct threats against Tskhai.

Pogosov's written statement was not returned, and the offer of a bribe was not accepted. The following day, the recruitment of agent Grigory was officially reported to the chief. A few days later, the phone rang in the office of the operative who had recruited Pogosov. The caller spoke from the Moscow FSB, on behalf of their own chief, politely recommending that Pogosov should be left in peace and threatening that if he weren't, there would be an investigation into money that had supposedly been stolen during the search at Pogosov's apartment. The operative never saw Pogosov again and never received any secret information from him. On April 12, 1997, at the age of thirty-nine, Tskhai died suddenly from cirrhosis of the liver, although he didn't drink or smoke. Presumably he was poisoned by the FSB, because he had discovered the identities of the true leaders of Lazovsky's group and realized exactly who had organized the explosions in Moscow. Poisons of a type that could have been used to kill Tskhai were made in a special FSB laboratory, which according to some sources was located at 42 Krasnobogatyrskaya Street in Moscow. The same building is also said to have been used for printing the high-quality counterfeit dollars used by the FSB to pay for contract killings and other counterintelligence operations. The laboratories had been in existence since Soviet times (the dollars were supposed to be printed in case of war).

On April 15, 1997, a funeral service was held for Tskhai, and he was buried at the Vagankovskoe Cemetery. After Tskhai's death, the investigation into Lazovsky's group deteriorated into a series of sporadic episodes. At the MUR, Lazovsky's case supposedly became the responsibility, by turn, of Pyotr Astafiev, Andrei Potekhin, Igor Travin, V. Budkin, A. Bazanov, G. Boguslavsky, V. Bubnov, and A. Kalinin, and it was also dealt with by the investigator for specially important cases Andrei Suprunenko, who first interrogated Lazovsky as early as 1996.

When Lazovsky was released in February 1998, he bought himself a luxurious mansion in an elite rural housing estate at Uspenskoe in the Odinovtsovsky district of Podmoskovie (the area round Moscow), which was reached by way of the Rublyovskoe Highway, and then set up a fund "for the support of peace in the Caucasus" under the title of "Unification," in which he took the position of vice president. Lazovsky continued his collaboration with the secret services. He was kept under observation following his release by Mikhail Fonaryov, an officer of the Criminal Investigation Department of the Moscow district, but no details are known of his activities during this period.

CHAPTER FOUR

Nikolai Patrushev
A Biographical Note

WHEREAS DURING the first Chechen war of 1994–1996, the state security forces had simply been attempting to forestall Russia's development towards a liberal-democratic society, the political goals of the second Chechen war were far more serious: to provoke Russia into war with Chechnya, and to exploit the ensuing commotion to seize power in Russia at the forthcoming presidential elections in 2000. The "honor" of provoking a war with Chechnya fell to the new director of the FSB, Colonel-General Patrushev.

Patrushev was born in Leningrad on July 11, 1951. In 1974, he graduated from the Leningrad Shipbuilding Institute and was assigned to the institute's design office, where he worked as an engineer. Just one year later, in 1975, he was invited to join the KGB, completed the one-year course at the Higher School of the KGB of the USSR, specializing in law, and joined the KGB's Leningrad branch. There, he served as junior operations officer, head of the city agency, deputy head of the regional agency, and head of the service for combating smuggling and corruption of the KGB Department for Leningrad and the Leningrad Region. By 1990, he had risen to the rank of colonel. Until 1991, he was a member of the Communist Party.

In 1990, Patrushev was transferred to Karelia, where he initially served as head of the local counterintelligence department. In 1992, he became Karelia's Minister of Security. In 1994, when the Leningrader Stepashin became director of the FSK, he called Patrushev to

Moscow to serve as head of one of the key divisions in the Lubyanka, the Internal Security Department of the FSK of the Russian Federation. The Internal Security Department of the FSK was counterintelligence within counterintelligence, the section which gathered compromising information on the FSK's own personnel. The head of the FSB had always been the FSK/FSB director's most trusted ally, reporting to him directly.

By moving Patrushev to Moscow, Stepashin saved him from the consequences of a serious scandal. In Karelia, Patrushev had gotten into difficulties over the theft and smuggling of precious Karelian birch timber, and the Public Prosecutor's Office of Petrozavodsk had initiated criminal proceedings against him, although he had initially only been a witness in the case. In the course of the investigation, facts had emerged which virtually proved his guilt as an accomplice. It was at this moment that Stepashin transferred Patrushev to a very high position in Moscow, well beyond the reach of the Public Prosecutor's Office of Karelia. Fortunately for Patrushev, the head of the FSB for the Republic of Karelia, Vassily Ankudinov, who could have told us a great deal about Patrushev and Karelian birch, died at the age of 56 on May 21, 2001.

In June 1995, Mikhail Barsukov replaced Stepashin as head of the FSK. In the summer of 1996, Nikolai Kovalyov replaced Barsukov. Neither Barsukov nor Kovalyov regarded Patrushev as their own man and did nothing to promote him. Then Vladimir Putin, who knew Patrushev from Leningrad, became the head of the president's Central Control Department and invited his old acquaintance to become his first deputy. Patrushev moved over to Putin's team.

Patrushev's subsequent rapid professional ascent is linked with Putin's own rise. When Putin became first deputy head of the President's Administration in May 1998, he promoted Patrushev to the vacant position of head of the president's Central Control Department. In October the same year, Patrushev returned to the Lubyanka, initially as Putin's deputy, a post to which he was appointed by Yeltsin in a decree of July 25, 1998, and later as First Deputy Director of the FSB.

On March 29, 1999, Yeltsin appointed Putin Secretary of the Security Council of the Russian Federation, while leaving him in position as director of the FSB, and on August 9 the same year, Yeltsin appointed Putin Prime Minister of Russia. In summing up the first few months of his administration, *Novaya Gazeta* wrote: "Long, long ago in a highly democratic country an elderly president entrusted the post of chancellor and prime minister to a young and energetic successor. Then the Reichstag went up in flames. . . . Historians have not yet given us an answer to the question of who set fire to it, but history has shown us who benefited." In Russia, however, "an elderly Guarantor [of the Constitution] entrusted the post of prime minister to a successor who had yet to be democratically elected. Then apartment blocks were blown up, and a new war began in Chechnya, and this war was glorified by arch-liars."

These events which shook the entire country were also linked with the ascendancy of one other man: on the day Putin became Prime Minister of Russia, Patrushev was given the directorship of the FSB. People with inside knowledge claim that Putin had no choice but to promote Patrushev, because Patrushev was in possession of compromising material about him. On August 17, 1999, Nikolai Patrushev was appointed director of the Federal Security Service of Russia. And then it began...

CHAPTER FIVE

The FSB Fiasco in Ryazan

*When someone commits a crime, it's very important
to catch him while the trail is still hot.*
Nikolai Patrushev on the events in Ryazan.
Itogi, 5 October 1999

IN SEPTEMBER 1999, monstrous acts of terrorism were perpetrated in Buinaksk, Moscow, and Volgodonsk.

We shall begin with the terrorist attack, which could have been the most terrible of them all, if it had not been foiled. On September 22, something unexpected happened: in Ryazan, FSB operatives were spotted planting sugar sacks containing hexogen in the bedroom community of Dashkovo-Pesochnya.

At 9:15 P.M., Alexei Kartofelnikov, a driver for the Spartak soccer club who lived in the single-entrance, twelve-story block built more than twenty years earlier at number 14/16 Novosyolov Street, phoned the Dashkovo-Pesochnya office of the Oktyabrsky Region Department of the Interior in Ryazan and reported that ten minutes earlier, he had seen a white model five or seven Zhiguli automobile with the Moscow license plate T534 VT 77 RUS outside the entrance to his apartment block, where there was a twenty-four hour "Night and Day" shop on the ground floor. The car had driven into the yard and stopped. A man and a young woman got out, went down into the basement of the building, and after a while came back. Then the car was driven right up against the basement door, and all three of the people in it began carrying sacks inside. One of the men had a mustache and the woman was wearing a tracksuit. Then all of them got into the car and drove away.

Note how quickly Kartofelnikov reacted. The police were less prompt in their response. "I spotted the model seven Zhiguli as I was walking home from the garage," Kartofelnikov recalled, "and I noticed the license plate out of professional habit. I saw that the regional number had been masked by a piece of paper with the Ryazan serial number '62'. I ran home to phone the police. I dialed '02' and got this lazy reply: 'call such-and-such a number.' I called it, and it was busy. I had to keep dialing the number for ten minutes before I got through. That gave the terrorists enough time to carry all of the sacks into the basement and set the detonators. . . . If I'd gotten through to the police immediately . . . the terrorists would have been arrested right there in their car."

When they arrived at 9:58 P.M. Moscow time, the policemen, commanded by warrant officer Andrei Chernyshov, discovered three fifty-kilogram sugar sacks in the basement of a residential block containing seventy-seven apartments. Chernyshov, who was the first to enter the mined basement, recalled:

> At about ten, we got a warning call from the officer on duty: suspicious individuals had been seen coming out of the basement of house number 14/16 Novosyolov Street. Near the house we were met by a girl who told us about a man who had come out of the basement and driven away in a car with its license plates masked. I left one officer in front of the entrance and went down into the basement with the other. The basement in that house is deep and completely flooded with water. The only dry spot is a tiny little storeroom like a brick shed. We shined the light in, and there were several sugar sacks arranged in a stack. There was a slit in the upper sack, and we could see some kind of electronic device: wires wrapped round with insulating tape, a timer. . . . Of course, it was all a bit of a shock for us. We ran out of the basement, I stayed behind to guard the entrance, while the guys went to evacuate the inhabitants.

After about fifteen minutes, reinforcements arrived, and the chief of the Regional MVD turned up. The sacks of explosives were removed by men from the Ministry of Emergencies in the presence of representatives of the FSB. Of course, after our bomb technicians had rendered them harmless. No one had any doubt that this was a genuine emergency situation.

One of the sacks had been slit open, and a homemade detonating device had been set inside, consisting of three batteries, an electronic watch, and a homemade detonating charge. The detonator was set for 5.30 A.M. on Thursday morning. The bomb technicians from the police engineering and technology section of the Ryazan Region MVD took just eleven minutes to disarm the bomb, under the leadership of their section head, police Lieutenant Yuri Tkachenko, and then immediately, at approximately 11 P.M., they conducted a trial explosion with the mixture. There was no detonation, either because the sample was too small, or because the engineers had taken it from the upper layers of the mixture, while the main concentration of hexogen might be in the bottom of the sack. Express analysis of the substance in the sacks with the help of a gas analyzer indicated "fumes of a hexogen-type explosive substance." It is important at this point to note that there could not have been any mistake. The instruments used were modern and in good condition, and the specialists who carried out the analysis were highly qualified.

The contents of the sacks did not outwardly resemble granulated sugar. All the witnesses, who discovered the suspicious sacks, later confirmed that they contained a yellow substance in the form of granules that resembled small vermicelli, which is exactly what hexogen looks like. On September 23, the press center of the Ministry of the Interior of Russia also announced that "analysis of the substance concerned indicated the presence of hexogen vapor," and that an explosive device had been disarmed. In other words, on the night proceeding September 23, local experts had determined that the detonator was live, and the "sugar" was an explosive mixture. "Our initial examination indicated the presence of explosive substances. . . . We believed there was a real danger of explosion," Lieutenant Colonel Sergei Kabashov, head of the Oktyabrsky Regional Department of the MVD, later stated.

House number 14/16 on Novosyolov Street was no chance selection on the bombers' part. It was a standard house in an unprestigious part of town, inhabited by simple people. Set up against the front of the house was a twenty-four hour shop selling groceries. The inhabitants of the house would surely not suspect that people unloading goods by the trap door of a twenty-four hour food store might be terrorists. The house stood on the edge of Ryazan close to an open area, which was known to local people as "the Old Circle," on a low rise. It was built of silicate brick. The sacks of explosives in the basement had been placed beside the building's main support, so if there had been an explosion, the entire building would have collapsed. The next house, built on the soft sandy soil of the slope, could also have been damaged.

So the alarm was raised, and the inhabitants of a house in Ryazan were roused from their beds and evacuated into the street in whatever they happened to be wearing at the time. This is how the newspaper Trud described the scene: "In a matter of minutes, people were forced to abandon their apartments without being allowed to gather their belongings (a fact which thieves later exploited) and gather in front of the dark, empty house. Women, old men, and children shuffled about in front of the entrance, reluctant to set out into the unknown. Some of them were not wearing outer clothing, or were even barefooted. . . . They hopped from one foot to the other in the freezing wind for several hours, and the invalids who had been brought down in their wheelchairs wept and cursed the entire world."

The house was cordoned off. It was cold. The director of the local cinema, the Oktyabr, took pity on the people and let them into the hall, and she also prepared tea for everyone. The only people left in the building were several old invalids, who were in no physical condition to leave their apartments, including one old woman who was paralyzed and whose daughter stayed all night with the police cordon expecting an explosion. This is how she recalled the event:

Between 10 and 11 P.M., police officers went to the apartments, asking people to get outside as quickly as possible. I ran out just as I was, in my nightshirt, with only my raincoat thrown over it. Outside in the yard, I learned there was a bomb in our house. I'd left my mother behind in the flat, and she can't even get out of bed on her own. I dashed over to the policemen in horror: "Let me into the house, help me bring my mother out!" They wouldn't let me back in. It was half past two before they started going to each of the flats with its occupants and checking them for signs of anything suspicious. They came to me too. I showed the policeman my sick mother and said I wouldn't go anywhere without her. He calmly wrote something down on his notepad and disappeared. And I suddenly had this realization that my mother and I were probably the only two people in a house with a bomb in it. I felt quite unbearably afraid. . . . But then suddenly there was a ring at the door. Standing on the doorstep were two senior police officers. They asked me sternly: "Have you decided you want to be buried alive, then, woman?" I was so scared my legs were giving way under me, but I stood my ground, I wouldn't go without my mother. And then they suddenly took pity on me: "All right then, stay here, your house has already been made safe." It turned out they'd removed the detonators from the "charge" even before they inspected the flats. Then I just dashed straight outside. . . .

All kinds of emergency services and managers turned up at the house. In addition, since analysis had determined the presence of hexogen, the cordon was ordered to expand the exclusion zone, in case there was an explosion. The head of the local FSB, Major-General Alexander Sergeiev, congratulated the inhabitants of the building on being granted a second life. Hero of the hour Kartofelnikov was told that he must have been born under a lucky star (a few days later, he was presented with a valuable gift from the municipal authorities for finding the bomb—a Russian-made color television). One of the Russian telegraph agencies informed the world of his fortunate discovery as follows:

TERRORIST BOMBING THWARTED IN RYAZAN: SACKS CONTAINING A MIXTURE OF SUGAR AND HEXOGEN FOUND BY POLICE IN APARTMENT HOUSE BASEMENT

First deputy staff officer for civil defense and emergencies in the Ryazan Region, Colonel Yuri Karpeiev, has informed an ITAR-TASS correspondent that the substance found in the sacks is undergoing analysis. According to the operations duty officer of the Ministry of Emergencies of the Russian Federation in Moscow, the detonating device discovered was set for 5:30 Moscow time on Thursday morning. Acting head of the MVD of the Ryazan Region, Alexei Savin, told the ITAR-TASS correspondent that the make, color, and number of the car in which the explosives were brought to the scene had been identified. According to Savin, specialists were carrying out a series of tests to determine the composition and explosion hazard posed by the mixture discovered in the sacks.... First deputy mayor of the region, Vladimir Markov, said that the situation in Ryazan is calm. The inhabitants of the building, who were rapidly evacuated from their apartments immediately following the discovery of the suspected explosives, have returned to their apartments. All the neighboring houses have been checked. According to Markov, it is the inhabitants themselves who must be the main support of agencies of law enforcement in their struggle with "this evil which has appeared in our country.... The more vigilant we are, the more reliable the defense will be."

At five minutes past midnight, the sacks were carried out of the basement and loaded into a fire engine. However, it was four in the morning before a decision was taken on where the explosives should be taken. The SWAT, the FSB, and the local military units refused to take in the sacks. In the end, they were taken to the yard of the Central Office for Civil Defense and Emergencies of Ryazan, where they were stacked in a garage, and a guard was placed over them. The rescuers later recalled that they would have used the sugar in their tea, except that the analysis had shown the presence of hexogen.

The sacks lay at the civil defense base for several days, until they were taken away to the MVD's expert center for criminalistic analysis in Moscow. The press office of the MVD of the Ryazan Region actually announced that the sacks had been taken to Moscow on September 23. At 8:30 in the morning, the work of removing the bomb and checking the building was completed, and the residents were allowed to return to their apartments.

On the evening of September 22, 1,200 policemen were put on alert and the so-called plan Operation Intercept was set in motion. Several eyewitnesses were identified, sketches were produced of three suspects, and roadblocks were set up on highways in the region and in nearby localities. The witnesses' testimony was quite detailed, and there was some hope that the perpetrators would be apprehended.

The governor of the region and the municipal authorities allocated additional funds to the counter-terrorist offensive. Members of the armed forces were used to guard apartment blocks, and at night a watch was organized among residents in all the buildings, while a further search was carried out of the entire residential district, especially of the apartment houses (by Friday, eighty percent of the houses in the town had been checked.) The city markets were deserted, with traders afraid to bring in their goods and customers afraid to go out shopping. According to the deputy mayor of Ryazan, Anatoly Baranov, "Practically no one in the town slept, and not only did the residents of that building spend the night on the street, so did the entire 30,000 population of the suburb of Dashkovo-Pesochnya in which it is located." The panicked response in the city grew stronger: there were rumors circulating that Ryazan had been singled out for terrorist attack, because the 137th airborne assault guards regiment which had fought in Dagestan, was stationed there. In addition, the Dyagilev military aerodrome, from which military forces had been airlifted to the Caucasus, was located near Ryazan. The main road out of Ryazan was jammed solid, because the police were checking all cars leaving the city. However, Operation Intercept failed to produce any results, the car used by the terrorists was not found, and the terrorists themselves were not arrested.

On the morning of September 23, the Russian news agencies broadcast the sensational news that "a terrorist bombing had been foiled in Ryazan." From eight in the morning, the television channels started broadcasting details of the failed mass murder attempt: Every TV and radio broadcasting company in Russia carried the same story: "According to members of the law enforcement agencies of the Ryazan MVD, the white crystalline substance in the sacks is hexogen."

At 1 P.M., the TV news program *Vesti* on the state's RTR TV channel carried a live interview with S. Kabashov: "So provisional guidelines have been issued for the detention of an automobile matching the description which residents have described. There are no results so far." *Vesti* announced that "bomb specialists from the municipal police have carried out an initial analysis and confirmed the presence of hexogen. The contents of the sacks have now been sent to the FSB laboratory in Moscow for definitive analysis. Meanwhile in Ryazan, the mayor, Pavel Mamatov, has held an extraordinary meeting with his deputies and given instructions for all basements in the city to be sealed off, and for rented storage facilities to be checked more thoroughly."

And so it turned out that the contents of the sacks were sent for analysis, not only to the MVD laboratory, but to the FSB laboratory.

Mamatov answered questions from journalists: "Whatever agencies we might bring in today, it is only possible to implement all the measures for sealing off attics and basements, repairs, installing gratings, and so on in a single week on one condition–if we all combine our efforts." In other words, at 1 P.M. on September 23, all of Ryazan was in a state of siege. They were searching for the terrorists and their car and checking attics and basements. When *Vesti* went on air again at 5 P.M., it was mostly a repeat of the broadcast at 1 P.M.

At 7 P.M., *Vesti* went on air with its normal news coverage: "Today, Russian Prime Minister Vladimir Putin spoke about the air strikes on the airport at Grozny." So while they were looking for terrorists in

Ryazan, Russian planes had been bombarding Grozny. The people of Ryazan were avenged. Those who were behind the terrorist attack would pay dearly for their sleepless night and their spoiled day.

Putin answered questions from journalists: "As far as the strike on Grozny airport is concerned, I can't make any comment. I know there is a general directive under which bandits will be pursued wherever they are. I'm simply not in the know, but if they were at the airport, that means at the airport. I can't really add anything to what has already been said." Evidently, as Prime Minister, Putin had known something the general public hadn't heard yet, that there were terrorists holed up at Grozny airport.

Putin also commented on the latest emergency in Ryazan: "As for the events in Ryazan, I don't think there was any kind of failure involved. If the sacks which proved to contain explosives were noticed, then there is a positive side to it, if only in the fact that the public is reacting correctly to the events taking place in our country today. I'd like to take advantage of your question in order to thank the public of our country for this. . . . This is absolutely the correct response. No panic, no sympathy for the bandits. This is the mood for fighting them to the very end. Until we win. And we shall win."

Rather vague, but the general meaning is clear enough. The foiling of the attempted bombing in Ryazan is not a mishandling by the secret services, who failed to spot the explosives being planted, but a victory for the entire Russian people who were keeping a vigilant lookout for their cruel enemies even in provincial towns like Ryazan. For that, the Prime Minister expresses his gratitude to the public.

This is a good point at which to draw our first conclusions. The FSB subsequently claimed that training exercises were being held in Ryazan, but this is contradicted by the following circumstances. On the evening of September 22, after the sacks of explosives had been discovered in the basement of the apartment building, the FSB made no announcement that training exercises were being held in Ryazan, that the sacks contained ordinary sugar, or that the detonating device was a mock-up. The FSB had a second opportunity to issue a statement concerning exercises on September 23, when the news agencies of the world carried the story of the failed terrorist attack in Ryazan. The FSB did not issue any denial, nor did it announce that training had been taking place in Ryazan. As of September 23, the Prime Minister of Russia and Yeltsin's successor in the post of president, Vladimir Putin, still supported the FSB version of events and sincerely believed (or at least pretended to believe) that a terrorist attack had been thwarted in Ryazan.

Let us imagine just for a moment that training exercises really were taking place in Ryazan. Could we possibly expect the FSB to say nothing all day long on September 23, while the whole world was buzzing with news of a failed terrorist attack? It's impossible to imagine. Is it possible to imagine that the Prime Minister of Russia and former director of the FSB, who, moreover, has personal links with Patrushev, was not informed about the "exercises?" It is quite impossible to imagine, even in your wildest dreams. It would be an open gesture of disloyalty to Putin by Patrushev, after which one or the other of them would have had to quit the political arena. The fact that at seven o'clock in the evening, on September 23, 1999, Putin did not make any statement about training exercises taking place in Ryazan was the weightiest possible argument in favor of interpreting events as a failed attempt by the FSB to blow up an apartment building in Ryazan.

The mayor of Moscow, Yuri Luzhkov, who has pretty good contacts among the departments of the armed forces and law enforcement, was not informed about any FSB "exercises" in Ryazan, either. On the contrary, on September 23, the Moscow authorities gave instructions for intensive precautions to be taken to prevent terrorist attacks in the capital, primarily because in the opinion of representatives of the agencies of law enforcement, the composition of the explosives found in Moscow and Ryazan, and the way they were planted, were similar. The Moscow police were given instructions to thoroughly inspect all premises, including non-residential, from top to bottom, and to carefully inspect every vehicle carrying goods into the city. In Moscow, the events in Ryazan were seen as a prevented terrorist attack.

But the most remarkable thing of all is that not even Vladimir Rushailo, the Minister of the Interior who headed the commission for combating terrorism and supervised the Whirlwind Anti-Terror operation, knew anything at all about exercises in Ryazan. Oleg Aksyonov, head of the information department of the MVD of Russia, later said: "For us, for the people of Ryazan, and the central administration, this is a total surprise; it was treated as a serious crime." On September 23, in his capacity as press secretary for the MVD, Aksyonov met the press several times. To Rushailo's shame, Aksyonov announced that, having familiarized himself with the situation, the minister had ordered that all the basements and attics in Ryazan should be checked once again in the space of a day and that vigilance should be increased. Aksyonov emphasized that the implementation of the order was to be closely monitored, since "people could pay for a minor slip-up with their lives."

Even on September 24, when he addressed the First All-Russian Congress for Combating Organized Crime, Rushailo spoke about the terrorist attack that had been thwarted in Ryazan and said that "a number of serious miscalculations have been made in the activities of the agencies of the interior" and that "harsh conclusions" had been drawn. Having pointed out the miscalculations of the agencies that had failed to spot the explosives being planted, Rushailo followed Putin in praising the people of Ryazan who had managed to foil the terrorist attack. "The struggle against terrorism is not the exclusive prerogative of the agencies of the interior," said Rushailo. A significant role in this matter was allotted to "the local authorities and administrations, whose work, however, also contains significant flaws." Rushailo recommended to his audience "the immediate creation of interdepartmental monitoring that would travel to the regions to check the implementation of decisions on site and to provide practical assistance." He pointed out that in the MVD such work was already being carried out and there had been definite improvements, such as the foiling of the attempt to blow up the apartment building in Ryazan. "The thwarting of new terrorist attacks and the punishment of the guilty parties in crimes already committed is the main task facing the MVD of Russia at the present stage," Minister of the Interior Rushailo emphasized with pride in the one thwarted terrorist attack he already had to his credit—in Ryazan.

If the minister himself regarded the Ryazan episode as a foiled terrorist attack, then what can we say about the regional MVD? The appeals composed in revolutionary style simply begged to be set to music:

The war declared by terrorism against the people of Russia continues. And this means that the unification of all the forces of society and the state to repel the treacherous foe is the essential requirement of the present day. The struggle against terrorism cannot remain a matter only for the police and the secret services. The most striking possible confirmation of this is the report of an attempt to blow up an apartment building in Ryazan which was thwarted thanks to the vigilance of the public. On September 23, in Ryazan . . . while checking the basement of an apartment building a police detachment discovered an explosive device consisting of three sacks of hexogen and a timing mechanism set for half-past five in the morning. The terrorist attack was thwarted thanks to the inhabitants of the building, which the criminals had chosen as their target. The evening before, they had noticed strangers carrying sacks of some kind into the basement from a Zhiguli automobile with its license plate papered over. The residents immediately contacted the police. Initial analysis of the contents of the sacks showed that they actually did contain a substance similar to hexogen mixed with granulated sugar. The sacks were immediately dispatched to Moscow under guard. Following expert analysis, the staff at the FSB laboratory will give a final answer as to whether this was an attempted terrorist attack or merely a diversionary ploy.

In this connection, the department of the interior for the region wishes to remind citizens yet again of the need to remain calm and to take an organized, business-like approach to ensuring one's own safety. The best reply to the terrorists will be the vigilance of us all. All this requires is to look a little closer at the people around you, pay attention to strangers noticed in the entranceway, in the attic, or the basement of your building, to abandoned automobiles parked directly beside apartment buildings. At the slightest suspicion phone the police.

Do not on any account attempt to examine the contents of any suspicious boxes, bags, and other unidentified objects, which you may find. In such situations you should restrict access to them by other people and call the police.

The establishment of house committees to organize the protection of buildings and surrounding territory during the night will also serve to reduce significantly the likelihood of terrorist incidents in our city. Remember, today it depends on every one of us just how effective the fight against evil will be.
—Regional MVD Information Group.

Unfortunately for him, on September 23, 1999, General Alexander Zdanovich, head of the Center for Public Relations of the FSB of Russia, was due to appear on the television program *Hero of the Day* on channel NTV. Thanks to this, we have yet another important piece of evidence that the FSB was planning to just sit it out and allow the people of Ryazan and the journalists to swallow the version of events as a failed terrorist attack by Chechens. It is obvious that prior to Zdanovich's appearance, the FSB had no intention of making any statement about "exercises." Their calculations were simple enough: the police had not found any terrorists from the FSB or the car. The story of the thwarted terrorist attack was still working, and, best of all, it suited everyone, since even Rushailo could claim a share of the credit for thwarting the bombing.

Zdanovich had, however, been instructed by his bosses to feel out the public reaction to the fairy tale about "exercises," in case something went wrong or there was a leak of information about the FSB's involvement in the terrorist attack in Ryazan. Note how gently

Zdanovich began hinting that no actual crime had been committed in the attempt to blow up the house in Ryazan, as if trying to convince people that there was nothing to get excited about. The press secretary of the FSB declared that the initial report indicated that there was no hexogen in the sacks discovered in the basement of one of the apartment blocks in the city, but that they contained "something like remote-control devices." Nor were there any detonating mechanisms, although it was now possible to confirm that "certain elements of a detonating mechanism" had been discovered.

At the same time, Zdanovich emphasized that the final answer would have to be given by the experts, his colleagues from the FSB laboratory in Moscow, who were Patrushev's subordinates. Zdanovich knew perfectly well just what "final answer" would be given by the FSB experts: it would be the one their boss ordered them to give (this answer would be communicated to us only after a certain delay, on March 21, 2000, a year-and-a-half after the foiled terrorist attack, and just five days before the presidential election).

But even so, at the beginning of the program *Hero of the Day*, Zdanovich was not in possession of any information to the effect that the FSB had apparently been carrying out "exercises" in Ryazan. He did not even hint at the possibility that training exercises might be involved. In his interview, Zdanovich did express doubts that the sacks contained explosives and that there was a live detonating device, but there was not a single word about any possible exercises. This discrepancy was yet another indication that the secret services had planned a terrorist attack in Ryazan. It is simply not possible to imagine that the leadership of the FSB had kept information on exercises already completed in Ryazan a secret from Zdanovich.

The evening of September 23 brought yet another absurdity. The *Novosti* news agency broadcast a recording of the NTV interview with General Zdanovich and announced that the Operation Intercept search for the white Zhiguli automobile was ongoing. "A lot of things about this entire story are unclear." In particular, the witnesses gave different descriptions of the color and make of the automobile. Doubts had even arisen about whether the car's license plate had been papered over. At the same time, as the press center remarked, the search for the car was being continued "in order to reconstruct an objective picture."

Despite Zdanovich's assurances that there had been no explosives or detonating device, the Ryazan FSB was still unable "to reconstruct an objective picture." On September 24, the morning newspapers carried details of how the terrorist attack in Ryazan had been foiled, but still no statement from the FSB about exercises.

Not until September 24 did FSB director Patrushev finally decide to issue a statement about the "exercises" which had been held in Ryazan. What could have made Patrushev shift tactics in this way? Firstly, the main clues, three sacks of explosives with a live detonating device, had been delivered into Patrushev's hands in Moscow, which was good news for Patrushev. Now he could substitute the sacks and confidently assert that the provincials in Ryazan had made a mistake, and the results of their analysis were wrong. There was also bad news: the Ryazan FSB had detained two terrorists.

Let's lend the FSB a hand in establishing the "objective picture" which was so zealously concealed from the people. In simplified form, the most brilliant part of the joint operation, conducted by the Ryazan police and the Ryazan Region FSB, went as follows.

Following the discovery in Ryazan of the sacks containing explosives and a live detonating device, Operation Intercept had been announced in the city. The senior officer responsible for public relations (press secretary) of the FSB of the Ryazan Region, Yuri Bludov, announced that Patrushev's statement had come as a complete surprise to the local members of the state security services. "Until the last moment, we worked across the board in close collaboration with the police, just as though the threat of a terrorist attack was real, we made up sketches of the suspected terrorists; on the basis of the results of the analysis, we initiated criminal proceedings under article 205 of the Criminal Code of the Russian Federation (terrorism); we conducted a search for cars and terrorists."

After the announcement of Operation Intercept, when the routes out of town were already closed off, the operational divisions of the

Ryazan MVD and Ryazan FSB attempted to determine the precise location of the terrorists they were seeking. They had a few lucky breaks. Nadezhda Yukhanova, an employee of the Electrosvyaz Company (the telephone service), recorded a suspicious call to Moscow. "Leave one at a time, there are patrols everywhere," replied the voice at the other end of the line. Yukhanova immediately reported the call to the Ryazan FSB, and it was a simple technical matter for the suspicious telephone to be monitored immediately. The operatives had no doubt that they had located the terrorists. However, difficulties arose, because when the bugging technology identified the Moscow telephone number the terrorists were calling, it turned out to be the number of one of the offices of the FSB in Moscow.

After leaving Novosyolov Street shortly after 9 P.M. on September 22, the terrorists had not risked driving straight to Moscow, because a solitary car is always noticeable on a deserted highway at night, and the chances of being stopped at a traffic police post were too high. Any car stopped at night would be noted in the duty officer's journal, even if the people sitting in it were members of the FSB or other secret services, and the next day when the news of the explosion was announced, the policeman would be bound to recall stopping a car with three people. If there also happened to be reports by witnesses in Ryazan, they would pick up the car and its passengers immediately. The terrorists had to wait until the morning, since they couldn't leave the target area until after the explosion had taken place, and their military mission had been accomplished. In the morning, there would be a lot of cars on the highway. For the first few hours after the attack, there would be panic. If witnesses had spotted two men and a woman in a car, the police would be looking for three terrorists, two men and one woman. One person alone in a car could always give any police cordon the slip.

That this was the way things really were is clear from the report of Operation Intercept in the newspaper *Trud*: "By now the situation in Ryazan was red hot. Reinforced patrols of police and cadets from the local military colleges walked the streets. All road routes out of and into the city were blocked by the patrols and sentries armed to the teeth and road traffic police. Miles-long traffic jams had built up with cars and trucks moving to and from Moscow. They searched all the cars thoroughly, looking for three terrorists, two men and a woman, whose descriptions were posted on almost every street lamp post."

Following instructions received, one of the terrorists set out towards Moscow in the car on September 23, abandoned the car in the area of Kolomna, and made his way to Moscow unhindered. One of the terrorists had now escaped the clutches of the Ryazan police and taken the car with him as well. Late in the day of September 23, less than twenty-four hours later, an empty car was found by the police on the Moscow-Ryazan highway close to Kolomna, about half-way to Moscow. It was the same car "with the papered-over license plates, which was used to transport the explosives," Bludov announced. The car turned out to be registered as missing with the police. In other words, the terrorists had carried out their operation in a stolen car (a classic feature of terrorist attacks).

The car had not been dumped near Kolomna by chance. If it had been stolen in Moscow or the Moscow Region, the police would have returned it to the owner at his home address, and it would probably never have entered anyone's head to think it might be the car used by unknown terrorists to transport hexogen for blowing up a building in a different region of the country, in Ryazan. Accordingly, they wouldn't have bothered to analyze the contents of the car for microparticles of hexogen and other explosive substances. The accomplice could go back for the two terrorists left behind in Ryazan the next day in a standard FSB operational vehicle and take them to Moscow without any risk of being caught. On the other hand, if it were discovered that the car found near Kolomna was the one used for the terrorist attack, the fact that it was abandoned halfway to Moscow would tell the Ryazan police that the terrorists had gotten away. The cordon in place around Ryazan would then be relaxed, which would make it easier for the remaining two terrorists to leave.

So now there were two terrorists left in Ryazan. From information provided by the Ryazan FSB, we know that the terrorists stayed over-night somewhere in Ryazan and didn't spend the night of September

22 hanging about in the hallways of buildings in a strange and unfamiliar town. The conclusion must be drawn that the terrorists had
arranged places to stay in advance, even if they themselves were not
from Ryazan. In that case, it is clear that they had time to choose their
target, which was far from random, and to prepare for their terrorist
attack. When they were caught by surprise by Operation Intercept
starting earlier than expected, the terrorists decided to wait it out in the
town. The arguments in support of this interpretation are as follows.

It is very important to note that the leaders of the Ryazan Region
were not aware of the explosion planned for Ryazan (or the "exercises," as the events are referred to diplomatically by all the officials
involved in them and by employees of the agencies of coercion). The
governor of the region, V. N. Lyubimov, announced this in an interview broadcast live on September 24, when he said: "Not even I knew
about this exercise." Mamatov, the mayor of Ryazan, was frankly
annoyed: "They've used us as guinea pigs. Tested Ryazan for lice. I'm
not against exercises. I served in the army myself, and I took part in
them, but I've never seen anything like this."

The FSB department for the Ryazan Region was also not
informed about the "exercises." Bludov stated that "the FSB was not
informed in advance that exercises were being conducted in the city."
The head of the Ryazan FSB, Major-General A.V. Sergeiev at first
stated in an interview with the local television company *Oka* that he
knew nothing about any "exercises" being held. It was only later, in
response to a question from journalists about whether he had in his
possession any official document confirming that exercises were held
in Ryazan, that he answered through his press secretary that he
accepted as proof of the exercises the television interview given by
FSB director Patrushev. One of the women living in house 14/16,
Marina Severina Street, recalled how, afterwards, the local FSB went
to each of the apartments apologizing: "Several people from the FSB
came to see us, led by a colonel. They apologized. They said that they
hadn't known anything, either." This is one case in which we can
believe the members of the FSB and accept their sincerity.

The Ryazan FSB realized that the people of Ryazan had been "set up" and that the Public Prosecutor's Office of Russia and the public might accuse the Ryazan FSB of planning the explosion. Shaken by the treachery of their Moscow colleagues, the Ryazan FSB decided to provide themselves with an alibi and announced to the world that the Ryazan operation had been planned in Moscow. There could be no other explanation for the statement from the Ryazan Region FSB, which appeared shortly after Patrushev's interview about "exercises" in Ryazan. We give the text of the statement in full.

It has become known that the planting on September 22, 1999 of a dummy explosive device was part of an ongoing interregional exercise. This announcement came as a surprise to us and appeared at a moment when the department of the FSB had identified the residences in Ryazan of those involved in planting the explosive device and was preparing to detain them. This had been made possible due to the vigilance and assistance of many of the residents of the city of Ryazan, collaboration with the agencies of the Ministry of the Interior, and the professionalism of our own staff. We thank everyone who assisted us in this work. We will continue in the future to do everything possible to ensure the safety of the people of Ryazan.

This unique document provides us with answers to the most important of our questions. Firstly, the Ryazan FSB had nothing to do with the operation to blow up the building in Ryazan. Secondly, at least two terrorists were discovered in Ryazan. Thirdly, the terrorists lived in Ryazan, if only temporarily, and evidently a network of at least two secret safe apartments were uncovered. Fourthly, just at the moment when arrangements were in hand to arrest the terrorists, the order came from Moscow not to arrest them, because the terrorist attack in Ryazan was only an FSB "exercise."

In order to remove any doubts that the Ryazan FSB statement was both deliberate and accurate, the leadership of the Ryazan FSB repeated it almost word-for-word in an interview. On May 21, 2000, just five days before the presidential election, when the failed explosion in Ryazan had been put back on the public agenda for political reasons by the parties competing for power, the head of the investigative section of the FSB for the Ryazan Region, Lieutenant Colonel Yuri Maximov, stated as follows:

> We can only feel sympathy for these people and offer our apologies. We also find the situation difficult. We took all the events of that night seriously, regarding the situation as genuinely dangerous. The announcement about exercises held by the FSB of the Russian Federation came as a complete surprise to us and appeared at a moment when the department of the FSB had identified the residences in Ryazan of those involved in planting the dummy (as it subsequently emerged) device and was preparing to detain them. This had been made possible due to the vigilance and assistance of the inhabitants of Ryazan, collaboration with the agencies of the Ministry of the Interior, and the professionalism of our own staff.

It was thus, twice confirmed in documentary form that the terrorists who had mined the building in Ryazan were employees of the FSB, that at the time of the operation they were living in Ryazan, and that the places where they lived had been identified by employees of the FSB for the Ryazan Region. This being so, we can catch Patrushev out in an obvious lie. On September 25, in an interview with one of the television companies, he stated that "those people who should in principle have been found immediately were among the residents who left the building, in which an explosive device was supposedly planted. They took part in the process of producing their own sketches, and held conversations with employees of the agencies of law enforcement."

The real facts were quite different. The terrorists scattered to different safe apartments. No sooner had the leadership of the Ryazan FSB reported in the line of duty by phone to Patrushev in Moscow, that the arrest of the terrorists was imminent than Patrushev gave the order not to arrest the terrorists and announced that the foiled terrorist attack in Ryazan was only an "exercise." One can imagine the expression on the face of the Ryazan FSB officer concerned: most likely Major-General Sergeiev was reporting to Patrushev in person when he was ordered to let the terrorists go.

Immediately after he put down the phone, Patrushev gave his first interview in those days to the NTV television company: "The incident in Ryazan was not a bombing, nor was it a foiled bombing. It was an exercise. It was sugar; there was no explosive substance there. Such exercises do not only take place in Ryazan. But to the honor of the agencies of law enforcement and the public in Ryazan, they responded promptly. I believe that exercises must be made as close as possible to what happens in real life, because otherwise we won't learn anything and won't be able to respond to anything anywhere." A day later, Patrushev added that the "exercise" in Ryazan was prompted by information about terrorist attacks planned to take place in Russia. In Chechnya several groups of terrorists had already been prepared and were "due to be advanced into Russian territory and carry out a series of terrorist attacks. . . . It was this information which led us to conclude that we needed to carry out training exercises, and not like the ones we'd had before, and to make them hard and strict. . . . Our personnel must be prepared; we must identify the shortcomings in the organization of our work and make corrections to its organization."

The *Moskovsky Komsomolets* newspaper managed to joke about it: "On September 24, 1999, the head of the FSB, Nikolai Patrushev, made the sensational announcement that the attempted bombing in Ryazan was nothing of the sort. It was an exercise. . . . The same day, Minister of the Interior Vladimir Rushailo congratulated his men on saving the building in Ryazan from certain destruction."

But in Ryazan, of course, no one was laughing. Obviously, even though Patrushev had forbidden it, the Ryazan FSB went ahead and arrested the terrorists, considerably roughing them up in the process. Who was arrested where, how many there were of them, and what else the Ryazan FSB officers found in those flats we shall probably never know. When they were arrested, the terrorists presented their "cover documents" and were detained, until the arrival from Moscow of an officer of the central administration with documents which permitted him to take the FSB operatives, who had been tracked down so rapidly, back to Moscow with him.

Beyond this point our investigation runs up against the old familiar "top secret" classification. The criminal proceedings instigated by the FSB for the Ryazan Region in connection with the discovery of an explosive substance under article 205 of the Criminal Code of the Russian Federation (terrorism) was classified, and the case materials are not available to the public. The names of the terrorists (FSB operatives) have been concealed. We don't even know if they were interrogated and what they said under interrogation. Patrushev certainly had something to hide. "There's nothing I can do, guys. The analysis shows explosive materials, I'm obliged to initiate criminal proceedings"—such was the stubborn reply made by the local FSB investigator to his Moscow colleagues, when they tried putting pressure on him. So then, people from the FSB's central administration were sent down and simply confiscated the results of the analysis.

On September 29, 1999, the newspapers *Cheliabinsky Rabochy* and *Krasnoyarsky Rabochy*, and on October 1, the *Volzhskaya Kommuna* of Samara carried identical articles; "We have learned from well-informed sources in the MVD of Russia that none of the MVD operatives and their colleagues in the FSB of Ryazan believes in any training involving the planting of explosives in the town. . . . In the opinion of highly placed employees of the MVD of Russia, the apartment building in Ryazan actually was mined by unknown persons using genuine explosives and the same detonators as in Moscow. . . . This theory is indirectly confirmed by the fact that the criminal proceedings under the article on terrorism have still not been closed. Furthermore, the results of the original analysis of the contents of the sacks, carried out at the first stage by local MVD experts, were confiscated by FSB personnel who arrived from Moscow, and immediately declared secret. Policemen who have been in contact with their colleagues in criminalistics, who carried out the first investigation of the sacks, continue to claim that they really did contain hexogen, and there is no possibility of any error."

Trying to put pressure on the investigation and declaring a criminal case classified were illegal acts. According to article 7 of the law of the Russian Federation, "On state secrecy," adopted on July 21, 1993, "information ... concerning emergencies and catastrophes which threaten the safety and health of members of the public and their consequences; ... concerning instances of the violation of human and civil rights and freedoms; ... concerning instances of the violation of legality by the agencies of state power and their officials ... shall not be declared a matter of state secrecy and classified as secret." The same law goes on to state: "officials who have made a decision to classify as secret the information listed, or to include it for this purpose in media which contain information that constitutes a matter of state secrecy, shall be subject to criminal, administrative, or disciplinary sanction, in accordance with the material and moral harm inflicted upon society, the state, and the public. Members of the public shall be entitled to appeal such decisions to a court of law."

Unfortunately, it looks as though those responsible for classifying a criminal case will not be held to account under the progressive and democratic law of 1993. As one of the residents of the ill-fated (or fortunate) building in Ryazan put it, they have "pulled the wool down hard over our eyes."

Certainly, in March 2000 (just before the presidential election), the voters were shown one of the three terrorists (a "member of the FSB special center"), who said that all three members of the group had left Moscow for Ryazan on the evening of September 22, that they had found a basement which happened by chance not to be locked; they had bought sacks of sugar at the market and a cartridge at the Kolchuga gun shop, from which they had constructed "mock-ups of an explosive device" on the spot, and "the whole business was concentrated together to implement the measure concerned. ... It was not sabotage, but an exercise. We didn't even really try to hide."

On March 22 (with four days left to the election), The Association of Veterans of the Alpha Group came to the defense of the story about FSB exercises in Ryazan, in the person of lieutenant-general of the reserve and former commander of the *Vympel* division of the FSB of Russia, Dmitry Gerasimov, and retired Major-General Gennady Zaitsev, the former commander of the Alpha group and a "Hero of the Soviet Union." Gerasimov declared that live detonating devices were not used in the exercises in Ryazan, and what was used instead was "a cartridge containing round shot," which was meant to produce "a shock effect." Since the impression produced by the detonating device really was shocking, from that point of view the "exercise" had been a success.

In Zaitsev's opinion, the story that live detonating devices had been involved in the exercise came about because the instruments used by the FSB for the Ryazan Region were faulty. He announced that members of *Vympel* had also been involved in the exercise in Ryazan, and that a special group had left for Ryazan in a private car on the eve of the events concerned, and had actually deliberately drawn attention to itself. A cartridge containing round shot was bought in the Kolchuga shop; "The ill-fated sugar, which some later called hexogen, was bought by the special group at the local bazaar. And, therefore, it could not possibly have been an explosive. The experts simply ignored basic rules and used dirty instruments on which there were traces of explosives from previous analyses. The experts concerned have already been punished for their negligence. Criminal proceedings have been initiated in connection with this instance."

The naiveté of the interview given by the "member of the special center" and the simple-mindedness of the statements made by Gerasimov and Zaitsev are genuinely astounding. First and foremost, it could well be true that three *Vympel* officers did set out for Ryazan in a private car on the evening of September 22, that they did buy three sacks of sugar and a cartridge from the Kolchuga shop. But exactly how did they try to attract attention to themselves? After all, it was sugar they were sold at the market, not hexogen. What was there to attract attention? A single shotgun cartridge bought in a shop?

Patrushev evidently also believed that in a country where sensational murders take place every day and houses with hundreds of inhabitants are blown up, suspicion should be aroused by people buying sugar at the market and a shotgun cartridge in a shop. "Everything that the supposed terrorists planted was bought in Ryazan, the sacks of sugar and the cartridges, which they bought without anyone asking them whether they had any right to do so." A minor point, of course, but now we have a mystery: just how many cartridges did the FSB operatives buy, one or several? (The purchases could have been an operation to cover for the real terrorists, who planted quite different sacks containing explosives in the basement of the building in Ryazan, sacks that had nothing to do with the *Vympel* group. In that case, the *Vympel* operatives themselves might not have known the purpose of the task they had been assigned of buying one cartridge and three bags of sugar.)

Finally, Zaitsev deliberately misled his readers by claiming that criminal proceedings had been initiated against Senior Lieutenant Yuri Tkachenko, the explosives technician at the engineering and technical section, for conducting the analysis incorrectly, when they had actually been initiated against the terrorists who had turned out to be FSB operatives. On September 30, Tkachenko and another Ryazan police explosives specialist, Pyotr Zhitnikov, had, in fact, been awarded a bonus for their courage in disarming the explosive device. Incidentally, Nadezhda Yukhanova, the telephone operator who intercepted the terrorists' telephone conversation with Moscow, was also paid a bonus for her assistance in capturing them.

The only thing that can be said in Zaitsev's defense is that a technical expert does bear criminal responsibility for the quality and objectivity of the results of his analysis, and if Tkachenko had carried out a flawed analysis and issued an incorrect result, then criminal proceedings would, indeed, have been taken against him. But as we know, this was not done, precisely because the result provided by the analysis was accurate: the sacks contained an explosive substance.

The testimony of the "member of the special center" and Zaitsev also suffers from serious inconsistencies of time-scale. The terrorists were spotted near the building in Ryazan only shortly after 9 P.M. On a weekday, they could not possibly have covered the 180 kilometers from Moscow to Ryazan in less than three hours, and then they still had to select a building in an unfamiliar town, buy the sacks of sugar, buy the cartridge at the Kolchuga shop, and put together the mock-up. On a weekday, the market in Ryazan closes at 6 P.M. at the latest. The Kolchuga shop closes at 7 P.M. So just when and how was the sugar bought? When was the cartridge bought? When did the terrorists leave Moscow? How long did the journey take? When did they arrive in Ryazan?

It is obvious that the entire story about the evening trip from Moscow by *Vympel* operatives is an invention from start to finish. Zaitsev himself provided legally valid proof of this. On September 28, 1999, a press conference was held by members of the departments of law enforcement and the armed forces in the office of the Kolomna security firm Oskord, at which the representative of the Alpha Group veterans' association, G. N. Zaitsev explained his position with regard to the "incident" in Ryazan: "Training exercises of this kind make me really angry. It's not right to practice on real people!" On October 7, a report on the press conference was published by the local Kolomna newspaper *Yat.* The only conclusion that can be drawn from Zaitsev's statement is that he had taken no part in the Ryazan escapade. But with only four days to go to the presidential election, when all forces were mobilized for Putin's victory, and the end justified any means, Zaitsev was forced to appear at a press conference and acknowledge his own blame and the involvement of *Vympel* operatives in the Ryazan "exercise." Naturally, those who involved Zaitsev in this propaganda show were not aware of his press conference in Kolomna.

Zaitsev's false testimony of March 22, 2000, served to emphasize an extremely important point: the employees of the secret services will lie if it is required by the interests of the agencies of state security, if they have been ordered to lie.

Commenting on Patrushev's statement about "exercises" in a live broadcast on the radio station *Ekho Moskvy*, chairman of the State Duma deputies' grouping "The Russian Regions," Oleg Morozov, said: "It seems monstrous to me. I understand that the secret services have the right to check up on what's being done, but not so much by us as by themselves." In addition, he said it was "difficult to imagine yourself in these people's places" (in Ryazan) and, therefore, "it wasn't worth it, there was no way such a price should have been paid for a check" on the activities of the FSB and the vigilance of the public.

Morozov declared that it might be possible to forgive the actions of the FSB, if the FSB promised there would be no more terrorist attacks. That was, in fact, the main point that he made: Russians had to be saved from the FSB terror. The subtle diplomat Morozov offered the terrorist Patrushev a deal: we don't punish you, and we close our eyes to all the explosions that have taken place in Russia, and you halt all operations in Russia for blowing up people's homes. Patrushev heard what Morozov was saying, and the explosions ceased. Patrushev was branded an idiot and allowed to remain at his desk. Perhaps the question of just who turned out to be the idiot in this situation should be regarded as undecided.

There were some people who were of the opinion that Patrushev was insane. On September 25, 1999, the newspaper *Novye Izvestiya* carried an article by Sergei Agafonov which, in view of the circumstances, failed even to offend Patrushev: "I wonder just how accurate an idea the head of the FSB actually has of what is going on? Does the head of the secret services have an adequate perception of surrounding reality? Does he not perhaps confuse colors, does he recognize his relatives? My soul is tormented by these alarming questions, since there seems to be no possible rational explanation for the FSB's all-Russian special training exercise using real people." Agafonov assumed that "General Patrushev is seriously unwell" and "he should be released from the excessive burdens of duty and given urgent treatment."

Of course, the FSB itself could not be unanimous in its attitude to Patrushev's operation. After the fiasco in Ryazan, even his own subordinates were prepared to criticize the head of the FSB (and Patrushev was prepared to tolerate this criticism abjectly). For instance, the press secretary of the FSB for Moscow and the Moscow Region, Sergei Bogdanov, called the "exercise" in Ryazan "crude and poorly planned work" (if they were caught, their work must have been crude). The head of the FSB for the Yaroslavl Region, Major-General A. A. Kotelnikov, replied as follows to a question about the "exercise": "I have my own point of view concerning the Ryazan exercises, but I would not wish to comment on the actions of my colleagues" (as if there were any way that he could!).

Note that not a single acting or retired senior member of the FSB made any attempt at a serious analysis of the actions of his "colleagues." The professionals of the armed services departments left that honorable task to the journalists, who did the best they could in the face of the attacks made on them by the FSB. They began, naturally enough, with the sugar.

The three sacks of sugar bothered everybody. Supposedly, the terrorists from the FSB (but probably it was a quite different group of FSB operatives) bought the sugar at the local market. They said that it was produced by the Kolpyansk Sugar Plant in the Orlov Region. But if it was just plain ordinary sugar from the Orlov Region, why was it sent off to Moscow for analysis? More importantly, why did the laboratory accept it for analysis? Not just one laboratory, but two in different state departments (the MVD and the FSB). And why was an additional analysis carried out later? Surely it should have been possible to recognize sugar the first time around? Further, why did it all take several months? It only made sense for Patrushev to have the sugar brought to Moscow for analysis, if he wanted to take the material evidence away from his colleagues in Ryazan, and only if the sacks did contain explosives. Why would Patrushev insist on sacks of sugar being sent to Moscow? His own men would have made him a laughing stock.

In the meantime, the FSB press office issued a statement saying that in order for the contents of the sacks from Ryazan to be checked, they were taken to an artillery range, where attempts were made to explode them. The detonation failed because it was ordinary sugar, the FSB reported triumphantly. "One wonders what sort of idiot would try to explode three sacks of ordinary sugar at an artillery range," the newspaper *Versiya* commented ironically. Why, indeed, did the FSB send the sacks to the artillery range if it knew that "exercises" were being conducted in Ryazan, and the sacks contained sugar bought at the local bazaar by *Vympel* operatives?

Then other sacks that did contain hexogen were discovered not far from Ryazan. There were a lot of them, and there was just a hint of a connection with the GRU. In the military depot of the 137th Ryazan regiment of the VDV, located on the territory of a special base for training intelligence and sabotage units close to Ryazan, hexogen was stored, packed in fifty-kilogram sugar sacks like those discovered on Novosyolov Street. In the fall of 1999, airborne assault forces (military unit 59236) Private Alexei Pinyaev and his fellow soldiers from Moscow were assigned to this very regiment. While they were guarding "a storehouse with weapons and ammunition," Pinyaev and a friend went inside, most probably out of simple curiosity, and saw sacks with the word "Sugar" on them.

The two paratroopers cut a hole in one of the sacks with a bayonet and tipped some of the state's sugar into a plastic bag. Unfortunately, the tea made with the stolen sugar had a strange taste and wasn't sweet at all. The frightened soldiers took their bag to their platoon commander. He suspected something wasn't right, since everyone was talking about the story of the explosions, and he decided to have the "sugar" checked out by an explosives specialist. The substance proved to be hexogen. The officer reported to his superiors. Members of the FSB from Moscow and Tula (where an airborne assault division was stationed, just like in Ryazan) descended on the unit. The regimental secret services were excluded from the investigation. The paratroopers who had discovered the hexogen were interrogated "for revealing a state secret." "You guys can't even imagine what serious business you've got tangled up in," one officer told them. The press was informed that there was no soldier in the unit with the name of Pinyaev and that information about sacks containing hexogen being found in the military depot had simply been invented by Pavel Voloshin, a journalist from *Novaya Gazeta*. The matter of the explosives was successfully hushed up, and Pinyaev's commander and fellow soldiers were sent off to serve in Chechnya.

For Pinyaev himself, they devised a more painful punishment. First, he was forced to retract what he had said (it's not too hard to imagine the kind of pressure the FSB could bring to bear on him). Then the head of the Investigative Department of the FSB announced that "the soldier will be questioned in the course of the criminal proceedings initiated against him." A female employee of the Public Relation Department of the FSB summed it all up: "The kid's had it. . . ." In March 2000, criminal proceedings were initiated against Pinyaev for the theft of army property from a military warehouse containing ammunition . . . the theft of a bagful of sugar! One must at least grant the FSB a sense of humor. But even so, it's hard to understand why the Investigative Department of the FSB should have been concerned with the petty theft of food products.

According to the engineers in Ryazan, explosives are not packed, stored, or transported in fifty-kilogram sacks, it's just too dangerous. Five hundred grams of the mixture is sufficient to blow up a small building. Fifty-kilogram sacks, disguised as sugar, could only be required for acts of terrorism. Evidently this was the warehouse which provided the three sacks, which were later planted under the load-bearing support of the building in Ryazan. The instruments of the Ryazan experts had not lied.

There was a sequel to the story of the 137th regiment of the VDV. In March 2000, just before the election, the paratroop regiment sued *Novaya Gazeta*, the newspaper that had published the interview with Pinyaev. The writ, which dealt with "the protection of honor, dignity and business reputation," was submitted to the Basmansky Intermunicipal Court by the regimental command. The commander himself, Oleg Churilov, declared that the article in question had insulted the honor not only of the regiment, but of the entire Russian army, since in September 1999, there had not been any such private in the regiment. "And it is not true that a soldier can gain entry to a warehouse where weapons and explosives are stored, because he has no right to enter it while he is on guard duty."

So Pinyaev did not exist, but he was still handed over for trial. The sacks contained sugar, but "a state secret had been breached." And the 137th regiment had not taken *Novaya Gazeta* to court over the article about hexogen, but because a private on guard duty has no right to enter the warehouse he is guarding, and any claims to the contrary were an insult to the Russian army.

The question of the detonating devices wasn't handled so smoothly, either. Despite all of Zdanovich's efforts to persuade people to the contrary, the device was genuine and live, as the chairman of the Ryazan regional Duma, Vladimir Fedotkin, firmly asserted in an interview with the Interfax news agency on September 24: "It was an absolutely genuine explosive device, nothing to do with any exercises."

The detonating device is a very important formal point. Instructions forbid the use of a live detonating device for exercises involving civilian structures and the civilian population. The device might obviously be stolen (and somebody would have to be held responsible), or it might be triggered by children or tramps, if they found it in the sack of sugar. If the detonating device was not live, then no criminal case could have been brought under article 205 of the Criminal Code of the Russian Federation (terrorism), the case would have been based on the discovery of the explosives and turned over to the MVD, not the FSB. In the final analysis, if we are talking about an "exercise," then the vigilance of the people of Ryazan was checked to see how promptly they would discover sacks containing explosives, not what they would do with a detonating device. The FSB could not have carried out such a check using a live device.

In order to find out whether this was really true, *Novaya Gazeta* turned for assistance to one of its military specialists, a colonel, and asked him the questions: "Are exercises conducted using real explosive substances," and "Are there any instructions and regulations which govern this kind of activity?" Here is the colonel's answer:

Powerful explosive devices are not used even in exercises involving live shelling. Only blanks are used. If it is required to check the ability to locate and disarm an explosive device, a mine for instance, models are used which contain no detonator and no TNT. Exercises on the use of explosives, of course, involve the real detonation of quite powerful explosive devices (the specialists have to know how to disarm them). But ... such exercises are conducted in restricted areas without any outsiders. Only trained personnel are present. There is no question of involving civilians. The whole business is strictly regulated. There are instructions covering the equipment required, instructions for clearing mines, appropriate instructions and orders. Undoubtedly, these are similar for the army and the secret services.

It is difficult for the uninitiated to appreciate the significance of the innocent phrase: "the initiation of criminal proceedings under article 205." Most importantly of all, it means that the investigation will not be conducted by the MVD, but by the FSB, since terrorist activity falls into the FSB's area of investigative competence. The FSB has more than enough cases to deal with, and it won't take on any unnecessary ones. In order to take on a case, it has to have very cogent reasons, indeed (in this case the cogent reasons were provided by the results of the analysis). The FSB investigation is supervised by the Public Prosecutor's Office, and the search for the perpetrators is conducted by the FSB jointly with the MVD. A crime for which criminal proceedings have been initiated is reported within twenty-four hours to the FSB of Russia duty officer at phone numbers (095) 224-3858 or 224-1869; or at the emergency line numbers 890-726 and 890-818; or by high-frequency phone at 52816. Every morning, the duty officer submits a report on all messages received to the director of the FSB himself. If something serious is going on, such as the foiling of a terrorist attack in Ryazan, the duty officer is entitled to phone the director of the FSB at home, even at night. Reports in the media about the FSB and its members are also presented every day in a separate report.

Within a few days of the instigation of criminal proceedings requiring investigation by the FSB, an analytical note is compiled on possible lines of action. For instance, the head of the section for combating terrorism at the Ryazan FSB draws up a note for the head of the Department for Combating Terrorism of the FSB. This note is then submitted via the secretariat of the deputy director of the FSB with responsibility for monitoring the corresponding department, and from there the note goes to the director of the FSB. All of which means that Patrushev knew about the discovery in the basement of a building in Ryazan of sacks containing explosives and a live detonating device no later than seven o'clock on the morning of September 23. When there are explosions happening everywhere, for a subordinate not to report to the top that a terrorist attack has been thwarted would be tantamount to suicide. The foiling of a terrorist attack is an occasion for rejoicing. It means medals and promotion and bonuses. And also, of course, public recognition.

This time, the apparent cause for celebration created a tricky situation. In connection with the incident in Ryazan, Zdanovich announced on September 24 that the FSB offered its apologies to the people of the city for the inconvenience and psychological stress they had suffered as a result of anti-terrorist exercises. Note that a day earlier, in his interview with NTV, Zdanovich had not apologized, which means that on September 24, Patrushev must have sent Zdanovich the directive to write everything off to sheer stupidity in order to avoid being accused of terrorism.

General Alexander Zdanovich today apologized to the inhabitants of Ryazan on behalf of the Federal Security Service of Russia for the inconvenience they had suffered in the course of antiterrorist exercises and also for the psychological stress caused to them. He emphasized that "the secret services thank the people of Ryazan for the vigilance, restraint, and patience they have shown." At the same time, Zdanovich called on Russians to take a tolerant view of the need to hold "hard-line" checks on the preparedness, in the first instance, of the agencies of law enforcement to ensure public safety, and also on the vigilance of the public under conditions of heightened terrorist activity. The general told us that this week, as part of the Whirlwind Anti-Terror operation, the FSB had implemented measures in several Russian cities designed to check the response of the law enforcement agencies, including the territorial divisions of the FSB itself, and of the population to "modeled" terrorist activity, involving the planting of explosive devices. The representative of the secret services observed that "serious shortcomings had been uncovered." "Unfortunately, in some of the cities tested, there was no response at all from the law enforcement agencies to the potential planting of bombs." According to Zdanovich, the FSB conducted its operation in conditions as close as possible to a real terrorist threat, otherwise there would have been no point to these checks. Naturally neither the local authorities nor the local law enforcement agencies were informed. Precisely for this reason, the results of the check provide an accurate picture of the degree to which the security of the Russian public is guaranteed in various cities in the country. The general emphasized that the last of these cities to be checked, Ryazan, proved to be by no means the last in terms of the vigilance of the public, but was, unfortunately, less successful in terms of the actions of the law enforcement agencies. The FSB is currently analyzing the results of the checks carried out in order urgently to introduce the necessary correctives to the work of the law enforcement agencies in ensuring the safety of the Russian public. Alexander Zdanovich assured us that once the results had been summed up and the reasons for the 'failures' in the operation itself explained, appropriate measures would be taken immediately.

In this way, the FSB issued an unambiguous statement that Ryazan was the last city in which exercises had been conducted. In actual fact, September 23 marked the beginning of the urgent organization by the FSB (despite Zdanovich's assurances) of an absolutely idiotically conceived exercise to check the vigilance of the public and the agencies of coercion. The press was full of reports of "practice bombings," which were quite impossible to distinguish from the hooligan escapades of telephone terrorists: mock-ups of bombs were planted in one crowded place after another, in post offices, in public institutions, in shops, and the following day, the media reported in graphic detail how the exhausted public had failed to pay any attention to them. This was Patrushev providing himself with an alibi, attempting to prove that the Ryazan "exercises" had been only one episode in a series of checks organized across the whole of Russia by the idiotic FSB.

The journalists had a field day, showering colorful epithets on the dimwitted FSB operatives who hadn't caught a single real terrorist, but kept thinking up stupid war games in a country where real terrorism was rampant. Headlines such as "FSB baseness and stupidity," "The Federal Sabotage Service," "Land of frightened idiots," "Man is Pavlov's dog to man. Let them hold these exercises in the Kremlin," or "The secret services have screwed the people of Ryazan," hardly even stood out against the general background. But the "base and stupid" leadership of the FSB demonstrated remarkable stubbornness, carrying out more and more "practice bombings" and for some reason failed to take serious offense at the journalists' new-found boldness— with only one exception, which was when they wrote about Ryazan.

Here are a few typical "training exercises" from late September and October 1999.

In Moscow, FSB operatives checking on police readiness arrived at a police station with a box on which the word 'bomb" was written. They were allowed inside, where they left their package in one of the offices and then left. The box was only discovered two days later.

A mock-up of an explosive device was planted in a pizzeria on Volkhonka Street in Moscow (it was not discovered).

In Balashikha outside Moscow, an abandoned building was selected, and exercises were conducted in and around it on rescuing the victims of an explosion that had supposedly already taken place in the building, with the involvement of the police, the FSB, and the MCHS.

In Tula and Chelyabinsk, there were repeated instances of mock bombs being planted, perhaps as an exercise, perhaps out of simple hooliganism.

In late October in Omsk employees of the Omsk Region department of the FSB for counterfeit documents drove a vehicle on to the grounds of the Omskvodokanal Company without encountering any obstacles, broke through the company's triple-level defenses, and "exploded" containers of liquid chlorine.

In Ivanovo, FSB operatives planted sacks containing sugar in the basement of a five-story apartment building (they were not discovered).

Also in Ivanovo, a mock-up of an explosive device was left in a trolley. Vigilant passengers immediately spotted the box with wires and handed it over to the driver, who put it in his compartment and drove around with it all night. Afterwards, he took the box to the terminus and dismantled it himself.

On another occasion in Ivanovo, a box containing a mock-up of a bomb was left in a taxi. The driver rode around with it all day long and then threw it out on to the edge of the road, where it lay for several more hours unnoticed by passing pedestrians.

On September 22, an explosive device was discovered in the toilet at the Central Market in Ivanovo. The market was cordoned off, and all the sales personnel and customers urgently evacuated. The military personnel who arrived at the market took an hour to work out what kind of bomb they were supposed to be dealing with. It turned out to be a mock-up. The law enforcement agencies began trying to identify who was responsible for such a professional "joke," especially since the bomb was located in a locked toilet reserved for the use of a small number of people working at the market. The entire personnel of the Ivanovo police was thrown into the search for the culprits. At the height of the operation, spokesmen for the FSB of Moscow officially announced that an exercise had been conducted at the market. Moscow FSB operatives had planted the mock-up.

In Toliatti, the Volga Automobile Plant was "mined." A mock-up of an explosive device was discovered and disarmed. Also in Toliatti, one of the hotels with about fifty people inside was "blown up." One-and-a-half hours were allowed for the "rescue." The exercise involved policemen, firemen, the MCHS, the emergency ambulance service, and the gas company. A practice bombing was also held at the meat factory. The employee who found the "explosive device" took it apart and kept the timing mechanism used in the mock-up for himself.

In Novomoskovsk in the Tula Region an FSB operative disguised as a saboteur gained entry to the Azot Chemical Combine, wrote the word "mined" on a tank of ammonia, and left without being observed. Two weeks before the exercise, a spokesman for Azot had told a session of the regional anti-terrorist commission that Azot did not have the personnel required to guard the plant and also had no money for external security.

Exercises conducted in St. Petersburg entailed consequences. A truck with a number from another town, filled with sacks of supposed explosives, was parked in the special parking lot on Zakharevskaya Street in front of the offices of the investigative department of the MVD and FSB of St. Petersburg and the Leningrad Region. The "terrorist" vehicle stood there for days without attracting any attention, although no one had ever seen a truck in the official parking lot before. The outcome of the exercise was the firing of the head of the MVD of St. Petersburg and the Leningrad Region major general of the police, Victor Vlasov (which was, in fact, the real reason for leaving the truck in the MVD parking lot).

Any abortive terrorist attack or straightforward incident of banditry could now easily be written off to possible FSB exercises. In early October, the residents were hastily evacuated from a nine-story house at number 4, Third Grazhdanskaya Street in Moscow. Someone had found four crates containing 288 mine detonators on the stone steps leading down into the basement. That was enough explosive to blow up the building.

According to the residents, two Zhiguli automobiles had stopped in the yard of their house, and several hefty men had taken four massive ironbound wooden crates out of the trunks of the cars, and left them on the basement steps before leaving again. Less than two minutes later, the first police units were already working at the scene. Another fifteen minutes later, the crates were being examined by explosives specialists from the FSB, and an "exclusion zone" had been established around the building.

The police were unable to establish who owned the cars from which the munitions had been unloaded, and they were not able to create sketches of the sturdy, fit-looking terrorists, either. In addition to the traditional explanation of the "Chechen connection," the police officers conducting the investigation came up with the alternative of a test of vigilance conducted by the secret services.

The work-rate of the law enforcement agencies in Ryazan was truly impressive during the days when Patrushev decided to hold his "exercises" there. From September 13 to September 22, the Ryazan special units responded to more than forty reports from local residents of sightings of explosive devices. On September 13, all the inhabitants of house number 18 on Kostiushko Street and the houses adjacent to it were evacuated in only twenty minutes. In only one-and-a half hours, the building was searched from the basements to the attics. The operation involved VDV cadets, police units, ambulance brigades, employees of the MCHS, and SWAT engineers. A similar evacuation also took place from a house on Internatsionalnaya Street. During this period the editorial staff of the newspaper *Vechernyaya Ryazan* and the pupils of school No. 45 had to be evacuated. Every case proved to be a false alarm. School children tossed a live RGD-22 shell into one of the entranceways of house No. 32 on Stankozavodskaya Street out of sheer mischief. There was also a bomb-clearance operation in the center of the city, on Victory Square. The suspicious object there proved to be a gas cylinder half-buried in the ground. In addition to all this, the "Dynamite" and "Foreigner" stages of the Whirlwind Anti-Terror operation were taking place in the city, with special detachments checking 3,812 city basements and 4,430 attics three times every day.

In the afternoon of September 22, Ryazan received a message from the Moscow FSB that, according to information received in Moscow, one of the houses on Biriuzov Street was mined, but which one was not known. In Ryazan, they immediately began checking all the houses along the street. Thousands of people were temporarily evacuated, and all the apartments were checked. Nothing was found. It was later established that it had been a false alarm from a telephone terrorist. Then at this point, Patrushev decided to check the vigilance of the people of Ryazan during the overnight hours.

For a number of formal reasons, the planting of the sacks in the apartment building in Ryazan could not have been an exercise. When a training exercise is held, there has to be a previously determined plan to work to. The plan must specify the manager of the exercise, his deputy, the observers, and the parties being tested (the inhabitants of Ryazan, the employees of the FSB for the Ryazan Region, and so on). The plan must list the items that are to be checked. The plan must have a so-called "plot," a specific scenario for the performance to be given. In the Ryazan incident, the scenario was the planting of sacks of sugar in the basement of an apartment building. The plan must define the material requirements of the exercise: vehicles, money (for instance, to buy three fifty-kilogram sacks of sugar), food (if a large number of people are taking part in the exercise), weapons, communications equipment, and coding systems (code tables), etc.

After all this has been included, the plan is approved by senior command and only then, on the basis of the approved plan, is a written instruction (it must be written) issued for the exercise, to be held. Immediately before the start of the exercise the individual who approved the plan for the exercise and issued the order for it to be held reports that it is beginning. After the completion of the exercise, he reports that it is over. Then a compulsory report is drawn up on the results of the exercise, identifying the positive outcomes and the shortcomings, individuals who have distinguished themselves are praised, and miscreants are identified. This same order lists the material resources consumed or destroyed in the course of the exercise (in the case of the Ryazan incident, at least three sacks of sugar and a cartridge for the detonator).

It is compulsory for the head of the local FSB to be notified of a planned exercise. He is directly subordinate to the director of the FSB, and no one has the right, for instance, to check on Sergeiev's performance without Patrushev's permission. Likewise, no one has the right to check up on Sergeiev's subordinates, the employees of the Ryazan FSB, without Sergeiev's permission. This means that Patrushev and Sergeiev must already have known on September 22 about any "exercises" which were due to be conducted. But Patrushev did not issue a statement to that effect until September 24, and Sergeiev has never issued one, because he knew nothing at all about the "exercises."

Under the terms of its statute, the FSB is only entitled to check on itself. It is not allowed to check the performance of other organizations or of private individuals. If the FSB carries out a check on the MVD (the Ryazan police, for instance), it has to be a joint exercise with the MVD, and the appropriate officials of the MVD in the center and the provinces have to be notified. If the exercise affects the civilian population (as was the case in Ryazan), then the civil defense service and the MCHS are also involved. In all cases, a joint plan of the exercise has to be drawn up and signed by the heads of all the relevant departments. The plan is approved by the individual who coordinates all the various agencies of coercion which are involved in the exercise. Exercises may be made as close as possible to real situations, such as exercises involving live shelling. However, it is absolutely forbidden to conduct exercises in which people might be hurt, or which might pose a threat of damage to the environment. There is a specific prohibition on holding exercises that involve members of the armed forces and military units on active service, or ships standing at battle station. If a frontier guard is on duty at his post, it is forbidden to imitate a breach of the frontier in order to test his vigilance. If a facility is under guard, it is forbidden to attack that facility as part of an exercise.

Active service differs from an exercise in that during periods of duty military goals are pursued with the use of live weapons. Each branch of the forces (and the police) has an active service charter which lays everything out in detail. On September 22–23 1999, the police patrols on the streets of Ryazan were on active service, carrying weapons and special equipment, which they were entitled to use to detain FSB operatives planting mysterious sacks in the basement of an apartment building. Following the series of explosions in Ryazan, the entire police force of the city was operating in an intensive regime in response to the real threat of terrorist attacks, which meant that unfortunate FSB operatives involved in unannounced exercises could quite simply have been shot.

That brings us to the initiation of criminal proceedings under article 205, which means that an investigator had issued a warrant for the location and arrest of the suspects, and that they could have been killed in the process of arrest. The basis for the instigation of criminal proceedings is clearly defined in the Criminal Procedural Code of the Russian Federation, which does not contain any points concerning the instigation of criminal proceedings during exercises or in connection with exercises. The unfounded or illegal instigation of criminal proceedings is in itself a criminal offense, as is their illegal termination.

And finally, exercises cannot be held without observers, who objectively assess the results of an exercise and then draw up reports on its successes and failures, apportion praise and blame, and draw conclusions. There were no observers in Ryazan.

If Patrushev were to have defied the existing regulations, charters and statutes and dared to order secret exercises, his action would have had to be regarded as a crime. Let us start from the fact that Patrushev would have violated the Federal Law on the Agencies of the Federal Security Service in the Russian Federation as adopted by the State Duma on February 22, 1995, and ratified by the president. Article No. 8 of this law states that "the activities of the agencies of the Federal Security Service and the methods and the means they employ must not cause harm to people's lives and health or cause damage to the environment." Article No. 6 of the law describes the responsibilities of the FSB and the rights of private individuals at length:

> The state guarantees the observance of human and civil rights and freedoms in the performance of their duty by the agencies of the Federal Security Service. No limitation of human and civil rights and freedoms shall be permitted with the exception of those cases specified by federal constitutional laws and federal laws.
>
> An individual who believes that the agencies of the Federal Security Service or their officers have infringed his rights and freedoms shall be entitled to make appeal against the actions of the aforementioned agencies and their officers to a superior

agency of the Federal Security Service, the Public Prosecutor's Office, or a court.

Agencies of the state, enterprises, institutions, and organizations, regardless of their form of ownership, and also public organizations and individuals shall be entitled in accordance with the legislation of the Russian Federation to receive an explanation and information from the agencies of the Federal Security Service in cases where their rights and freedoms have been restricted. . . .

In a case of the infringement of human and civil rights by employees of the agencies of the Federal Security Service, the head of the respective agency of the Federal Security Service, public prosecutor, or judge is obliged to take measures to restore such rights and freedoms, make good any damage caused, and call the guilty parties to account as specified under the legislation of the Russian Federation.

Officers of the agencies of the Federal Security Service who have committed an abuse of power or exceeded the bounds of their official authority shall be held responsible as specified under the legislation of the Russian Federation.

The criminal acts described in article 6 of the Federal Law on the FSB fall under the following articles of the Criminal Code of the Russian Federation:

Article 286. Exceeding the bounds of official authority.

Acts committed by an officer which clearly exceed the bounds of his authority and have resulted in violation of the rights and legitimate interests of individuals or organizations...The same action committed by an individual occupying an official state post of the Russian Federation . . . with the use of force or threat of its use; with the use of a weapon or special means; resulting in grave consequences . . . shall be punishable by a term of imprisonment of from three to ten years and deprivation of the right to hold specified posts or engage in specified forms of activity for a period of up to three years.

Article 207. Deliberate provision of false information concerning an act of terrorism.

The deliberate provision of false information concerning a planned explosion, act of arson, or other actions which constitute a threat to the lives of individuals and a danger of substantial damage to property . . . shall be punishable by a fine . . . or by imprisonment for a term of up to three years.

And finally, article 213. "Hooliganism, a gross violation of public order clearly expressive of disrespect for society . . . shall be punishable . . . by imprisonment for a term of up to two years."

An officer occupying an official state post, FSB director Patrushev, issued orders for the use of special means (sacks with unidentified contents and a shotgun cartridge) for the forcible exclusion of residents from a building in Ryazan for the entire night. This absolutely illegal action, which has no basis in any military or civil charters or statutes, and certainly not in any laws, entailed grave consequences in the form of damage to health and severe psychological stress suffered by individuals, specifically the serious cold contracted by one child whose mother was ordered by the police to take him outside straight from his bath without any chance to dress him properly, as well as heart attacks and hypertensive crises suffered by several of the residents.

At least two medical experts provided opinions concerning the psychological consequences of the "exercise" for the people who were driven out of their homes. In the opinion of Nikolai Kyrov, head of administration of the psychotherapeutical support service of the Moscow Public Health Committee, the residents of the building in Ryazan were subjected to serious psychological trauma: "It is comparable with what people would have suffered during a genuine terrorist attack. And people who have survived an explosion are changed forever; they've been taken right up to the boundary between life and death. The mind never lets go of such significant moments. At least some time in the middle of the experiment, the inhabitants of the house should have been informed that it was not a real emergency, but only an exercise." Yuri Boiko, Moscow's senior psychotherapist, drew an even gloomier picture: "The result of uncertainty and fear will be a sharp increase in the consumption of nicotine, alcohol, and simply food. Part of the public is already turning for help to non-professionals: people's interest in all sorts of sects, magicians, and fortune-tellers is on the increase." (The penalty on this charge is from three to ten years, with exclusion from holding office for three years.)

Although supposedly aware that an exercise was being conducted in Ryazan, Patrushev failed to inform the public and the inhabitants of the building in Ryazan for one and a half days, which is tanta-mount to deliberately providing false information concerning an act of terrorism. (We can settle for the fine on this charge—and then, under the terms of article 2 1 3, add two years for flagrant disrespect for society.)

Let us also note that, under the terms of part IV of the Statute on the Federal Security Service of the Russian Federation of July 6, 1 9 9 8, "the director of the F S B of Russia bears personal responsibil-ity for the achievement of the objectives set for the F S B of Russia and the agencies of the Federal Security Service." Perhaps the General Public Prosecutor of Russia will take up the case? He has already rejected the instigation of criminal proceedings for terrorism.

An exercise could not legally have been conducted using a stolen car. According to the Criminal Code of the Russian Federation the theft of an automobile is a crime, and a person who has committed such a crime bears criminal responsibility. Under the terms of the law on the F S B, the service's operatives have no right to commit a crime, even when in pursuit of military objectives. Only the F S B's own vehicles are used in operational exercises involving agents (including opera-tional passenger automobiles, of which the F S B has two full parking lots for its central administration alone). If one of these cars is stopped by police, for instance, for speeding on the Moscow-Ryazan highway, or detained by the Ryazan police because paper has been pasted over the Moscow license plate, obscuring it in a suspicious manner, the car can immediately be identified as one that is specially registered. Any policeman will recognize this as indicating that the car is one of the operational vehicles belonging to the agencies of law enforcement or the secret services.

Exercises would have been conducted using operational vehicles. However, the FSB could not use operational vehicles to commit an act of terrorism. The car might be noticed (as it was) and identified (as it was). It would look really bad if terrorists blew up a building in Ryazan using a car registered to the FSB transport fleet, but if terrorists blew up the building using a stolen car that would only be normal and natural. On the other hand, if FSB operatives driving in a stolen car by day (not by night) were stopped for a routine check or for speeding, they would simply present their official identity cards or "cover documents" and after that, no policeman would bother to check the documents for the car, so he would never know it was wanted by the police.

FSB agents on operational duty often carry a MUR identity card, printed in the special FSB laboratory as a "cover document." On the occasion of his arrest, Khinshtein, a *Moskovsky Komsomolets* journalist, famed for his remarkable and far from accidental knowledge concerning cases residing in the safes of the secret services, presented MUR identity card No. 03726 of a certain Alexander Matveiev, a captain in the criminal investigation department, issued by the Moscow MVD. In addition Khinshtein was carrying a special pass forbidding the police to search his car. When the police asked him where the documents came from, he replied honestly that they belonged to him and were his "cover documents."

If official identity cards of that kind were found on someone like Khinshtein, one can imagine what an array of "cover documents" was carried by the FSB operatives setting out to blow up the building in Ryazan. And if the car's documents were checked, and it was discovered to be stolen, they could always say they'd just found it and were returning it to its owner.

The car in which the terrorists arrived was the only clue left after the attempt to blow up the apartment building, the beginning of the only trail that might lead back to the perpetrators. The car is the weakest link in the planning and implementation of any act of terrorism. It was only possible to blow up the building in Ryazan if a stolen car was used.

In conclusion, we would like to quote the opinion expressed by former Public Prosecutor General of Russia, Skuratov in an interview with the Russian-language Paris newspaper *Russkaya Mysl* for October 29, 1999:

> I was very much disturbed and alarmed by what happened in Ryazan. In this case, it certainly is possible to construct a scenario with the secret services themselves involved in planning an explosion in Ryazan, and making very clumsy excuses when they were caught out. I am amazed that the public prosecutor's office never did get to the bottom of the business. That's its job.

So we are left with no indication that an exercise was being carried out in Ryazan, except the oral statements of FSB chief Patrushev, his subordinate Zdanovich, who is bound in the line of duty to support everything Patrushev says, and several other FSB officers. All the facts, however, indicate that a terrorist attack was, indeed, thwarted in Ryazan. Those who commissioned, planned, carried out, and abetted this crime have yet to be tried and convicted. But since we know the suspects' names, positions, work and home addresses, and even their telephone numbers, arresting them should not be too difficult.

CHAPTER SIX

The FSB Resorts to Mass Terror
Buinaksk, Moscow, and Volgodonsk

THE PERPETRATORS of the terrorist attacks in Buinaksk, Moscow, and Volgodonsk were never found, and we can only guess at who was behind the attacks by analogy with the events in Ryazan. In these three towns, the Ryazan-style "exercises" were carried through to their intended conclusion, and the lives of several hundred people were abruptly cut short or completely devastated.

In August 1999, all the members of Lazovsky's group were at large in society, including Vorobyov. At that time, yet another military operation was just approaching its conclusion in Dagestan, into which the Chechen separatists had made an incursion. A lot has been said and written since that time about this Chechen encroachment into Dagestan. It has been claimed that the invasion was planned in the Kremlin and deliberately provoked by the Russian secret services. The Russian media were full of articles about a conspiratorial meeting in France, between Shamil Basaev and the head of the president's office, Alexander Voloshin, organized by the Russian intelligence agent, A. Surikov, in France. We are not in possession of enough facts to draw absolutely definite conclusions. Let us begin with Surikov's interview.

On August 24, 1999, the newspaper Versiya—a part of the holding company *Sovershenno Sekretno* that was headed by Artym Borovik, who died in a plane crash together with the Chechen businessman Ziya Bazhaev on March 9, 2000—published an interview with Colonel

Surikov of the GRU, a person close to Yevgeny Primakov on the one hand and to Yuri Maslyukov on the other. During the Georgian–Abkhazian conflict, Surikov served under Abkhazian Defense Minister Sultan Sosnaliev. In the course of the war he became acquainted with Basaev. From then on, he was considered an expert on the Caucausus. In the editorial note that preceded the interview, Versiya reported that it was Surikov who had organized the "secret meeting with the head of the president's office, Voloshin." Neither Surikov nor Voloshin denied this statement. Surikov reported that:

> Shamil Basaev and Hattab created fortified areas in Dagestan on a scale not even suspected by the press. They dug trenches, erected fortifications, established arms and ammunition supply lines from Chechnya. They also established communication and transportation networks between each other and Chechnya. Mine fields surround the fortified areas. My professional opinion is that using artillery and aviation alone, as the federal troops have been doing in the mountains of Dagestan, is not enough. So far the federation's actions have been ineffective and have not caused damage to the enemy's forces or fortifications. In order to liquidate the fortified areas, a ground offensive with air support is necessary. . . .
>
> The federal formations being organized in Dagestan are made up of odd scraps. Policemen from the Urals, SWAT from Murmansk, various components from the Defense Ministry, large numbers of conscripts. According to my sources, conscripts constitute one third—contrary to the generals' assurances that conscripts aren't sent to Dagestan. It is pointless to talk about "stream-lining" such a diverse crowd for active duty. There are as many as thirty generals in the region at the moment, although a single well-coordinated regiment would be sufficient to liquidate the Chechen fighters. And with co-ordinated activity and unified command in place, a single colonel could be in charge of the entire operation. At the

moment, all of these generals are simply making a huge mess of the chain of command since they belong to different departments.

Therefore, in the current situation a military operation would cause great casualties among our soldiers and policemen. I would predict that 300–400 of our men would die in an attack, and we already have approximately 250 dead and wounded. Despite the generals' assertions to the contrary, the Chechen fighters have suffered minimal losses–about 40 people. They might lose about as many in an assault. In general, reports about losses on the Chechen side—thousands killed in one day—remind me of reports from the Chechen War of 1995–1997.

Our generals evidently fail to take into account the fact that Shamil Basaev is an experienced guerrilla fighter who became an expert in sabotage long before the war in Chechnya. He went through a complete training course in one of the Russian intelligence agencies. This was during the peak of the Georgian–Abkhazian war. At that time, Moscow took a cowardly stance, and instead of acting in defense of Abkhazia, where a genocide was taking place, the only thing that the Russian forces did was to offer unofficial assistance to the volunteer detachments that went off to war. Pavel Grachyov, who was Minister of Defense at the time, pretended not to know about this. And one fourth of these volunteers, who came to fight in Abkhazia, were Chechens. And their leader was Shamil Basaev.

Basaev is now making significant tactical improvements to the military actions in Dagestan. He's holding down a fortified area in Botlikha, but this is merely a diversionary maneuver. He's starting to establish a guerrilla movement. Along with sabotage, this is the most effective means to conduct a war in a forested mountainous region. Now his tactics consist of short attacks on columns of federal forces, organizing ambushes, mining roads, shelling strategic targets with RPGs. . . .

The Kremlin knew that Dagestan was about to be invaded

by the Wahhabists. They could not not have known it. They were warned about it by the secret services. Even Versiya wrote about it. So why did they blow it? Because there are people in the Kremlin who seriously believe that individuals such as Basaev can be paid to do anything that Moscow tells them. . . .

On the whole, the Russian secret services also slept through Basaev's invasion of Dagestan. Because our secret services are now at that stage of decay when it becomes hard to deal with direct obligations on account of business commitments. They're only capable of bulldozing reporters like Pasko, and even then unsuccessfully. The situation in the Caucausus can still be salvaged. But there's no one to salvage it.

What is remarkable is not that Surikov gave Versiya an interview, but that his interview was given three weeks after Versiya's publication of the original materials about the meeting between Voloshin and Basaev. Had Surikov thought that Versiya's earlier article did not correspond to reality, he would have either refused to grant Versiya an interview or else made use of the opportunity to refute it.

Versiya's original article was titled "The Agreement." It was published on August 3, 1999:

A luxurious villa in the French town of Beaulieu, situated between Nice and Monaco, has been watched by the French secret services for a long time. The villa belongs to the international arms dealer Adnan Khashoggi. And although nothing can be said against Khashoggi from the perspective of the French criminal code, the Saudi billionaire has a suspicious reputation.

Versiya was informed about the heightened interest in Khashoggi by a source in the French secret services whose name we will not publish. He is a professor of political science and at the same time an expert in Russian defense, security, and organized crime issues. He frequently speaks out in the press and takes part in investigative reporting. He works under contract for French government agencies, including French counterintelligence.

This source has reported that the French put the villa under close surveillance at the beginning of July, when the Venezuelan banker Alfonso Davidovich moved in there with his young black secretary. In the Latin American press, Davidovich is described as a money launderer for the left-wing insurgent organization FARC (Fuerzas Armadas Revolucionarias de Colombia), which has been engaged in a military conflict with the official authorities for several decades. FARC's principal source of funds is believed to be the drug trade.

It soon turned out that one of Davidovich's rather frequent visitors was a certain French businessman of Israeli-Soviet origin, the Sukhumi-born 53-year-old Yakov Kosman. After a while, Kosman arrived at the villa with six people who had come through Austria with Turkish passports. One of these Turks was identified by the secret services as Tsveiba, who had at one time so distinguished himself in the Georgian–Abkhazian war that he is still charged with war crimes by the authorities in Tbilisi, including massacres of the civilian population. All six moved into the villa and did not leave its confines for three weeks.

Finally, the secret services were able to observe Kosman together with Tsveiba and one other guest—presumably an Abkhazian—departing for the local airport in Nice. At the same time, two people arrived at the airport in a private plane from Paris. One of them—Sultan Sosnaliev—had been the Abkhazian Minister of Defense during the years of the Georgian–Abkhazian war and effectively the number two man in the republic after Vladislav Ardzinba. The second person who came out of that airplane was another individual from Sukhumi—Anton Surikov. During the years of the war in Abkhazia, Surikov had served under Sosnaliev. Operating under the assumed name "Mansur," he was responsible for organizing acts of sabotage. Subsequently, under his real name, Surikov occupied a key post in the administration of Yevgeny Primakov, although his official title was merely assistant to First Deputy Prime Minister Yuri Maslyukov. Both of them proceeded to the villa in Beaulieu.

In the middle of July, two days after the couple's arrival, the private British yacht "Magia" arrived in the port of Beaulieu from Malta. Two "Englishmen" came ashore from the boat. If their passports are to be believed, one of these "Englishmen" was a certain Turk by the name of Mehmet, formerly a consultant to the Islamist Prime Minister of Turkey, Erbakan, a rather influential figure in Turkish, Middle Eastern, and Caucasian Wahhabist circles. The second person, to the surprise of the secret services, was the well-known Chechen field commander Shamil Basaev. Incidentally, he had also at one time been Sosnaliev's deputy and headed the Chechen forces in Abkhazia. The French intensified their surveillance. And for good reason. Late in the evening, on an airplane belonging to one of Russia's oil companies, a man arrived at the Nice airport. The man was balding, had a beard, sharp eyes, and bore a strong resemblance to the head of the Kremlin administration. After passing through French passport control, this individual looked around intently. He was dressed in a formal suit, with a suitcase and without any bodyguards. The balding man calmed down only when he saw the people who were there to meet him—two Abkhazians and Surikov. All of them got inside a Rolls Royce and drove off to the villa in Beaulieu.

That entire night, something went on at the villa. The villa's security was especially vigilant, and there was so much magnetic radiation in the area surrounding the villa that cell phones within a radius of several hundred yards stopped working. In the morning, the same Rolls Royce drove to the airport and the person who resembled Voloshin flew back to Moscow. The following day, all of the guests at the villa departed.

It should be noted that Versiya turned out to be remarkably unyield-
ing, even stubborn, in insisting on the theory that the invasion of
Dagestan in August 1999 was organized by Russian secret services.
In particular, on February 29, 2000, a few days before the deaths of
Borovik and Bazhayev and the presidential election that brought
Putin to power, the newspaper published an article titled "Khasbula-
tov's Conspiracy":

> After Khasbulatov informs the Kremlin about the coup d'etat
> being prepared [in Chechnya], the head of the president's
> office Alexander Voloshin, according to certain sources, hur-
> ries to a meeting with Shamil Basaev in France. This meeting
> is organized for Voloshin by Anton Surikov, a GRU colonel
> close to the authorities, or more concretely, close to the circle
> of Yevgeny Primakov, the former head of federal intelligence.
> Immediately after the talks in France, Shamil Basaev invades
> Dagestan. Then come the apartment-house bombings in
> Moscow and other Russian cities. And then the second
> Chechen campaign. That is how wars start.

The bibliography of the meeting between Voloshin and Basaev would
not be complete without a reference to "Conspiracy-2," the final article
in this series. The article was published—again in Versiya—on July 2,
2000, after Putin's election victory, outside the context of any election campaign. It represented an expanded version of the earlier article,
"Conspiracy," with new excerpts:

> The meeting supposedly took place at the villa of the interna-
> tional arms dealer Adnan Khashoggi in the village of Beaulieu
> near Nice on July 4, 1999.... Earlier, sources in the French
> and Israeli secret services, which had provided this informa-
> tion, reported that "there exists a video of the meeting at the
> villa in Beaulieu." However, they offered no evidence. At the
> end of June, Versiya received a large mail envelope without a
> return address. The envelope contained a photograph of three

men. Pictured on the left was an individual resembling Anton Surikov, assistant to former First Deputy Prime Minister Yuri Maslyukov. Pictured in the middle was a person bearing a very close resemblance to the head of the Kremlin office, Alexander Voloshin—balding and with a similar beard. Next to these two individuals was a squatting person wearing shorts—balding, but with a more substantial beard. After some time, *Versiya* received a phone call, and the caller, without introducing himself, said: "This is a photograph of the meeting between Voloshin and Basaev. Voloshin is easy to recognize. Basaev is the bearded man on the right." The unidentified caller specified that the photo was printed from a still-frame, and that the recording was made on an analog video camera. . . .

At the time of the meeting, Surikov was a consultant to the general director of MIG Company. At present he is still working with Maslyukov, but now heads the Committee on Industry, Construction, and Scientific Technology in the Duma. . . .

According to verifiable information from the French and Israelis, the private British yacht *Magia* arrived at the Beaulieu port from Malta on July 3. Two passengers disembarked. If their passports are credible, one of these "Englishmen" was a certain Turk by the name of Mehmet. . . . The second person, to the surprise of the intelligence officers, was Chechen field commander Shamil Basaev. . . .

Late in the evening of July 4, a man arrived at the Nice airport in a private plane belonging to one of Russia's oil companies. The man was balding, with a small beard, sharp eyes, and resembled the head of the President's Administration. . . .

Whether by coincidence or not, some time later—in August—Shamil Basaev's group invaded Dagestan. The resignation of Prime Minister Sergei Stepashin soon followed. The former head of the FSB replaced him. After this, federal troops successfully repulsed the attack on Dagestan, and in pursuit of the Chechen fighters, once again entered rebellious Chechnya. The "anti-terrorist operation" in the Chechen Republic has been going on since that time and is unlikely to end in the near future. It should be noted that different sources have given different explanations of the purpose of the visit to Beaulieu by individuals resembling Voloshin and Basaev. According to one hypothesis, the subsequent invasion of Dagestan constituted a public relations stunt within the framework of the operation "Heir." According to a contrary hypothesis, the man resembling the head of the President's Administration had learned from the Russian secret services about Basaev's intentions and had asked individuals who had once worked with him —presumably Anton Surikov—to arrange a meeting with Basaev, in order to attempt to prevent the invasion.

Ilyas Akhmadov, the Chechen minister of foreign affairs in the government of Aslan Maskhadov, believed that the operation in Dagestan was provoked by Moscow:

> The leadership of Chechnya has condemned the Dagestan campaign. For us this is really a big problem. But remember what happened in July, when the Russian army destroyed our fortified position and then an entire battalion of Russian soldiers invaded our territory. Surely, that is provocation? Pilgrims from Dagestan came to Basaev and asked him to free them from 'the Russian yoke,' then when he began the campaign, they began saying on television that they didn't want it, and they wanted to live in Russia. It's an obvious set-up.

According to Abdurashid Saidov, founder and former chairman of the Islamic Democratic Party of Dagestan from 1997 onwards, following the adoption by the Dagestan Parliament of its famous law "On the struggle against Islamic fundamentalism," members of the religious minority (the Wahhabites) were deliberately forced out of Dagestan into Chechnya. Persecution and threats of physical violence simply made it impossible for Wahhabis to live in Dagestan. At the same time, the Dagestan leadership was well aware that the Wahhabis would be greeted with open arms in Chechnya. Once forced out of Dagestan into Chechnya the Dagestan Islamists joined the opposition and were prepared in time to return to Dagestan in the new capacity of rulers of the state. Rumors of a forthcoming invasion from Chechnya had circulated in Dagestan in 1997 and 1998, at a time when Russia had left the borders with Chechnya in the Tsumadin, Botlikha, and Kazbek districts of Dagestan exposed. Active members of the radical Dagestan opposition moved freely between the territories of the two republics, but there was no reaction from the FSB, which at that time was headed by Putin. It is possible that the retinue of the leader of the Dagestan Islamist radicals, Bagaudin, who had sought refuge from pursuit in Chechnya, included provocateurs operating on the orders of certain Russian departments of coercion, and they were the ones who, when the right moment came, pushed Bagaudin, and through him Basaev and Hattab, into the invasion of Dagestan.

From May to June 1999, every market trader in Grozny already knew that an invasion of Dagestan was inevitable. For some reason, only the Russian secret services knew nothing about it. From July, there were several hundred armed Dagestan Wahhabis in the Dagestan village of Echeda in Russia, where they had dug themselves in and reinforced their positions in the inaccessible ravines on the Russian border with Chechnya and Georgia. Long before the arrival in the Tsumadin Region of the Islamist rebels, the area was bristling with weapons. In late July, at the height of a fuel crisis in the region, heavy tankers delivered fuel, tons at a time, to the guerrilla camps in the hills above the very windows of the Regional MVD and FSB of the Tsumada district. The FSB failed to react, because the prospective armed conflict between the Chechens and the Dagestanis would be to the Kremlin's advantage.

At the same time, Bagaudin was receiving encouraging reports from his agents: "There's no one in Tsumada apart from policemen, and they won't go against their own. We'll be in the regional center in no time at all. This is your home region, the people are waiting for you, support is guaranteed, so push on!" And Bagaudin fell into the trap. On the eve of the invasion, Basaev actually suggested joint operations with Bagaudin, but the offer of help was refused, so that Basaev and Hattab were forced to act separately, advancing in the direction of Botlikha, which was most opportune for the Russian leadership, indeed perfectly timed for the organizers of Putin's election campaign. At this precise point in time, Russia was hit by an unprecedented series of terrorist attacks.

The motivation behind the September attacks was provided by the FSB itself. An official information release from the FSB for Moscow and the Moscow region, formulated the goals of the terrorists, who blew up apartment houses in Moscow in September 1999, as follows: "One of the main explanations under consideration by the investigators was the perpetration of a terrorist attack intended to destabilize the situation in Moscow, intimidate the public, and influence the authorities into taking certain decisions, which are in the interests of the organizers of the attack." The very same idea was formulated in the language of satirical polemic by the newspaper *Vechernyaya Moskva*: "The terrorists' main aim is to create a heinously oppressive atmosphere in society. To make me turn into a coward so that I slap my neighbor from the Caucasus across the face, and he pulls out his dagger, and then it all starts. . . . So that the party of idiots can emerge from underground, and the mass arrests can start—only don't ask what party this is, and where this underground is located."

It's clear enough which kind of "particular decisions" the authorities could be influenced into taking by the bombings, and which kind they could not. The explosions could easily result in a decision to introduce troops into Chechnya. But there was absolutely no way terrorist attacks could produce the decision the Chechens wanted on granting Chechnya formal independence (by this time it had already achieved informal independence). In other words, the bombings were needed by the Russian secret services, in order to start a war with Chechnya, but not by the insurgents in Chechnya to encourage the legal recognition of their independent republic. Future events confirmed that this was indeed the case: the war began, the secret services came to power in Russia, and Chechen independence came to an end.

And all as a result of the terrorist attacks carried out in September.

On August 31, a trial bombing took place in the Okhotnyi Ryad shopping center on Manezh Square in the center of Moscow. One person was killed, and forty were injured The government immediately put forward the "Chechen connection" as an explanation, although it was hard to imagine that the Chechen terrorists would attack a shopping complex where the director was the well-known Chechen, Umar Djabrailov. The person later arrested for planning and carrying out the terrorist attack was "a certain Ryzhenkov," who according to the FSB "impersonated an FSB general." In fact, however, as early as 1996, Nikolai Zelenko, head of military intelligence in General Lev Rokhlin's 8th Army Corps, had reported to the FSB that FSB General Ryzhenkov was "definitely working" for terrorists.

Military intelligence engages in operational activity, both inside and outside Russia, and it has its own staff of secret agents. The 8th Army Corps was stationed at Volgograd, had fought in Chechnya, and was especially active in recruiting agents among the Chechens. Shamil Basaev underwent training at the GRU firing range in Volgograd before the conflict between Georgia and Abkhazia, and it was military intelligence that trained him. If Zelenko had learned something about who was behind the bombing at the Okhotnyi Ryad shopping complex, and about Ryzhenkov, he certainly must have reported it to General Rokhlin, who was chairman of the Defense Committee of the State Duma. At the time, however, Ryzhenkov was not detained. On the contrary, it was Zelenko who was arrested.

Zelenko had served almost all of his time in the army in the Caucasus. He'd been in all the hot spots: Karabakh, Baku, Tbilisi, Abkhazia, Dagestan, and Chechnya. He only missed out on Grozny itself, because he had been seriously wounded. FSB employees turned up to see Zelenko twenty days after he'd had a heart operation at the Burdenko Hospital in Moscow. They accused him of possessing an unregistered pistol and planning to kill a certain businessman, and they took him as far away from Moscow as possible, to the prison in Chelyabinsk.

So why was Zelenko arrested? Rokhlin was on good terms with the head of the FSB's military intelligence at the time, Vladimir Petrischev, and would have been obliged to report to him any information received from Zelenko. That was when strange things started to happen: first Zelenko was arrested, and then on July 3, 1998, General Rokhlin was murdered.

The FSB itself effectively confirmed that the arrest of Zelenko, the murder of Rokhlin, and the terrorist attacks in Russia were all interconnected. All of the cases were handled by the same investigator from the office of the Public Prosecutor General, N. P. Indiukov, who had a great deal of experience in the investigation of fixed cases, in which it was important to make sure that the investigation was directed along a false trail. Indiukov was appointed to conduct the investigation into the case of Tamara Rokhlina, who was accused of murdering her husband. The various stages of this great masterpiece of Russian jurisprudence are well known. Tamara Rokhlina was arrested after the general's murder, and in November 2000, she was sentenced to eight years' imprisonment. In December, the length of her sentence was halved. On June 7, 2001, the Supreme Court of the Russian Federation quashed Rokhlina's conviction, and on June 8, she was released from custody. Indiukov made no attempt whatsoever to investigate claims that the general had been killed by three unknown men wearing masks.

However, the most remarkable thing in all of this is that Zelenko's case, following his arrest on completely unrelated charges of common criminal activity, was also investigated by Indiukov, and that the case never even reached the courts. Zelenko was quietly released without any publicity following General Rokhlin's death.

These strange killings, dubious investigations and deliberately provoked incursions into foreign territory provided the background to the blowing up of a residential building in the district of Buinaksk in Dagestan. Sixty-four of the building's residents were killed. This terrorist attack was deliberately linked with the defeat of the Chechen rebel detachments in Dagestan, even though there were no Chechens among the perpetrators of the attack, and those accused of planning the bombing claimed that they were innocent. On the same day, a

ZIL-130 automobile loaded with 2,706 kilograms of explosives was found in Buinaksk. The car was in a parking lot in a region containing residential buildings and a military hospital. An explosion was only averted thanks to the vigilance of local people. In other words, a second terrorist bombing in Buinaksk was foiled by members of the public, not the secret services.

During the night of September 8–9, the nine-story apartment house at number 19 Guryanov Street in Moscow was torn apart by an explosion. The blast killed ninety-four people and injured 164 more. The first account put forward was an explosion due to a gas leak. The following day, the FSB for Moscow and the Moscow Region announced that "the collapse of the third and fourth entranceways was induced by the detonation of about 350 kilograms of a high-explosive mixture. The explosive device was located at ground level. Physical and chemical investigation of items removed from the site of the occurrence revealed traces ... of hexogen and TNT on their surfaces."

It was apparent immediately after the first bombing of an apartment block that the attack was the work of professionals, not so much from the actual implementation of the terrorist attack itself as from its planning and preparation. A massive terrorist bombing, which involves the use of hundreds of kilograms of explosives, several vehicles, and a number of people is hard to put together in a hurry. Many former and serving members of the secret services including, a former GRU employee, retired Colonel Robert Bykov, believe that the terrorists must have shipped the explosives into Moscow in several batches over a period of four to six months. Modeling of terrorist attacks has shown that it would have been impossible to prepare for an explosion of this type any quicker. The model was constructed to take account of all the stages of the operation: finalization of the contract, making initial calculations based on the plan of the building, visiting the site, adjusting the initial calculations, determining the optimal composition of the explosives, ordering its manufacture, making final calculations adjusted according to the actual composition of the explosives, renting storage space, and shipping in the explosives, etc. This meant that the preparations would have had to begin in the spring of 1999. During that period, the Chechens could not have been preparing terrorist attacks in response to the counter-offensive by Russian forces in Dagestan, since the Chechens had not yet made their own incursion into Dagestan territory.

Rumors about imminent terrorist attacks had been circulating long before the first explosions occurred. On July 2, 1999, the journalist Alexander Zhilin obtained possession of a certain document dated June 29, 1999. He believed that it originated from the Kremlin and that the leak had been arranged by Sergei Zverev, deputy head of the president's office, which was why he was removed from his post.

The contents of the document were baffling, but even so Zhilin passed it on to Sergei Yastrzhembsky, vice premier in the government of Moscow. Yastrzhembsky, however, failed to react to it (some time later Yastrzhembsky left Luzhkov's administration, which is hardly surprising; however, he was then taken on by Putin, which really is surprising). If the document had been published after the explosions, everyone would have believed it was a fake produced after the fact. But the newspaper *Moskovskaya Pravda* went ahead with the publication of the document under the headline "Storm in Moscow" on July 22, before the explosions had occurred:

Confidential

Certain information concerning plans with regard to Yu. M. Luzhkov and the situation in Moscow.

The following information has been received from reliable sources. One of the analytical groups working for the president's office has developed a plan for discrediting Luzhkov by means of acts of sabotage intended to destabilize the public mood in Moscow. The plan is known by the planners as "Storm in."

According to our sources, the city can expect serious upheavals. For instance, it is planned to carry out sensational terrorist attacks (or attempted terrorist attacks) against a number of state institutions: buildings of the FSB and MVD, the Council of the Federation, the Moscow Municipal Court, the Moscow Arbitration Court, and a number of buildings. The abduction of well-known people and ordinary citizens by "Chechen guerrillas" is envisaged.

A separate chapter is devoted to "armed criminal" activities directed against commercial organizations and businessmen who support Luzhkov. The order has been given to dig up and also manufacture "operational" material on Kobzon, Gusinsky, and the Most-Media group, Djabrailov, Luchansky, Tarpischev, Tarantsev, Ordjonikidze, Baturina (Luzhkov's wife), Gromov, Yevtushenkov, P. Gusev, and others. In particular, incidents in the close vicinity of Kobzon's office and [the company] "Russian Gold" have supposedly gone off according to the plan in question. The purpose is to create the firm conviction that the businesses of those who support Luzhkov will be destroyed and that the safety of his confederates themselves is not guaranteed.

A separate program has been developed in order to set the organized criminal groups active in Moscow against each other and provoke war between them, which the authors of the report believe will, on the one hand, create an intolerable crime wave in the capital and, on the other hand, provide a screen for the planned terrorist attacks against state institutions in the form of a settling of accounts between criminals, and general chaos.

These "measures" pursue several goals: creating an atmosphere of fear in Moscow and the illusion of entirely unfettered criminal activity; initiating the process of removing the present head of the MVD of Moscow from his post; instilling in Muscovites the conviction that Luzhkov has lost control of the situation in the city.

In addition, according to information from our sources, while all of this is going on, the press will be swamped with information about who in the government of Moscow has links with the mafia and organized crime. The particular individual

represented as the major controller for organized criminal
groups will be Mr. Ordjonikidze, who will be linked in the
press, amongst others, with Chechen criminals "who have
been granted use of the Kiev railway station, the Radisson–
Slavyanskaya Hotel, the shopping complex on the Manezh
Square," etc. Material will be placed in the "red" and "patriotic" press about the domination of Moscow by people from
the Caucasus, about their wild excesses in the capital and the
damage done to the security and material welfare of Muscovites. The statistics on this are already being put together in
the MVD. In addition, the same channel will be exploited for
materials already fabricated concerning "Luzhkov's links with
international Zionist and sectarian organizations."

Several days before the explosions took place State Duma deputy
Konstantin Borovoi had a meeting with a GRU officer who gave him a
list of the names of participants in a terrorist attack. Borovoi immediately passed on the list to the FSB, but his warning met with absolutely
no response. Borovoi believes that he was not the only channel
through which the secret services received warnings about imminent
terrorist attacks, but no measures were taken to prevent them. It
would be possible to dismiss Borovoi's opinion if only it did not coincide with the opinion of one of the most famous Russian specialists in
sabotage and terrorist activity, retired colonel and former GRU officer
Ilya Starinov. He declared that it was simply impossible for his department not to have known about the planned explosions. This fatal disre-
gard by the FSB of warnings of imminent terrorist attacks can only be
explained by the fact that the FSB itself was planning the attacks.

One of the organizers of the explosions in Moscow was FSB
Major Vladimir Kondratiev. On March 11, 2000, he sent a letter of
penitential confession entitled "I bombed Moscow!" via the Internet
to the electronic publication of the Free Lance Bureau. It should be
emphasized at this point that, as patriotic citizens should, the
employees of the site immediately informed the FSB about the letter,
and its contents were reported to Patrushev. Two computer special-

ists from the FSB promptly arrived, downloaded the letter, and promised to get to the bottom of the whole business. No one ever saw them again. Here is an extract from that letter:

Yes, I was the one who blew up the house on Guryanov Street in Moscow. I am not a Chechen or an Arab or a Dagestani, I am a genuine Russian, Vladimir Kondratiev, a major in the FSB, a member of the top secret Department K-20. Our department was set up immediately after the signing of the Khasavyurt Accords. We were set the task of planning and carrying out operations to discredit the Chechen Republic, so that it would not receive international recognition. For this purpose, we were granted very extensive powers and access to virtually unlimited financial and technical resources.

One of the first operations we planned and carried out successfully was called Kovpak. It essentially consisted in our traveling round all of Russia's [penal] colonies and recruiting criminals (preference was given to individuals from the Caucasian nationalities), assembling them into groups, giving them weapons and money, and then transporting them to Chechnya, and setting them free with a single specific goal, to abduct people, in particular foreigners. And it should be said that our pupils handled it very well.

Maskhadov and his people were traveling all over the world, trying in vain to obtain foreign support, and at the same time, foreigners were disappearing in their republic. The most effective points of this operation were the abduction and murder of British and Dutch engineers, carried out on our orders.

In June last year, our section was set a new task, provoking general hatred in Russia for Chechnya and the Chechens. We worked up some ideas through the effective use of brainstorming. One of our brainstorming sessions produced several ideas, including distributing leaflets with threats from the Chechens throughout the country, murdering the country's favorite singer Alla Pugachova, blowing up apartment buildings, and then throwing all the blame on to the Chechens. All of these suggestions were reported to the leadership of the FSB, which selected the final one as the most effective, and gave the 'go-ahead' for its implementation.

We planned bombings in Moscow, Volgodonsk, Ryazan, Samara, as well as in Dagestan and Ingushetia. Specific buildings were picked, the type of explosive was selected, and the amount calculated. The operation was given the code name "Hiroshima." I was made directly responsible for its implementation, since I was the only explosives expert in our section, and I also had quite a lot of experience. Although in my heart, I did not agree with the idea of blowing up apartment blocks, I could not refuse to carry out the order, because ever since our section was set up, every member of it has been put in a situation, which means he has had to obey any order. Otherwise, he was simply silenced for all eternity. So I carried out the order!

The day after the bombing, I went to the site of the operation, intending to assess its implementation and analyze the results. I was shaken by what I saw there. I have already mentioned that I had blown up buildings before, but they were not people's houses, and they were not in Russia. But here I'd blown up a Russian house and killed Russian people, and the Russian women weeping over Russian corpses were cursing the one who'd done this in my native language. And standing beside them, I could physically feel the curses enveloping me, sinking into my head and my chest, filling my body, infusing every cell. And I realized that I WAS CURSED!

Going back to the section, instead of reporting on the implementation of the operation, I wrote out a statement requesting to be transferred to another section on grounds of mental and physical exhaustion. In view of the state I was in, I was temporarily suspended from all operations, and the second bombing, which was planned for Monday, was entrusted to my partner. To make sure I couldn't do anything to prevent it, they decided to eliminate me.

On Saturday, in order to be alone and think over what I should do and gather my thoughts, I went out of town to my dacha. On the way, I felt the brakes fail in my car, which I had always taken good care of and which had never let me down.

"I realized they had decided to get rid of me in the classic way used in my department, and I did exactly what we'd been taught to do in such situations and drove the car into water, since there happened to be a small river on my route. That very day, I used operational channels to get out of Russia.

Now I live thousands of kilometers away from my homeland. My documents are in order—I am now a citizen of this small country. I have a non-Russian name, and no one here has any idea who I really am. I know that the FSB is capable of anything, but I hope my colleagues will not find me here.

In my new country, I have set up a small business, I have money, and now I can live here in peace for the rest of my days. So why am I writing all of this to you and risking exposure? (Even though I have taken precautions by having the letter sent from a third country by a third party.)

I have already mentioned Samara as one of the towns planned for a bombing. The victims there were to have been the residents of a house on Novovokzalnaya Street. Although I think it is possible that after the failed attempt to blow up the building in Ryazan, our section might have completely given up operations like this, even so I consider it my duty to warn you about it.

Following the publication of Kondratiev's letter on the Internet, the Association of Alpha Veterans issued a denial just a few days before the presidential elections, stating among other claims that there was no section K-20 in the secret services. It is, therefore, worth our while to take a moment to trace the history of Department K's creation.

Back in 1996, an Antiterrorist Center was established in the FSB on the basis of the Department for Combating Terrorism. The Antiterrorist Center included an Operations Department, which built up information on terrorists and tracked them down, and a Department for the Defense of the Constitutional Order (Department K), the former Fifth Department of the KGB, which built up information on political and religious groups, organizations, and dissidents. Later, the Antiterrorist Center was transformed (or rather simply renamed) into the Department for Combating Terrorism and the Department of Constitutional Security (Department K). On August 28, 1999, before the September wave of bombings began, it went through yet another transformation, becoming the Department for the Protection of Constitutional Order and Combating Terrorism.

These numerous reorganizations should not be regarded as simple coincidence. In restructuring various "departments" and "offices," the FSB was simply attempting in the most primitive manner to cover its tracks. In the face of such frequent transformations, it seemed absolutely impossible for any outsider to figure out who was in charge of what, who gave the orders, and who was subordinate to whom. These complicated and confusing titles, so similar to each other, were created quite deliberately. All this also served to throw journalists off the scent. In reality everybody stayed in his own job, and to this day, officers of the state security service sit in their offices on the seventh and ninth floors of the building at number 1 Bolshaya Lubyanka Street, just as Sudoplatov sat there in Stalin's time. Nothing has changed.

The head of the new department was Vice Admiral German Ugriumov, who died in his office in Khankala in Chechnya on May 31, 2001. Immediately after his death, information began to circulate that Ugriumov had committed suicide. It was reported that a man dressed in civilian clothes had entered Ugriumov's office at 1 P.M. and left half an hour later. The vice-admiral supposedly shot himself fifteen to twenty minutes after that.

If former members of the Fifth Department of the KGB were entrusted with the task of combating terrorism and defending the constitutional order of democratic Russia, we may be sure that the only business conducted by Department K was organizing terrorist attacks and opposing democracy. As Sobchak (the mayor of St. Petersburg) said, these were people for whom the words "legality" and "democracy" simply had no meaning. "Nothing exists for them except orders, and for them laws and rights are a mere hindrance." Does this mean that apart from the secret section K-20 mentioned by Major Kondratiev, there were at least another nineteen special groups?

Remarkably enough, even state security agents believed that the terrorist attacks were the work of the FSB. Erik Kotlyar, a journalist at the newspaper Moskovskaya Pravda, described one particular instance in an article of February 10, 2000: "Last fall I happened to have a meeting with a member of a super-secret service. . . . And this is what he told me: 'That evening I got back late. There was no one at home. My wife, daughter and mother-in-law were at the dacha. I'd just cracked some eggs into the frying pan, when there was a deafening explosion outside the window. Lumps of glass came flying straight into the room together with clouds of fumes and dust! I dashed out onto the landing, my neighbors were out there in a panic. For some reason they were trying to call the lift. I shouted at them: 'Go down the stairs, the lift might fall!' 'I dashed out on to the street, and there was almost nothing left of the middle section of the house opposite! The next day I got answers to a few questions and made a firm decision: I'm taking my family out of Russia, it's dangerous to live here, and I've only got one daughter!' 'But it was the Chechens who planted the bombs in Moscow. . . .' 'The Chechens had nothing to do with it,' he said gesturing his hand angrily." Kotlyar drew the conclusion that his acquaintance knew something.

On September 10, the governor of the Altai Region, Alexander Surikov, announced that "the explosions in Moscow were echoes from Dagestan," but that the people who were interested in terrorist attacks were in Russia and in Moscow. Alexander Surikov proposed holding an extraordinary session of the Council of the Federation to discuss the declaration of a state of emergency in the country.

During the night of September 12–13, the newspaper *Moskovsky Komsomolets* set up for printing an article entitled "The secret account of a bombing." It attempted to analyze what had happened.

Chechen guerrillas took no direct part in the preparations for the terrorist attack. To judge from the general picture of the explosion, the bomb was planted by specialists who had been trained in Russian secret service departments. It also happens that all the previous terrorist attacks, with trails generally supposed to lead back to Chechnya, were carried out according to exactly the same scenario: a car bomb exploding close to a building. The car is usually parked in front of the intended target only a few hours in advance. The detonator is equipped with a timing mechanism. Even if the car bomb is discovered, explosives experts have only a matter of minutes to disarm it (as they did last Sunday outside the military hospital in Buinaksk). This love of car bombs is very easy to explain. Explosives are very expensive nowadays, and terrorists pay for every kilogram of TNT or any other substance in cash. And planting the bomb at the target even one day before the deadline is fraught with the danger of failure, the risk of the bomb being discovered is too great. . . . However, the general picture of the explosion on Guryanov Street suggests that it was planned by people who are not used to economizing, i.e., members of the secret services. . . . Experts have determined that the main charge in the house on Guryanov Street was planted in the rented storage facility of a shop on the ground floor. And moreover, the explosive device was there a long time before the explosion took place. The criminals were evidently wasting no time on trifles, and if the explosives were discovered the attack would simply have been transferred to another district of the capital. This tactic is similar to the use of the secret addresses so beloved of secret services the whole world over. When one of them is exposed, the operation simply takes place in a different area. During the days of the

USSR, specialists capable of carrying out such a terrorist attack served in both the KGB and the Second Central Department of the General Staff (better known as the GRU).

In other words, *Moskovsky Komsomolets* was hinting, ever so gently, that the FSB was behind the bombings.

On September 12, the Moscow police received a phone call from the inhabitants of house number 6/3 on Kashirskoye Highway: "Something's not right in our basement," the concerned members of the public reported. A squad of policemen arrived. At the entrance to the basement, they were met by a person they took to be an employee of the district housing management office (REU), who told them that everything was in order in the basement, and "our people" were in there. The policemen lingered at the door to the basement for a while without going in and then went away.

Early next morning, just as the edition of *Moskovsky Komsomolets* with the article "The secret account of a bombing" was being delivered to Moscow's news kiosks, the eight-story building at number 6/3 Kashirskoye Highway was blown into the air, the same building where the polite "REU employee" had spoken with the policemen outside the entrance. He had been right, everything in the basement was in order—for a terrorist bombing.

A few days later, Moskovsky Komsomolts attempted to track down the resourceful "REU employee": "I had a meeting with the housing managers of the Kashirskoye Highway ditrict," the newspaper's correspondent related. "As yet we are unable to work out which REU employee had covered for the man who subleased the basement of house number 6 on the sly. No one admits to it. It's either an engineer or foreman or a district manager." Neither the REU employee nor those who actually sublet the basement were ever found.

By 2 P.M. on September 13, the rubble of the house which was bombed on Kashirskoye Highway had yielded 119 dead bodies and thirteen fragments of bodies. The dead included twelve children. The experts quickly established that the two Moscow explosions were absolutely identical in nature, and the composition of the explosive device was the same in both cases. A thorough check of buildings, attics, and basements was launched. At one address, number 16/2 on Borisovskie Prudy Street, a cache of explosives was discovered. Together with the hexogen mixture and eight kilograms of plastic explosives, used as a detonator, they also found six electronic timers made from Casio wristwatches. Five of them were already programmed for specific times. All the terrorists had to do was take the timers to their sites and attach them to the detonators. One of the mined houses was on Krasnodor-skaya Street.

The last house they were planning to destroy was the one on Borisovskie Prudy Street, at five minutes past four in the morning of September 21. It is remarkable that the FSB, which was hunting terrorists in Moscow, chose not to set an ambush at Borisovskie Prudy Street to apprehend the terrorists—who undoubtedly would have sooner or later come for the detonators—but instead hurried to inform the criminals via the mass media that the cache at Borisovskie Prudy Street had been discovered. It is absolutely impossible to assume that the FSB's announcement about the discovery of the secret terrorist cache was an accident. Not even a beginning investigating officer could have made such a mistake.

The information about the explosives discovered after the terrorist attacks and the quantity discovered was not consistent. In Moscow, they found thirteen tons of explosives. There were three or four tons in the house on Borisovskie Prudy Street, even more at a cache in the district of Liublino, and four tons in a car shelter in Kapotnya. Some time later, it was discovered that six tons of heptyl (a rocket fuel of which hexogen is one of the components) had been taken from the Nevinnomyssk Chemical Combine in the Stavropol Region. Six tons of heptyl could have been used to produce ten tons of explosives. But there's no way to process six tons of heptyl into ten tons of explosives in a kitchen, a garage or an underground laboratory. The heptyl was evidently processed at an army depot. Then the sacks had to be loaded into a vehicle and driven out under the eyes of the guards, with some kind of documents being presented. So transporting the material required drivers and trucks. Overall, an entire group of people must have been involved in the operation, and if that's the case, information must have been received through the FSB's secret agents and the agents of military counterintelligence.

The explosives were packed in sugar sacks bearing the words "Cherkessk Sugar Plant," but no such plant exists. If "sugar" had been carried throughout the whole of Russia in sacks like that, especially with counterfeit documentation, the chances of discovery would have been too great. It would have been simpler to draw up documentation for the "sugar" from a plant that actually exists. Several conclusions can immediately be drawn from this fact, for instance, that the terrorists wanted to point the investigation in the direction of the Republic of Karachaevo-Cherkessia, since it was obvious that sooner or later, at least one sack from the "Cherkessk Sugar Plant" would fall into the hands of the investigators; also that the terrorists were not afraid of transporting sacks with a false name and documents into Moscow, since they were clearly quite certain, both they themselves and their goods were safe. Finally, it is reasonable to assume that the explosives were packed in the sacks in Moscow.

It would have been hard to finance the terrorist attacks without leaving any tracks. The intelligence services must have heard something, at least about a large sale of heptyl or hexogen from the depots, since no one would have given terrorists explosives for free. Only the agencies of state security or military officers could have gotten hexogen from a factory or a store without paying for it.

Such were precisely the conclusions reached by many reporters and specialists, trying to figure out the clever plan by which the hexogen could have been delivered to Moscow. The plan turned out to be exceedingly simple, since it had been worked out by the FSB itself. It consisted of the following steps.

On October 24, 1991, the scientific research institute "Roskonversvzryvtsenr" opened in Moscow. The institute was located in the center of the city—Bolshaya Lubyanka 18, building 3—and it was created for the "utilization of convertible explosive materials in national agriculture." The head of the institute from 1991 to 2000 was Yu. G. Schukin. In reality, the institute was a cover, a front"—a link between the army and the "consumer"—and its business was illegal trade in explosives. Hundreds of thousands of tons of explosive substances, mainly TNT, passed through the institute. The institute purchased explosives from the military for utilization and conversion, or from chemical factories for "research." It then sold explosives to consumers, which included real and legitimate commercial enterprises, such as the Belarus's government enterprise "Granit." Naturally, the institute had no right to sell explosives. But for some reason no one seemed to notice, including the heads of the security agencies, least of all Patrushev.

Among the numerous large contracts for shipments of hundreds of thousands of tons of TNT and TNT charges, brokered by the institute between the supplier (the army) and the consumer (the commercial enterprises), there occasionally appeared small orders for one-two tons of TNT charges. These orders contained detailed descriptions of the obligations of both sides, although the sale of a ton of "goods" brought no more than $300–350, barely enough to cover trucking expenses. In reality, these small orders for the delivery of "TNT charges" were contracts for hexogen shipments. Through the institute hexogen was purchased from the army and delivered to the terrorists for the bombing of buildings in Moscow and other Russian cities. These deliveries were possible only because Schukin's scientific research institute "Roskonversvzryvtsenr" had been created by the secret services, and the terrorists who received the "TNT charges" were agents of the FSB.

The hexogen, packed in 50-kilogram sacks labeled "Sugar," was stored in the only place where it could have been stored—in military warehouses, guarded by armed soldiers. One such warehouse was the warehouse of the 137th Ryazan Airborne Regiment. One of its guards was private Alexei Pinyaev. For the price of TNT charges—namely, 8900 rubles per ton (roughly $300–350)—the institute purchased hexogen from the military warehouse, nominally for research. In the invoices the hexogen was treated as TNT. Order forms were made out to "recipient"-the link between the institute and the terrorists. In the order forms the TNT charges went under the innocent label A-IX-I.

Only an extremely narrow circle of people knew that the label A-IX-I denoted hexogen. It is possible that the go-betweens who drove the hexogen out of the military warehouses in their own vehicles did not know about it.

The small shipments of "TNT charges" (hexogen) transported from the military warehouses literally vanished (were given to the terrorists). In the overall flow of hundreds of thousands of tons of TNT charges, small orders in the range of $300–600 were impossible to trace.

Reporters have tried to understand how exactly the terrorists transported the hexogen across the expanse of Russia. But there was no need to transport it. The hexogen was used were it was found. Thus, the hexogen from the warehouse of the 137th Ryazan Airborne Regiment was used on Novosyolov Street in Ryazan. The hexogen from the military warehouses outside of Moscow ended up in Moscow. The system was ingeniously simple. Everything had been foreseen, except, perhaps, entirely accidental omissions, which, certainly, were not worth taking into account: the observant driver Alexei Kartofelnikov, the curious private Alexei Pinyaev, the fearless *Novaya Gazeta* reporter Pavel Voloshin. And what was absolutely impossible to foresee was the departure for London, with documents and video footage in hand, of FSB agent and member of the consultation board of the State Duma commission for fighting corruption N.S. Chekulin, who, as fate would have it, served as director of the "Roskonversvzryvtsenr" institute in 2000–2001.

Meanwhile, after two buildings had been bombed, the checks on housing in the capital continued. In a single day, the Moscow police checked 26,561 apartments. Special attention was paid to non-residential spaces on the ground floors of buildings, basements and semi-basements, in other words to places that are often used for storage. The number of such locations checked was 7,908. Public buildings were also checked: 180 hotels, 415 hostels, and 548 places of entertainment (casinos, bars, cafes). The work was conducted under the pretext of a search for those suspected of involvement in the terrorist attacks in Moscow. Taking part in the checks were 14,500 employees of the MVD and 9,500 members of the interior ministry's armed forces, including a separate operational division (the former Dzerzhinsky Division). Employees of the MVD worked twelve hours a day with no days off.

Locations in which the terrorists had planted bombs were identified. According to the official version of the investigation (which may have absolutely nothing in common with the truth), they had been rented by Achemez Gochiyaev (Laipanov). The genuine Laipanov was a native of the Republic of Karachaevo-Cherkessia, who had been killed in a car accident in Krasnodar in 1999. The dead Laipanov's documents became "cover documents" for the real terrorist. A former GRU employee, who spent all his life building up a network of secret agents abroad, commented: "This kind of practice is the usual approach employed to legalizing agents in all the secret services in the world. It's a classic, described in all the textbooks. It's as though the dead man is granted a second life."

As early as July 1999, Gochiyaev-Laipanov had inquired at one of the Moscow rental agencies on Begovaya Street and received information about forty-one sites. After the first explosion, thirty-eight of these locations were checked by investigators for explosives.

"Laipanov's" young partner was also identified. The FSB claimed that he was Denis Saitakov, a twenty-year-old forced emigrant from Uzbekistan and former novice at the Yoldyz Madrasah (Islamic Seminary) in Naberezhnye Chelny in Tatarstan, who had a Russian mother and a Bashkiri father. The FSB believed that during the preparations for the terrorist attack, he and "Laipanov" rented a room in the Altai Hotel and telephoned firms that rent out trucks. Although on the second day after the attack, the KGB of Tatarstan, at Moscow's insistent request, began looking for Saitakov. No one in the KGB of Tatarstan was convinced that Saitakov was involved in the bombings. In any case deputy chairman of the KGB of Tatarstan, Ilgiz Minullin, emphasized that "no one can declare Saitakov a terrorist until his guilt has been proved. . . . At the present time, the agencies of state security are not in possession of any facts which indicate the involvement in terrorist attacks in Moscow . . . of students of the Yoldyz Madrasah."

The KGB of Naberezhnye Chelny also issued a statement, indicating that accusations against inhabitants of Tatarstan of complicity with terrorists were groundless, and that the Tatarstan KGB had no information indicating the involvement of residents of the republic in the bombings.

The terrorists who set up the September explosions followed the line of least resistance. First they used their "cover documents" to rent several basement and semi-basement rooms, including the ones on Guryanov Street and Kashirskoye Highway. Then they moved in the explosives, stacking sacks of sugar and tea and packages of plumbing supplies around the crates of hexogen (at least that's the way they did it on Guryanov Street). The targets for sabotage were ideally selected. The chances of encountering the police in front of buildings in the unfashionable dormitory districts are not usually very high, and usually there are no caretakers in the entranceways. Starinov announced that "the location of these buildings and the environment around them met the two conditions most essential for terrorist bombers—vulnerability and accessibility."

The terrorists planted the right amount of explosive required for the total demolition of their targets. The saboteur Starinov believed that three men could have carried out the bombings. The terrorists seemed to have been well trained, not just in sabotage, but also in intelligence work: they knew how to avoid surveillance and live under assumed identities. Even a year's course at the very best special training center is not long enough to learn all of this. So it seemed that Muscovites had fallen victim to professional terrorists. And the only professional terrorists working in Russia were in the structures of the FSB and GRU.

Petra Prohazkova, a Czech journalist who was interviewing Hattab at the time of the bombings, remembered Hattab's astounding reaction to the announcement of the terrorist attacks in Moscow. His face suddenly assumed an expression of genuine fright. It was the sincere fright of a front-line soldier who realizes that now he's going to get the blame for everything. Everybody who knows Hattab agrees that he is no actor and could not possibly have feigned astonishment and fear.

The Chechens knew it was not in their interests to carry out any terrorist attacks. Public opinion was on their side, and public opinion, both Russian and international, was more valuable to them than two or three hundred lives abruptly cut short. That was why the Chechens could not have been behind the terrorist attacks of September 1999. And the Chechens must be given credit for always denying their involvement in these bombings. Here is what Ilyas Akhmadov, minister of foreign affairs in Aslan Maskhadov's government, had to say on that point:

QUESTION: In France you talk as though everybody knows that the terrorist attacks in Moscow and Volgodonsk were set up by the Russian secret services. . . . Do you have any proof?

ANSWER: Of course. Throughout the last war, we never showed the slightest inclination for that sort of thing. But if it had been organized by Basaev or Hattab, I can assure you that they wouldn't have been shy about admitting it to Russia. What's more, everybody knows that the failed bombing in Ryazan was organized by the FSB. . . . I myself served in the army as a demolition officer at a military proving ground, and I know perfectly well what a great difference there is between explosives and sugar.

Here is the opinion of another interested party with whom it is hard to disagree, the Chechen minister of defense and commander of the presidential guard, Mahomet Khambiev:

Now for the explosions in Moscow. Why are the Chechens not committing acts of terrorism now, when our people are being annihilated? Why did the Russian authorities pay no attention to the hexogen incident in Ryazan, when the police had detained a member of the secret services with this explosive? There's not a single piece of evidence for the so-called Chechen connection in these bombings. And the bombings were least of all in the interest of the Chechens. But what is hidden will certainly be revealed. I assure you that the perpetrators and planners of the bombings in Moscow will become known, when there's a change of political regime in the Kremlin. Because those who ordered the bombings should be sought in the corridors of the Kremlin. These bombings were necessary in order to start the war, in order to distract the attention of Russians and the whole world from the scandals and dirty intrigues going on in the Kremlin.

Suspicions arose that the bombings were being carried out by people attempting to force the government to declare a state of emergency and cancel the elections. A number of politicians rejected the idea: "I don't agree with the statements of certain analysts who connect this series of terrorist attacks with somebody's intentions to declare a state of emergency in Russia and cancel the elections to the State Duma," declared former Russian minister of the interior Kulikov in an interview with *Nezavisimaya Gazeta* on September 11. The Chechens could not have had any interest in presidential elections or the declaration of a state of emergency in Russia. In 1996, it was the Korzhakov–Barsukov–Soskovets group and the secret services standing behind them that supported the cancellation of the election. So who was attempting to provoke the declaration of a state of emergency in 1999?

Minister of Defense Igor Sergeiev thought it possible that military patrols might appear on the streets of Moscow. "Soldiers could take part in patrolling the city together with the MVD's forces," he declared to journalists after a meeting with Boris Yeltsin. The military had been "set the task" of participating in the protection of the public against terrorist activity, Sergeiev stated. He also said that the GRU was "working intensively" to identify all possible contacts between those who had planned the explosions in Russian towns and international terrorists (a hint at foreign saboteurs!). The use of soldiers to protect peaceful citizens against terrorists looked rather like the introduction of military law. Igor Sergeiev spoke out "for the introduction of wide-reaching anti-terrorist measures and anti-terrorist operations." In other words, the Russian Ministry of Defense was calling for war against an unnamed enemy, but, in fact, it was clear to everyone that he was calling for a war against Chechnya.

The final decision on all of these questions remained with President Yeltsin. The secret services, however, had practically unlimited opportunities for filtering or falsifying the information presented to the president. This was confirmed in an interview given on November 12, 1999 by Eduard Shevardnadze, the president of Georgia and former head of the Georgian MVD, when he spoke about the Chechen problem: "Reference is usually made to the fact that the GRU has information of this kind. I know what information the GRU has historically used, how it is assembled, how it is reported at first to the General Staff, then to the Minister of Defense, then to the Supreme Commander. I know that there is large-scale falsification."

Former Prime Minister Yevgeny Primakov, another well-informed contemporary politician, who was a presidential candidate in the 2000 election, formulated his doubts differently. When Primakov was asked for his comments on the terrorist attacks in Moscow, he said that he thought the Moscow bombings would not be the end of the matter, there could be more explosions right across Russia, and one of the reasons for the situation that had arisen lay in the links between people in the agencies of law enforcement and the criminal underworld.

In effect, Primakov admitted that bombings in every part of Russia were the work of people connected with the secret services. This was also confirmed by Georgian President Eduard Shevardnadze in an address broadcast on national television on November 15, 1999: "Already at the meeting in Kishinev, I informed Boris Yeltsin that his secret services had contacts with Chechen terrorists. But Russia does not listen to its friends." Diplomatic etiquette did not permit a more forthright statement. The president of Georgia could not say that by "Chechen terrorists" he simply meant terrorists.

It is obvious, however, that Shevardnadze suspected the Russian secret services of committing the bombings. Information in his possession even suggested that the Russian secret services had been involved in two attempts on Shevardnadze's own life. In order to avoid making unsubstantiated claims, we can quote the former director of the United States National Security Agency (NSA), retired Lieutenant-General William Odom. In October 1999, he stated that Prime Minister Putin and his entourage from the military were using this Chechen campaign to put Shevardnadze under severe pressure. They had already made one attempt to dismember Georgia by taking Abkhazia and southern Ossetia away from it and now, Odom said, they wanted to exploit the Chechen events to position their forces there, which was opposed by the current president of Georgia. Beginning with Primakov's term as Prime Minister, the Russian government had made at least two attempts on Shevardnadze's life. The Georgian leadership had provided the governments of a number of foreign countries with convincing evidence of this. Primakov himself was personally involved. He had used secret agents of the Russian foreign intelligence service in Belarus, and in May an attempt was made with his knowledge on the life of Shevardnadze and several members of his entourage. The American government is in possession of tape recordings of conversations made by the actual killers involved in the attempt. A year before that, a first attempt to kill Shevardnadze was made, not by amateurs, but by genuine professionals, well-prepared military groups who could only have been trained in Russia. There is, in addition, a mass of material evidence collected at the scene of the crime which confirms all of this.

What Shevardnadze hesitated to say about the bombings in Moscow was openly stated by Lebed, in answer to a question from the French newspaper *Le Figaro*: "Do you mean to say that the present regime is behind the bombings?" The general replied: "I'm almost convinced of it." Lebed pointed out that the force that could be discerned behind the bombings of residential buildings in Moscow and Volgodonsk was not the Chechen terrorists, but "the hand of power," that is the Kremlin and the president, who were "up to their necks in shit," totally isolated, and together with Yeltsin's "family" had "only one goal, to destabilize the position in order to avoid elections."

On September 14, the FSB and MVD issued the statement for which the FSB had carried out the bombings: Zdanovich announced that the law enforcement agencies had no doubt that the series of explosions from Buinaksk to a house on Kashirskoye Highway in Moscow represented "a large-scale terrorist operation launched by Basaev and Hattab's guerrillas in support of their military action in Dagestan." Igor Zubov, the deputy minister of foreign affairs, confirmed the suggestion: "We can now state without the slightest doubt that Basaev and Hattab are behind these bombings."

The statements by Zdanovich and Zubov did not reflect the true situation. A day later, the head of the MVD's Central Office for Combating Organized Crime, Vladimir Kozlov, announced that "a number of people involved in these terrorist attacks have been identified," and explained that he meant a group of terrorists with connections in Moscow and the regions and towns surrounding the capital. Kozlov did not even mention Chechnya or Dagestan. Zdanovich was openly disseminating false information.

The FSB's conclusions did not sound convincing, and the attempts of the security forces to capture the culprits looked farcical. In the atmosphere of anti-Chechen hysteria in Moscow a few days after the second explosion, members of the FSB and MVD arrested two suspects for the terrorist attacks, and their names were immediately made public, without any concern for possible prejudice to the investigation: they were thirty-two-year-old Timur Dakhkilgov and his father-in-law, forty-year-old old Bekmars Sauntiev.

Timur Dakhkilgov was an Ingushetian who was born in Grozny, and lived there before he moved to Moscow. He was a dyer in a textile combine. On September 10, immediately after the terrorist attack on Guryanov Street, Sauntiev went to see the Dakhkilgovs and said that they all had to go to the Northern Butovo police station for re-registration.

At the station, Timur Dakhkilgov and his wife Lida were photographed, their fingerprints were taken, swabs were taken from the palms of their hands, and they were released. Soon after the second bombing, MVD operatives turned up at Sauntiev's and the Dakhkilgov's apartments, said that there were traces of hexogen on Timur Dakhkilgov's hands (he was a dyer, after all!), and arrested him. There was no hexogen on Sauntiev's hands, so, instead, they found a revolver under his bath, and discovered traces of hexogen on the handle of the door to his flat (on the outside, that is, in the stairwell).

The suspects were questioned for three days. Sauntiev was later released and the pistol found in his apartment was apparently forgotten. Timur Dakhkilgov was taken to the MUR department on Petrovka Street, where he was accused of possessing explosives and terrorism. The entire process was reported openly on television, and Rushailo even reported to the Council of the Federation that a terrorist had been caught.

According to Dakhkilgov, three investigators worked with him, but they were never introduced to him, and they never called each other by name. To himself the suspect called them Old Man, Ginger, and Nice Guy. The latter earned his nickname by never actually hitting Dakhkilgov. The interrogation lasted for three days, after which Dakhkilgov was transferred to the FSB detention center at Lefortovo.

It was very important for the FSB to keep Dakhkilgov in prison for as long as possible, since the Ingushetian was their only justification for the "Chechen connection." They began working on Dakhkilgov in his cell, in ways which he knew nothing about. An inside agent who was supposedly an "authoritative" criminal was planted in the cell with him. The agent won the Ingushetian's confidence, and Dakhkilgov told him the circumstances of his case, saying that he had nothing to do with the bombings. Some time later, Dakhkilgov was released. An analysis of the swab taken from his hand had confirmed the presence of hexane, a solvent used at the fabric combine for cleaning wool. There was no hexogen on his hands. The "Chechen connection" had been broken. But the war with Chechnya was now already in full swing, so Dakhkilgov had not spent his time in prison in vain.

On March 16, 2000, when the leadership of the FSB was giving an account to the public of progress made in investigating the September bombings, one of the journalists asked the deputy head of the investigative department of the FSB, Nikolai Sapozhkov: "Can you please tell me why Timur Dakhkilgov spent three months in prison as a terrorist?" The reply given by Sapozhkov, who had already spent several months investigating the terrorist attacks as a member of a group of many dozens of investigators, depressed the journalists, since it made it clear that the investigation was following a false trail:

> "I can explain. There was direct testimony against him from the people who brought the sugar and explosives to Moscow. . . ."
>
> "So they gave his name?"
>
> "No they . . . I mean it was direct testimony, they identified him by sight as a man who had helped to unload those sacks. Afterwards, you know, when we did a more thorough. . . Well, you know that he had hexogen on his hands, and then the other details which at the time unambiguously provided a basis for treating him as a suspect. Later we did a very thorough job on the Dakhkilgov connection. We had to check everything out again and present him for identification in a calm situation. And we were convinced that the features by which he'd been identified, they were for Slavic persons identifying so-called Caucasians, but they raised doubts for those who had identified him, and by thorough investigation and establishing his alibi, we reached the conclusion that he was not involved in this crime. The case was considered jointly with employees of the Public Prosecutor's Office, and they agreed with our conclusions."

We must apologize to our readers for the quality of Sapozhkov's language. What Sapozhkov had planned to say was as follows. When the investigators arrested Dakhkilgov and began showing him to the residents of the bombed houses, so that they could decide whether he was the one who had planted the sacks of explosives with the timers and detonating devices, the residents, to whom all Caucasians look the same, identified him as a man involved in the terrorist attacks. They "did a thorough job" on Dakhkilgov (we know that they interrogated him, beat him, tortured him, put polyethylene bags over his head, choked him, and planted an agent in his cell). The most important thing for them was to drag out the whole process as long as possible. After three months, Dakhkilgov was not needed any longer, and with the consent of the Public Prosecutor's Office, he was released, and the case against him was closed.

So Dakhkilgov spent his time inside for two reasons. Firstly, the crowd identified him as one of the culprits, and secondly, hexogen was supposedly found on his hands. But the FSB managed to get its explosives confused. Soon after, the bombing reports began appearing in the media that "according to the FSB the hexogen story is a diversionary ploy. In actual fact, in all of the bombings the terrorists used a different explosive substance." Western commentators pointed out that the rubble of the houses bombed in Moscow was cleared and removed with lightning speed (for Russia, in only three days) These suspicious-minded foreigners thought that anyone in Russia working as diligently as that must be covering up their tracks. In any case, the FSB's ploy was merely for public consumption. The terrorists themselves knew perfectly well what explosives they used and there was no point in concealing the components of the explosives from them.

The question of exactly what was used as an explosive in the September bombings should not be regarded as still unanswered. Hexogen was produced in Russia at restricted military plants. "Hexogen is carefully guarded, and its use is carefully controlled" was the assurance given in September 1999, at the Russian research and production enterprise Region, where they worked with hexogen. At the plant, they were convinced that any leak of hexogen from secret defense plants, known only by their numbers was, virtually impossible.

Since hexogen was used by the terrorists in large quantities, it would have been easy to determine just who had bought or been given the substance, espcially since the experts could always determine exactly where any particular batch had been produced. It was impossible for tens of tons of hexogen to have been stolen. Thousands of tons of TNT-hexogen mixture were kept at military depots and in the warehouses of munitions factories for inclusion in rocket warheads, mines, torpedoes, and shells. But hexogen extracted from finished munitions had a distinctive appearance, and extracting it was difficult and risky. Here are a few examples.

On October 8,1999, one of the Russian information agencies announced that the Central Military Prosecutor's Office had insti-gated proceedings against a number of officials in the central admin-istration of the Anti-Aircraft Defense Forces. The senior military prosecutor, Yu. Demin, stated that over a period of several years, high-ranking military officers had abused their official positions by forging and falsifying documents, in order to steal spares for a range of anti-aircraft rocket-launchers, which were sold to commercial companies and private entrepreneurs. Just a few of this group's many criminal escapades had cost the state a total of more than two million dollars. It is easy to imagine what kind of "commercial organizations and pri-vate entrepreneurs" bought stolen spare parts for rocket-launchers. It is quite obvious that without the involvement of the FSB and the GRU, it would not have been possible to continue stealing over a period of several years.

On September 28, 1999, employees of the Ryazan Department for Combating Organized Crime arrested the head of an automobile repair shop in an air-strike technology depot, twenty-five-year-old Warrant Officer Vyacheslav Korniev, who served at the military aero-drome in Dyagilev where bombers were based. At the time of his arrest, he was discovered to be in possession of eleven kilograms of TNT. Korniev confessed that the TNT had been stolen from a military depot, and that a group of employees to which he belonged had extracted it from FAB-300 high-explosive bombs that were stored outdoors at the depot.

The same day, the military court of the Ryazan garrison pro-nounced sentence on the head of the field supplies depot of the Ryazan Institute of the VDV, A. Ashbarin, for stealing more than three kilograms of TNT, with the intention of selling it for three thousand dollars. Although the appropriate article of the Criminal Code of the Russian Federation stipulated a sentence of from three to seven years' imprisonment, the soldier was fined 20,000 rubles.

Clearly, stealing TNT-hexogen mixture in small amounts was difficult. In contrast, removing it by the truckload was easy, but only with the appropriate permits, which meant you were bound to leave a trail, and a trail like that might lead back to the FSB. After the bombings, numerous representatives of the Russian military–industrial complex stated that such a large amount of explosives could only be stolen with the connivance of highly placed officials. On September 15 Vladimir Kozlov, confirmed that the explosion on Guryanov Street had not been caused by a homemade pyrotechnic mixture, but by industrial explosives.

So in order to throw pushy journalists and conscientious criminal investigation officers off the scent, the FSB had fed the media its story about hexogen as a diversionary ploy; in actual fact, they said, the explosive used was ammonium nitrate, a fertilizer. The point was that ammonium nitrate could have been bought, transported, and stored quite openly. It made good bombs, and if hexogen, TNT, or aluminum powder was added, it became a powerful explosive. It was true, however, that it required a complicated detonating device, a device not every terrorist would be able to work with.

Why was the hexogen story used initially? Because the houses were blown up by one group of FSB officers, the explosive was analyzed by a second and the propaganda (or public relations, to use the current term) surrounding the event was handled by a third. The first group carried out the terrorist attacks successfully (with the exception of Ryazan). The second easily determined that they had used hexogen. The third suddenly realized that hexogen is produced in Russia at restricted military plants, and it was a simple job to determine exactly who had bought the hexogen which had been used to blow up the houses, and when it was bought. At this point, panic set in. In three days, all the material evidence (the bombed houses) was removed, and stories were urgently planted in the media about ammonium nitrate. On March 16, 2000, the first deputy head of the Second Department (for the Protection of the Constitutional Order and Combating Terrorism, i.e., Department K) and the operations and investigation department of the FSB, Alexander Shagako, told a press conference that the explosives used in absolutely all the bomb-ings in Russia had been identified, and that the explosives were nitrate:

> I'd like to observe that as a result of criminalistic investigations carried out by FSB experts, Russia has received confirmation that the composition of the explosives used in Moscow and the composition of the explosives which were discovered in the basement of the house on Borisovskie Prudy Street in Moscow, and also the composition of the explosive substances which were discovered in the town of Buinaksk on September 4 in an unexploded ZIL-130 automobile, are identical, i.e., the com-position of all of these substances includes ammonium nitrate and aluminum powder, in some cases hexogen has been added, and in some cases TNT has been added....

All that remained was to determine where the nitrate in Moscow and the other Russian cities had come from. Shagako and Zdanovich, who were also at the press conference, dealt successfully with that problem. "Were there any cases of theft of these explosives from state plants where they are produced using specific technologies?" Zdanovich asked and then answered himself: "I can say straight away that there were not, or at least the investigation is not in possession of any such information."

It is impossible to determine who has bought and sold nitrate for nefarious purposes. There is just too much of it all over the country, including in Chechnya. Small amounts of TNT, hexogen, and alu-minum powder could have been stolen by anybody from any military depot (a matter on which, with the assistance of the FSB and the Central Military Prosecutor's Office, several reports appeared in the media). In misinforming public opinion concerning the composition of the explosives, the FSB was trying to deflect suspicions that it had planned and carried out the terrorist attacks. All that still needed to be done was to find a warehouse of chemical fertilizers somewhere in Chechnya. It turned out that it had also already been dealt with, which was very timely, since it allowed the investigation to be completed a few days before the presidential election:

In this connection I would also like to point out to you," said Shagako, "that two months ago employees of the Federal Security Service in Urus Martan discovered a center for training demolition operatives. On the territory of this center five tons of ammonium nitrate were discovered. At the same site trigger mechanisms, identical to the mechanisms which were used in the explosions I listed earlier, were also discovered. . . . The trigger devices discovered in the ZIL-130 automobile in the town of Buinaksk and also the trigger devices discovered in the basement on Borisovskie Prudy Street in Moscow, in the course of criminalistic analysis, were proved to be identical. In all of these trigger devices, a Casio electronic watch was used as a delay mechanism. In all of these trigger devices, light diodes of identical design were used, the electronic circuit boards, even the colors of the wires which were used for welding, they're the same color in all the mechanisms. In this connection I wish to point out that several days ago, employees of the Federal Security Service in Chechnya discovered several trigger mechanisms among the possessions of guerrillas who had been killed while attempting to break out of the encirclement of the city of Grozny. Investigations carried out by specialists of the Federal Security Service demonstrated that the design was the same for the trigger mechanisms removed from the ZIL-130 automobile in Buinaksk and the trigger mechaisms removed from Borisovskie Prudy Street in Moscow. They are all identical to each other. . . . In March in the settlement of Duba-Yurt, an isolated building was discovered in which literature in Arabic on mine laying and demolition and military training instructions were discovered, and in addition at the same address, instructions for the use of a Casio watch. This kind of watch, as I told you earlier, was used by the criminals in all of the bombings. In March, in the settlement of Chiri-Yurt, an isolated building was discovered which was surrounded by an iron fence inside which fifty sacks of ammonium nitrate were sighted, identified, and discovered—that's something in the region of two-and-a-half tons.

If the terrorists had really used ammonium nitrate, the investigators would not have looked for hexogen on Dakhkilgov and Sauntiev's hands, they would have focused on nitrate. The police looked for hexogen on the hands of their detainees, precisely because the official conclusion which the experts had provided to the investigation was that hexogen was used to blow up the houses. No subsequent expert analysis could have been more accurate, including the repeat analysis which was later carried out by the investigative agencies of the FSB and made public in March 2000, just a few days before the presidential election. On the contrary, there is every reason to believe that in March 2000, a few days before the presidential election, the FSB was deliberately dispensing misinformation.

On September 13, 1999, in Moscow, Luzhkov signed three sets of regulations which contravened the Constitution and the laws of the Russian Federation. The first of them proclaimed the re-registration of refugees and migrants in Moscow. The second document demanded the expulsion from the capital of people who violated the regulations on registration. The third put a halt to the registration in Moscow of refugees and migrants. On the same day, the governor of the Moscow Region, Anatoly Tyazhlov, signed instructions for the arrest of individuals who were not registered as residents of Moscow or the Moscow Region. Of course, none of these regulations made any mention of Chechens, or even of Caucasians.

On September 15, joint police and military patrols were introduced in Moscow, and the Whirlwind Anti-Terror operation was launched throughout Russia with the participation of the forces of the Ministry of the Interior. Muscovites were not yet aware that the wave of terror in the capital had ended at this point. Now it was the turn of the provinces. Early in the morning of September 16, an apartment block was blown up in Volgodonsk in the Rostov Region. Seventeen people were killed.

At an extraordinary session of the Council of the Federation held in camera on September 17, with the participation of the Prime Minister and the armed forces and law enforcement ministries, the Council approved a proposal for the creation of "civil security councils" in the Russian regions. Chairman of the Council of the Federation Yegor Stroev remarked that the senators intended "to offer a political assessment of events and put forward concrete economic and social measures in the conflict zone, including measures in support of the civilian population and the army." The speaker of the house remarked that "the explosion in Volgodonsk strengthened the senators' mood on the need for more decisive and hard-line action for the struggle against terrorism." Stroev did not accuse the Chechens of the terrorist attacks, but he quite obviously drew a connection between the "conflict zone" in Dagestan and the "struggle against terrorism."

Prime Minister Vladimir Putin delivered a report to the extraordinary session of the Council of the Federation. As "measures of defense against terrorism" he proposed establishing a safety cordon along the entire Russian–Chechen border and also intensifying the aerial and artillery bombardment of Chechen territory. In this way, Putin declared the Chechen Republic responsible for the terrorist attacks and called for military action to be taken against Chechnya.

At the conclusion of the session, Putin declared that the members of the Council of the Federation had supported action "of the most hard-line character" by the government for resolving the situation in the Northern Caucasus, including the "proposal to introduce a quarantine around Chechnya." Answering questions from journalists, Putin emphasized that preemptive strikes "have been delivered and will be delivered" against bandit bases in Chechnya, but that the possibility of introducing Russian forces into the territory of the Chechen Republic had not been discussed.

Putin emphasized that "the bandits must be exterminated, no other action is possible here." By bandits Putin meant the Chechen army, not terrorists. In other words, the government had settled for a single account of the bombings, the Chechen version, and was willing to use the bombings as an excuse for war.

The leaders of the various regions of the North Caucasus understood that Russia was setting up a new war against the Chechen Republic. On September 20, at a meeting in Magas in Ingushetia, the President of Ingushetia, A. Dzasokhov, and the President of Northern Ossetia, R. Aushev, supported A. Maskhadov's suggestion that talks were needed between Maskhadov and Yeltsin. Dzasokhov and Aushev also intended to arrange a meeting between the president of Chechnya and Russian Prime Minister Putin in Nalchik or Pyatigorsk no later than the end of September 1999. All of the leaders from the North Caucasus were supposed to attend the meeting.

Clearly, political negotiations might have prevented the war and cast light on the terrorist attacks that had taken place in Russia. For this very reason the FSB did everything in its power to prevent the meeting of leaders from the North Caucasus regions taking place. Before the end of September the FSB intended to blow up residential buildings in Ryazan, Tula, Pskov, and Samara. As always happens when a large terrorist attack involving groups of terrorists is being planned, there was a leak of information. "According to the information we received, it was Ryazan which had been singled out by the terrorists for the next bombing, because of the Ryazan VDV training college," said the mayor of Ryazan, Mamatov. This "next bombing" would be the failed attempt to blow up the house on Novosyolov Street on September 22.

On September 23, Zdanovich announced that the FSB had identified all the participants in the terrorist attacks in Buinaksk, Moscow, and Volgodonsk. "There is not a single ethnic Chechen among them." Not a single one. Following which, of course, the FSB general apologized to the Chechen people and the Chechen diaspora in Russia. No, nothing of the sort! Instead, with the stubbornness of a classroom dunce, Zdanovich set out himself to discover a "Chechen connection." To give him his due, he managed to find one. He thought it possible that after carrying out the bombings the terrorists, who had after all been planning their attacks since mid-August, might have had escape routes. They could possibly have taken refuge in the Commonwealth of Independent States (CIS) countries, but it was most probable that they had withdrawn to Chechnya. In short, the Chechens were being bombed because in Zdanovich's opinion the terrorists (among whom there were no ethnic Chechens) had probably retreated to Chechnya. But then why didn't they bomb the countries of the CIS?

"We have definite sources of information inside Chechnya, and we know what is going on there," Zdanovich emphasized. From 1991 to 1994, the FSK conducted hardly any operational work at all in this republic, but later "we did certain work. We know about those people who develop terrorist operations, make the financial input, recruit the mercenaries, and prepare the explosives. Nowadays in our country it's easy to obtain information on how to produce an explosive device, and apart from that there are many people who have fought in the hot spots who have the necessary knowledge and skills. Many of them have fought in Karabakh, Tajikistan, and Chechnya. This does not mean that anyone is accusing the population of Chechnya or Aslan Maskhadov. We accuse specific criminals, terrorists who are located in Chechnya. That's where the name 'the Chechen connection' came from," concluded Zdanovich, without actually naming a single "specific criminal."

To use the "probable" withdrawal of the terrorists to Chechnya as an excuse for launching a war against the Chechen people, while acknowledging that the bombings were not carried out by Chechens, is the height of cynicism. If Putin's government considered it possible to start the second Chechen war because of such a "probability," we must conclude that the bombings were no more than an excuse, and the war was an operation planned long in advance at General Staff HQ. Stepashin threw some light on this question in January 2000, when he announced that the political "decision to invade Chechnya was taken as early as March 1999," that the intervention had been "planned for August-September" and that "it would have happened even if there had been no explosions in Moscow." "I was preparing for active intervention," Stepashin said. "We were planning to be north of Terek in August-September." Putin, "who at that time was director of the FSB, was in possession of this information."

The testimony of former head of the FSK and former Prime Minister Stepashin does not match the testimony of former head of the FSB and former Prime Minister Putin:

> Last summer we launched a campaign, not against the independence of Chechnya, but against the aggressive impulses which have begun to manifest themselves on its territory. We are not attacking. We are defending ourselves. And we have pushed them out of Dagestan. . . . And after we gave them a good thrashing, they blew up houses in Moscow, Buinaksk, and Volgodonsk.
>
> QUESTION: Did you make the decision to continue the operation in Chechnya before the houses were bombed or after?
>
> ANSWER: After.
>
> QUESTION: Do you know that according to one account the houses were deliberately blown up in order to justify the start of military operations in Chechnya? That is, it was supposedly done by the Russian secret services?
>
> ANSWER: What? We blew up our own houses? You know. . . Rubbish! It's raving nonsense! There are no people in the Russian secret services who would be capable of such a crime against their own people. The very suggestion is immoral and essentially it's nothing more than an instance of the war of information against Russia.

At some stage, when the archives of the Ministry of Defense are opened up, we shall see these military documents: maps, plans, directives, orders of the day for air strikes, and the deployment of land forces. They will have dates on them. We shall discover for certain just how spontaneous was the Russian government's decision to start land operations in Chechnya, and whether the General Staff had finished planning the military operations before the first September bombing. We shall ask ourselves why bombings took place before the election campaign and before the incursion into Chechnya (when they were not in the Chechens' interests), and ceased following Putin's election as president and the beginning of all-out war against the Chechen Republic (the very time when the Chechens ought to have taken revenge against their invaders). We shall only receive the final and complete answers to these questions and many more after power has changed hands in Russia.

CHAPTER SEVEN

The FSB Against the People

SO FAR THE TERRORISTS had not been identified, or rather they had been identified as not being Chechens. The failed bombing attempt in Ryazan prompted the public to think that the FSB might be behind the bombings. For the "party of war" this was just one more indication that a full-scale war in Chechnya had to be started as soon as possible. The date of September 24 was no coincidence, for if the bombing in Ryazan had succeeded, Putin and the heads of all the military and law enforcement ministries were scheduled to make hard-line speeches in response.

On September 24, like a chorus in some well-planned stage performance, Russian politicians began demanding war. Patrushev announced that the terrorists who blew up the apartment houses in Moscow were in Chechnya. We know this is a lie. Patrushev did not identify his sources, since he had none. Patrushev did not offer any proof. His press secretary Zdanovich had spoken only of the possible or probable withdrawal of the terrorists to Chechnya (or to the countries of the CIS). But Patrushev needed to start a war, and so he claimed that Chechnya had been transformed into a hotbed of terrorism.

Rushailo claimed that organized crime inside and outside Russia had used the "Chechen bridgehead to unleash a wide-reaching campaign of subversion against Russia. . . . The law enforcement agencies and the armed forces have adequate potential to defend the interests of Russia in the Northern Caucasus. . . The federal forces are prepared to mount armed operations." In other words, the MVD was preparing to wage war against Chechnya as part of the effort to combat organized crime, including criminal groups. As though the fight against crime was going perfectly well on all the rest of Russia's territory!

The situation in the Northern Caucasus and the possible consequences for Russia were outlined by the chairman of the Security and Defense Committee, Alexander Ryabov, in an interview he gave to the newspaper *Segodnya*. In his opinion the world was undergoing a new geopolitical division under the cover of Muslim slogans. For Russia's enemies, the most important thing was to create a weak zone in Russia's "soft underbelly." This theory is reminiscent of the conspiracy of the Elders of Zion, except that this time the elders are Muslim, not Jewish. "A new geopolitical division of the world" is serious business. It will take a serious war to sort it out.

The newspaper *Vek* published an interview with the vice president of a Collegium of Military Experts, Alexander Vladimirov, who expressed the belief that the best solution right now would be a small victorious war in Chechnya. In his opinion the safety cordon around Chechnya proposed by Putin was a good idea, but it should be only the first step, since a cordon for its own sake is a pointless exercise. (Vladmirov's opinion must certainly have been noted, since they actually started with the second step, full-scale war.)

The final, decisive word in support of war was spoken by Prime Minister Putin in Astan: "The Russian state does not intend to keep things on hold. . . . The recent unprovoked attacks which have taken place against territories contiguous with Chechnya, the barbarous acts which have resulted in casualties among the peaceful population have set the terrorists not only outside the law but outside he framework of human society and modern civilization." Air strikes were taking place "exclusively against the guerrillas' bases, and this will continue wherever the terrorists may be located. . . . We shall pursue the terrorists everywhere. And if, pardon my language, we catch up with them in the toilet, then we'll wipe them out in the johns."

The mood of the public in those days can best be characterized by the fact that after his inspired phrase about "squelching them in the johns" Putin's ratings actually improved. The propaganda campaign mounted by the supporters of war had produced the desired result. According to an opinion poll conducted by the All-Russian Central Public Opinion Institute almost fifty percent of Russians were convinced that the explosions in Russian cities had been carried out by Basaev's guerrillas and another thirty-three percent blamed the Wahhabites and their leader Hattab. Eighty-eight percent of the people questioned were afraid of falling victim to a terrorist attack. Sixty-four percent were in agreement that all Chechens should be deported, and the same proportion was in favor of the mass bombing of Chechnya.

The bombings of the houses had broken down the resistance of public opinion. A small victorious war now seemed like the only natural response in the fight against terrorism. The stupefied country was not yet aware that the terrorists were not Chechens, and the war would be neither small nor victorious.

Note the absolutely glaring lack of logic here. The Chechen leadership denies it was involved in the terrorist attacks. Zdanovich confirms that there are no Chechens among the culprits, but states that the terrorists have "probably" gone into hiding in Chechnya. This "probably" is enough to fit the terrorists up with a "Chechen trail," which in turn provides a pretext for starting to bomb Chechnya. Aslan Maskhadov declares that he is willing to hold negotiations. But he is not heard. It is important for the FSB to drag Russia into a war as quickly as possible, so that the presidential election can be held against the background of a major armed conflict, and so that after the new president comes to power, he can inherit the war together with all the political consequences which it implies the president's dependence on the structures of coercion. Only through war can the FSB finally seize power in the country. It is a simple little matter of a conspiracy with the goal of allowing the former KGB to seize power under the banner of the fight against Chechen terrorism. On October 4, the coup ended in victory for the conspirators. That was the day when Russian forces crossed the border of Chechnya. Most of the population of Russia supported the decision taken by former director of the FSB Vladimir Putin; director of the FSB, Patrushev; and FSB general Sergei Ivanov.

During this difficult period for the Russian political elite, those who spoke out decisively against war defined their position. Novaya Gazeta should be named as one of the most principled opponents of war against the Chechen Republic: "The KGB lieutenant colonel mouthing criminal jargon who finds himself by some miracle at the head of a great country, is losing no time in exploiting the effect produced. Any general or politician planning a military campaign always attempts to minimize the number of his enemies and maximize the number of his allies. Putin is deliberately bombing Grozny in order to make negotiations with Maskhadov impossible, in order to bury all of the regime's previous crimes under the bloody slaughter. The outgoing regime is attempting to use the crime currently in preparation —the genocide of the Chechen people—to bind the entire Russian people in blood, to make it the regime's accomplice and hostage. It is still not too late to call a halt on the road to Russia's destruction."

Konstantin Titov, the governor of the Samara Region, believed that land operations in Chechnya were a catastrophe for Russia. "I am no believer in purely coercive methods of resolving global problems. And in Samara I shall never allow the kind of ethnic purges they have in Moscow." (Konstantin Titov, of course, was not aware that during those days full preparations had been set in place for the bombing of an apartment house on Novovokzalnaya Street in Samara, but the FSB had halted the terrorist attacks after the fiasco in Ryazan).

The mood of the apprehensive section of the democratic public at this time was described by the well-known Russian lawyer, Anatoly Kucherena:

WHEN THE GUNS ROAR,
THE PUBLIC PROSECUTORS FALL SILENT.

The clearest possible illustration is provided by the "exercises" conducted by the FSB in Ryazan. This act bears witness to the most profound degradation, primarily moral, of the Russian secret services. The secret services continue to think of themselves as "a state within a state." Their leaders seem to think that they are not subject to any laws and act exclusively on the basis of political expediency, as they did in those glorious times when the agencies organized abductions and political assassinations in foreign states, created the "legends" for non-existent anti-Soviet organizations, and wrote the scripts for show trials.

The numerous 'spy cases' of recent years (Platon Obukhov, Grigory Pasko, captain Alexander Nikitin), operation "Face in the Snow," various unlawful acts committed on the eve of the presidential elections of 1996, such as the attempt to "seal up" the State Duma, the escapade in which members of the Russian army were recruited for the storming of Grozny by the forces of the so-called anti-Dudaev opposition in 1994—all of this bears witness to the fact that unlawful tendencies have remained a part of the activity of the secret services to this very day.

One gets the impression that both the present party of power and the so-called opposition believe that Russia's democratic project is dead and buried. The authorities are not capable of imposing order founded in the law, it is beyond their ability to build a society governed by law. The alternative to a society governed by law is a bandit-and-police state, a situation in which the actions of terrorists and bandits on the one hand and the agencies of law enforcement on the other are indistinguishable either in terms of their objectives or the methods they employ. Among the public the mass conviction is gaining ground that democracy has failed to deliver as a form of government.

And since nothing has come of the democratic project, many political players are tempted to have done with it once and for all. So each of them pursues his own goals, but in objective terms the vectors of their efforts coincide. Some are frightened by the impending redistribution of property, some wish to avoid responsibility for committing unlawful acts, some see themselves as the new Bonaparte or Pinochet and are impatient to grasp the "rudder" with an iron hand.

Government through democratic institutions has failed yet again in Russia. A time of rule by means of fear is beginning. A time of terror by both bandits and the state. Could this perhaps be the present regime's "political project" for Russia?

While Kucherena formulated the apprehensions of the democratic section of the population, the goals and plans of the conspirators who successfully canvassed for the invasion of Chechnya were revealed on March 8, 2000, in the article "The country needs a new KGB" by State Duma deputy and former head of the SBP, Korzhakov:

There is one feature of the preparations for the presidential elections which is of fundamental importance. In characterizing the number one candidate for the highest state position, Vladimir Putin, virtually no one expresses dissatisfaction at the fact that his background is in the secret services, more specifically, from deep within the KGB. Only a few years ago, it was impossible to imagine such a thing, but now public opinion is openly sympathetic to a politician who began his career in one of the secret services. Vladimir Putin's high rating is testimony first of all to the fact that people see him, a product of the KGB, as a politician capable of straightening the country out and organizing the work of all the power structures so that at long last we can really start to pull out of social and political crisis. The nomination of a former KGB officer for the highest state position gives me a reason once again to draw attention to certain aspects of the activities of the secret services and the roles they play in general at the present stage of our economic and political development. . . .

The well-known bombing incidents in houses in Moscow and other towns in the country which have resulted in the death of dozens of peaceful and entirely innocent people, the continuing export of the nation's wealth, the flourishing corruption in state structures, cases of slave-dealing and trading in children—all of this provokes the legitimate anger of our citizens.

People ask in bewilderment: where are our secret services, which exist in order to fight this kind of phenomenon? We have enough manpower and secret services—the FSB, the MVD, GRU, SVR, FAPSI—all of these are capable of solving the most complex problems. The real problem is that the secret services act separately, like an open hand, not a clenched fist.

There was a time when our democratic society was terribly frightened by the existence of the KGB. Then they decided to destroy the "monster" so that it would not be capable of any surprises. It seemed to some that it would be easier to control the activity of the secret services that way. However, the control did not turn out quite as they had intended and the co-ordination of action by the secret services didn't get very far. This is confirmed by the textbook mistakes and failures suffered in the fight against Chechen and international terrorists. Now even the most vehement opponents of the KGB are beginning to realize that the destruction of that structure has not produced anything useful. Alexander Solzhenitsyn was right when he remarked to a small circle of acquaintances that what we need now is the KGB.

There is also another real factor. Nobody will ever voluntarily return our national wealth which has been stolen and exported to other countries. Not a single foreign special service will pass up a chance to acquire important secrets in science or other important areas if we do not block off their access to these secrets. Corruption will continue to exist just as long as the relevant services, whose job it is to expose bribe-takers, continue to act separately, each for itself. Stealing from the treasury will continue just as long as our laws remain humane towards those who love to stick their fingers into the state purse.

In supporting Vladimir Putin's candidacy for the post of president our people are sending the authorities a signal, the meaning of which is perfectly clear: it is high time to gather the secret services together into a single fist and strike out with it at those who prevent us from building a normal life. Russia needs its own KGB! The time has come to speak of this without inhibition! Sharing this opinion, I believe that the first step on the path to the creation of a new Committee of State Security must be the formation of a Secret Services Coordinating Committee attached to the Security Council and subordinated directly to the head of state. This will make it possible to formulate the structure of the future KGB and define its functions and objectives. If the Coordinating Committee were to be set up in the immediate future it would make possible a more effective solution to the problem of bringing illegally exported capital back into the country. I say this with confidence, since at one time the President's Security Service did start working along these lines and produced concrete results. The Service demonstrated in practice that bringing capital back into the country is not only necessary, but possible if the job is taken seriously.

A second high-priority task is the fight against terrorism using specific methods and means, excluding the use of large-scale armed forces and deaths among the peaceful population. Nobody doubts that the Chechen and international terrorists will be destroyed. However, the terrorist threat will not disappear then. It should not be forgotten that in Chechnya a generation of young people has already grown up in conditions of war and hatred of Russians. The aspiration of today's young Chechen boys to avenge themselves on the "offenders" any way they can will find outlets not just inside Chechnya. It is no longer possible to use the army to combat local manifestations of terrorism, such possibilities have been exhausted. The secret services will be dealing with it.

A third task is to expose cases of the illegal privatization of facilities of strategic importance and the contrived bankruptcy of factories, plants, and mines, so that they could be grabbed as private property. Experience has shown that we cannot manage without the participation of the secret services in this work either.

Kucherena believed that Russia's woes were caused by a bandit-and-police state. Korzhakov claims that all of the misfortunes were due to the lack of a strong hand of power, since the secret services acted "like an open hand, not a fist." Korzhakov suggested clenching the hand into a fist, setting up a Secret Services Coordinating Committee and subordinating it to the secretary of the Security Council (FSB General Sergei Ivanov). We can assume that at the head of this new agency Korzhakov saw himself, since he emphasized that the SBP, which he used to head, had been working along exactly these lines and had achieved concrete results. In other words, Korzhakov acknowledged that he abused his power and exceeded his official authority, which is regarded as a crime under Russian law and is punishable by imprisonment (Korzhakov's formal functions consisted of guarding the president and members of this family).

This statement by Korzhakov alone makes it clear what the SBP was doing for all those years under Korzhakov's leadership and what Korzhakov himself was doing afterwards as a private individual with contacts in the structures of coercion. Let us call things by their real names. Having found themselves outside the structures of power and discharged from the secret services, Soskovets and the retired generals Korzhakov and Barsukov, with help from organized criminal structures which they had formerly used themselves, such as Stealth, attempted to become involved in the redistribution of property in Russia and establish control over businesses for purposes of personal gain. The Izmailovo organized criminal group funded their activities. Underground and operational work was carried out by various private security firms. Information and propaganda backup were provided by a number of media outlets, either controlled or bought. Combat support was provided by organized criminal groups and individual fighters from the ranks of former employees of the special sections of the MO, FSB, and MVD.

Bringing back capital from abroad "à la Korzhakov" is nothing more than the extortion of money from businessmen living in Russia. In practice, this meant that having obtained financial information via the secret services, Korzhakov summoned businessmen to see him, told them he knew about the money they had exported, and demanded that they return the money to Russia. Only it is very important to understand that the businessmen did not return the money to the state's coffers, but to accounts named by Korzhakov.

Korzhakov also revealed the political goals of his structure. The first was to subordinate all the secret services to the President's Security Service (or his new structure, the Coordinating Committee). The second was to allow carte blanche for punitive acts throughout the country, i.e., dictatorial powers. In addition, Korzhakov openly declared that the genocide of the Chechen people should be Russian state policy. Let us take another look at what he said: "It should not be forgotten that in Chechnya, a generation of young people has already grown up in conditions of war and hatred of Russians. The aspiration of today's young Chechen boys to avenge themselves on the 'offenders' in any way they can will find outlets not only inside Chechnya." It seems that Korzhakov wanted to shoot all the "young Chechen boys" everywhere in Russia so that they would never reach an age where they would be able to avenge their murdered fathers and ruined homeland.

That Korzhakov's appeal "The country needs a new KGB" was not an isolated chance gesture, but a symptom of a genuine trend was demonstrated in July 2001, by FSB staff member and director of the Institute for Problems of Economic Security, Yu. Ovchenko. In a meeting with a small group of journalists, he informed them that a number of officials "with access to the president" and connections with the structures of coercion, including deputy director of the FSB Yu. Zaostrovtsev, intended to change the government's economic policy fundamentally and move "from an oligarchic system to a national one." According to the newspaper *Argumenty i Facty*, Ovchenko literally said the following:

> The secret services have a particularly important role in the process of de-privatization and the investigation of illegally exported capital. Control over the process of the change of ownership must be transferred to the FSB system. The functions of

monitoring the results of privatization must be transferred to the Security Council, where the secretary must be a man from the FSB system. . . . In order to halt any further leakage of capital, the systems of the Central Bank and the State Customs Committee must be transferred into effective control. . . . Representatives of the economic security service must be introduced into the management staff of these agencies and must be in possession of complete information on resources already exported and capable of talking to the oligarchs in a language they understand. . . . Even though the proposed measures . . . will be extremely popular with the public, their implementation will require the establishment of state control over the main electronic media. It would be appropriate to make it illegal for private capital to own controlling blocks of shares in broadcasting channels and newspapers with a print-run of over 200,000 copies.

When asked how long the plan would take to implement, Ovchenko replied: "Changes will be made by the end of the year. But it could be sooner if conditions are ripe."

Society was divided. Some demanded the construction of new secret services. Others believed that the old ones were worse than any terrorists. The public was crazed and stupefied by the Moscow bombings and the escapade in Ryazan. In a country where there were no laws, it was impossible to do anything anyway. The whole business got no further than acrimonious newspaper articles. Lawyer Pavel Astakhov tried to submit a question to the FSB about which operational activities had been the reason for the infringement of liberty suffered by the citizens of Ryazan, who were sent out into the street on that cold autumn evening. The FSB referred him to its own law "On operational and investigative activity." It turned out that according to this law, the FSB had the right to conduct exercises wherever it wanted whenever it wanted, and the people had no recourse against this FSB law.

However, the incident in Ryazan did not in fact comply with the requirements of federal legislation and exceeded the competence of the FSB. "The Federal Law on the Federal Security Service" stated that the activity of the agencies of the FSB "shall be conducted in accordance with the law of the Russian Federation 'On operational and investigative activity in the Russian Federation,' the criminal and criminal procedural legislation of the Russian Federation and also in accordance with the present federal law." Not one of these documents, including the law "On operational and investigative activity" indicated that exercises could be carried out to the detriment and in violation of the civil rights of the population at large. And in addition article 5 of the law "On operational and investigative activity" formally guaranteed members of the public against possible abuse by the agencies of law enforcement:

Agencies (officials) who engage in operational and investigative activity must, when carrying out operational and investigative measures, ensure the observance of the human and civil rights to the inviolability of private life . . . the inviolability of the home. . . . It is not permitted to carry out public operational and investigative activity for the achievement of goals and implementation of tasks which are not specified in the present Federal Law. An individual who believes that the actions of agencies engaging in operational and investigative activity have resulted in the infringement of his rights and freedoms shall be entitled to make appeal regarding such actions to a superior agency engaging in operational and investigative activity, a public prosecutor's office, or a court of law. . . . If the agency (or official) engaging in operational and investigative activity has infringed the rights and legitimate interests of individuals and legal entities, the superior agency, prosecutor, or judge is obliged under the terms of the legislation of the Russian Federation to take measures for the restitution of such rights and legitimate interests and the provision of compensation for damage inflicted. Violations of the present

Federal Law committed in the course of operational and investigtive activity shall be punishable as prescribed by the legislation of the Russian Federation.

Zdanovich and Patrushev had, therefore, both lied openly when referring to Russian law.

Putin and Patrushev were not allowed to forget the Ryazan incident right up to the presidential elections. During the night of October 3, 1999, three GRU officers disappeared without a trace in the Nadterek district of Chechnya: Colonel Zuriko Ivanov, Major Victor Pakhomov, and Senior Lieutenant Alexei Galkin, together with a GRU employee of Chechen nationality, Vesami Abdulaev. The leader of the group, Zuriko Ivanov, had graduated from the Ryazan VDV College and gone into special missions intelligence, serving in the Fifteenth Special Missions Brigade, which was famous from the Afghan war, and then in the Northern Caucasus military district. He managed the personal bodyguard of Doku Zavgaev, who had connections in Moscow. Shortly before the beginning of the second Chechen war, Ivanov was transferred to the central administration in Moscow. His new duties did not include raids behind enemy lines, but as soon as preparations for ground operations in Chechnya began, Ivanov was needed in the zone of conflict.

On October 19, in Grozny, the head of the press center of the armed forces of Chechnya, Vakha Ibragimov informed the assembled journalists on behalf of the military command that GRU officers who had gone over to the Chechens had "established contact with Chechen soldiers of their own initiative" and had expressed the wish to co-operate with the Chechen authorities. Ibragimov stated that the GRU officers and their agent were prepared to supply information about the organizers of the bombings in Moscow, Buinaksk and Volgodonsk. The Russian Ministry of Defense called this statement from the Chechen side a provocation intended to discredit the internal policy of the Russian leadership and the actions of the federal forces in the Northern Caucasus. However, in late December 1999, the GRU officially acknowledged the death of the leader of the group,

Ivanov: the federal forces were given the headless corpse of a man and the blood-soaked identity pass of Colonel Zuriko Ivanov (the officer's severed head was discovered later). On March 24, 2000, Zdanovich announced that the entire group of GRU operatives had been executed by the Chechens.

On January 6, 2000, the London newspaper *The Independent* published an article by its correspondent Helen Womack entitled "Russian agents behind Moscow flat bombings":

The Independent has obtained a videotape on which a Russian officer, captured by the Chechens, "confesses" that Russian secret services committed the Moscow apartment-block bombings that ignited the latest war in Chechnya and propelled Vladimir Putin into the Kremlin. On the video, shot by a Turkish journalist last month before Grozny was finally cut off by Russian forces, the captured Russian identifies himself as Alexei Galkin of the GRU (Russian military intelligence service). The bearded captive acknowledges as his own papers displayed by the Chechens that identify him as a "Senior Lieutenant, Armed Secret Services, General Headquarters for Special Forces of the Russian Federation." The Ministry of Defense was checking yesterday whether there was indeed such a GRU officer. "Even if he exists, you understand what methods could have been used on him in captivity," said a junior officer, who asked not to be named.

Colonel Yakov Firsov of the Ministry of Defense said on the record: "The (Chechen) bandits feel their end is near and so they are using all manner of dirty tricks in the information war. This is a provocation. This is rubbish. The Russian armed forces protect the people. It is impossible that they would attack their own people."

On the video, Senior Lieutenant Galkin said he was captured at the border between Dagestan, and Chechnya while on a mine-laying mission. "I did not take part in the destruction of the buildings in Moscow and Dagestan but I have information about it. I know who is responsible for the bombings in Moscow (and Dagestan). It is the FSB (Russian Security Service), in cooperation with the GRU, that is responsible for the explosions in Volgodonsk and Moscow. He then named other GRU officers. Nearly 300 people died when four multi-story apartment blocks were destroyed by terrorist bombs in September. The attacks provoked Mr. Putin, appointed Prime Minister the month before, to launch a new war in Chechnya.

Sedat Aral, a photographer with ISF News Pictures, said he shot the video in a bunker in Grozny, where he met Abu Movsaev, head of Chechen rebel intelligence. Mr. Movsaev said the Chechens could prove they were not responsible for the apartment-block bombings.

The Russian public backs the "anti-terrorist campaign" in Chechnya, which has so boosted the popularity of its author, Mr. Putin, that Boris Yeltsin has retired early to make way for his chosen successor. However the war started, the beneficiary is clearly Mr. Putin. The former head of Russia's domestic intelligence service is now poised to realize his presidential ambitions.

Commenting on the article, BBC correspondent Malcolm Haslett confirmed that the hypothesis of a secret services conspiracy had existed since the time when the explosions had occurred, since the FSB could have planted the bomb in order to justify the military operation in Chechnya. In this context, Haslett remarked that the authorities had still not provided convincing proof of Chechen involvement in the bombings, and Shamil Basaev, one of the people accused of these heinous crimes, categorically denied having anything to do with them. Haslett supposed that on the eve of the presidential elections, Putin could be badly damaged by the scandal over Galkin's videotaped testimony, since the popularity of this little-known officer of the FSB had improved considerably after military operations began in Chechnya.

The French newspaper *Le Monde* also wrote about the danger to Putin of exposés of the secret services' involvement in the September bombings: "Having reinforced his popularity and emerged victorious in the elections to the State Duma as a result of the war unleashed against the Chechen people, Vladimir Putin understands that there are only two things capable of preventing him from becoming president in the elections in March. These are major military failures and losses of personnel in Chechnya, and the recognition that the Russian secret services might have been involved in the bombing of residential buildings, which cost about 300 people their lives in September of last year and served as the official pretext for the beginning of the 'anti-terrorist operation' in Chechnya."

It is interesting that in connection with the bombings in Moscow neither Lazovsky nor any of his people were questioned, although it would have been reasonable to assume that the people behind these terrorist attacks were the same as those behind the attacks of 1994–1996. Not until spring 2000 did the public prosecutor consent to Lazovsky's arrest. The people behind Lazovsk—and it is obvious that the most important people standing behind Lazovsky were the Moscow FSB—decided not to allow Lazovsky to be arrested. According to operational information, Lazovsky was killed immediately after the order for his arrest was issued. He was shot on April 28, 2000, on the threshold of the Cathedral of the Assumption, from a Kalashnikov automatic rifle with a silencer and an optical sight. The four bullets, one of which struck him in the throat, proved fatal. They were fired from a clump of shrubs about 150 meters away. For some reason, the jeep in which Lazovsky's bodyguards constantly followed him around, was nowhere nearby. The killer abandoned his weapon and went into hiding. Someone took the bloody corpse to the nearby hospital and put it on a bench. The local police used a doctor from the Odintsovo polyclinic to identify the body. The records of the examination of the murder victim and the inspection of the scene of the incident were drawn up in an extremely sloppy and unprofessional manner, which provided a pretext for claiming that it was not Lazovsky who had been killed but his double.

On the evening of May 22, 2000, a small detachment of guerrillas fell into a trap set by GRU special missions in the region between the villages of Serzhen-Yurt and Shali. The brief battle left ten guerrillas dead and the others were scattered. The dead included thirty-eight-year-old field commander and head of Chechen military counter-intelligence, Abu Movsaev, who had interrogated Senior Lieutenant Galkin and probably also possessed other information about the bombings. Local residents said that in May, Movsaev had several times secretly come to spend the night with relatives who lived in Shali. One member of the local authorities had reported this to the FSB representative, who did nothing about it. When a GRU special missions group had attempted to seize the field commander, the FSB had opposed them. A scandal blew up, and the case was transferred to Moscow, where it was decided to bring Movsaev in. However, he was not brought in alive.

On March 9, 2000, an airplane with nine people on board crashed on takeoff in Moscow. The nine were Artym Borovik, president of the holding company *Sovershenno Sekretno*, Ziya Bazhaev, a Chechen national who was head of the holding company Alliance Group, two of the latter's bodyguards, and five members of the crew. The YAK-40 plane, rented by the holding company *Sovershenno Sekretno* about a year earlier from the Vologda Aviation Company via the Moscow Aviation Company Aerotex, should have flown on to Kiev. The report from the commission for the investigation of incidents in air transport stated that the Vologda aviation technicians had not sprayed the plane with special deicing liquid before take off and its wing-flaps had only been extended by ten degrees, whereas for takeoff twenty degrees was required. However, on the morning of March 9, it was only four degrees below zero at Sheremetevo Airport, and there had not been any precipitation. There was no need to spray the plane with the Arktika deicing fluid. Furthermore, the YAK-40 could have taken off and flown with its wing-flaps extended by only 10 degrees; the run-up would simply have been longer, and it would have handled a bit sluggishly. Judging from the fact that the plane crashed at about the center of the runway, which at Sheremetevo is 3.6 kilometers long, the plane's run-up was the standard length of about 800 meters. On learning of the tragedy, Grigory Yavlinsky, leader of the *Yabloko* political party and State Duma deputy stated that recently Borovik and his team had been conducting an independent investigation into the bombings in Moscow. We can only guess at what conclusions Borovik would have reached.

Former KGB General Oleg Kalugin had his own opinion on the matter. He believed that the FSB, as an organization, was not directly involved in organizing the terrorist attacks and that the bombings had been ordered by one of the "Russian power blocs," which was interested in improving Putin's rating. Those who ordered the acts of terror might well have made use of individual specialists from the FSB or the old KGB, but the FSB itself only became involved in the operation after the fiasco in Ryazan, and it provided a cover story for the failed operation and its organizers.

Of course, this version raises the question of what sort of "bloc" it was, and who was its leader, if after the failure in Ryazan the entire FSB, and other state departments too, were thrown into the "cover story for the failed operation and its organizers." It is clear that only Putin could have been in control of such a "bloc" and that the "Russian power bloc," attempting to improve Putin's rating, consisted primarily of Putin himself, Patrushev, everyone who had striven to unleash war in Chechnya, and those who wished to clench the secret services into a solid fist.

Several unidentified FSB employees expressed their opinions on the failed bombing in Ryazan in an interview with journalists from *Novaya Gazeta*: "If the bombing in Ryazan really was planned by the secret services, then a highly clandestine group (five to six people) must have been put together for it, including fanatical officers of two categories. The first, the frontline operatives, would have had to be eliminated immediately. And of course, the bosses wouldn't have given them any instructions directly." In addition "there is also a certain unlikely but in our conditions entirely possible account of the events in Ryazan. The decay within the secret services led to the formation within, say, the FSB of a group of patriotic officers which got out of control. (The present degree of co-ordination of action within this structure makes such a supposition possible.) Let us assume the group was sufficiently clandestine and autonomous, that it carried out specific secret tasks, but in addition to its main activities, it became involved in work of its own. For instance, certain similar 'autonomous groups' may operate as elusive criminal groups in their free time. But out of certain political considerations, these wanted to blow up a house in order to improve the nation's fighting spirit, etc. Even if the leadership of the FSB does discover the unsanctioned activities of such a breakaway group, it will never acknowledge the fact of its existence. Of course, the schismatic will be declared wanted men, and in the end they'll be liquidated, but without any unnecessary fuss. This secret, if it existed, would have been kept with special zeal. And they would have reacted to attempts to expose it just like they're acting now."

Even so, the theory of a conspiracy within the FSB cannot account for the obvious patronage from the very top of the FSB and the state. It is not right to assume that the FSB would have failed to spot such a major conspiracy within. To reach the rank of FSB general means going through hell and high water and developing an intuition so subtle that you can spot any conspiracy among subordinates from a mile away. Apart from that, internal informing is established on a very wide scale within the FSB. A group of five or six men cannot possibly conspire to commit a terrorist act, and carrying out bombings in four cities requires far more than that number.

State Duma Deputy Vladimir Volkov also believed that the September bombings were the ork of the secret services: "This is the second time in a row that presidential elections have apparently by accident coincided with a change for the worse in Chechnya. This time the Chechnya campaign was preceded by terrorist attacks in Moscow, Buinaksk, Volgodonsk, Rostov. . . . But for some reason the bombing of a residential building in Ryazan failed and is now being described as an exercise. As a military man, I know that no exercise is ever carried out using genuine explosive devices, and that the local police and FSB must have known about any exercise. Unfortunately, what happened in Ryazan was something else, and the press is already openly saying that all the 'Chechen' terrorist attacks in Russian cities were committed by the secret services, who were preparing a 'small war' to suit Putin. The search for an answer to these suspicions has not yet begun, but it is already clear even today that instead of a white charger, Putin has been handed a steed stained red with the spilled blood of the people."

In their own distinctive celebration of the anniversary of the bombings in Buinaksk, Moscow and Volgodonsk, on August 8, 2000, two FSB employees, named in their "cover documents" as Major Izmailov and Captain Fyodorov, carried out a terrorist attack on the pedestrian subway at Pushkin Square in Moscow. Thirteen people were killed, and more than a hundred received injuries of varying degrees of severity. Not far from the site of the explosion, specialists from the Moscow FSB discovered another two explosive devices and fired on them from a water cannon.

The explosion on Pushkin Square was a shot in the heart. "The still-unidentified evildoers were very careful in choosing their location," wrote Vitaly Portnikov in the Kiev newspaper *Zerkalo Nedeli* on August 12. "In order to understand what Pushkin Square means to a resident of the Russian capital, one must be a Muscovite. Because Red Square, Alexandrovsky Garden, the underground complex in Okhotny Ryad, Staryi Arbat Street—all of these are places for sightseeing. But when Muscovites make plans to meet, they meet in Pushkin Square. . . . Pushkin Square is not simply the center of the city, the square or the metro stop. It is a whole environment. . . . To blow up an environment is more important for a terrorist than to plant a bomb inside a residential building. Because the building can turn out to be your neighbor's, but the environment is always yours."

Yuri Luzhkov was quick to attempt to pin this bombing on the Chechens as well: "This is Chechnya, no doubt about it." This time, weary of the constant accusations, the Chechens decided to call the mayor to order. The head of the Chechen administration, Akhmad Kadyrov, expressed his indignation that the Chechens were once again being accused of a bombing without any proof. Kadyrov's representative to the Russian government, the former minister of foreign affairs in the government of Djokhar Dudaev, Shamil Beno, threatened that

Chechens would demonstrate in Moscow, and chairman of the State Council of Chechnya, Malik Saidulaev, promised an impressive reward for information about the real organizers of the bombing. Aslan Maskhadov also disassociated himself from the terrorist attack and offered Russians his condolences.

On August 12, 2000, a group of twelve members of Andrei Morev's special group, having just arrived at 38 Petrovka Street for a briefing before another operation, had witnessed a conversation between Izmailov and Fyodorov about a job on Pushkin Square. The terrorist attack took place just three days later, and Morev recognized two FSB officers from the sketches.

Years will go by, maybe even decades. Russia will change, of course. It will have a different political elite, a different political leadership. If we're still alive, our children will ask us: why didn't you say anything? When they were bombing you in Moscow, Volgodonsk, Buinaksk, and Ryazan, why didn't you say anything? Why did you behave like guinea pigs in a laboratory?

We did say something. We screamed and yelled, we wrote. . . . The inhabitants of house number 14/16 on Novosyolov Street tried to take the FSB to court. A letter sent to the General Public Prosecutor of Russia said: "We have been used for a monstrous experiment, in which two hundred and forty entirely innocent people were cast in the role of extras. All of us suffered not only severe psychological trauma, but also irreversible damage to our health." The people of Ryazan were supported by the Ryazan regional authorities, but despite that, the case never got beyond empty words, and the collective application to the prosecutor's office was mislaid.

On March 18, Sergei Ivanenko and Yuri Schekochikhin, both Duma deputies belonging to the *Yabloko* faction, drafted the text of a Duma resolution for a parliamentary question to the acting General Public Prosecutor, Vladimir Ustinov, entitled "On the discovery in the city of Ryazan on September 22, 1999, of an explosive substance and the circumstances of its investigation." Ivanenko and Schekochikhin proposed that the deputies of the State Duma should be given answers to the following questions: What stage has been reached in the criminal case of the discovery of an explosive substance in Ryazan on September 22, 1999? Has an analysis been carried out of the substance that was discovered? Who gave the order to hold an exercise and when, what were the aims and objectives of the exercise? What equipment and substances—explosives or imitations thereof—were used in the course of the exercise? Check material published in *Novaya Gazeta* (No.10, 2000) about hexogen packed in sugar sacks being stored at the weapons and munitions depot of a VDV training unit.

The draft questions also mentioned the fact that during the first two days after the incident, the FSB changed its official position. According to its first account, issued on September 22, 1999, a terrorist attack had been foiled. According to the second, exercises designed to check the readiness of the law enforcement agencies had been taking place in Ryazan. "A number of the facts adduced cast doubt on the official version of the events that took place in Ryazan" the text of the question stated. Information related to the exercise was restricted. The materials of the criminal case initiated by the FSB of the Ryazan Region in connection with the discovery of explosive substance were inaccessible. The individuals who planted the imitation explosive substance had not been named, nor had the persons who issued the order to hold the exercise. "The statement by the leadership of the FSB that the substance found in Ryazan consisted of granulated sugar does not stand up to examination." In particular, the instrument used to analyze the substance that was found indicated the presence of hexogen and was in perfect working order, and the detonator of the explosive device was not an imitation.

Unfortunately, a majority of the members of the Duma voted not to put the question. Those who opposed the putting of the question included Unity, the pro-government party, the People's Deputies group, part of the Regions of Russia faction, and part of the Liberal-Democratic Party of Russia. Those who voted for the question were *Yabloko*, the Union of Right Forces, the Communists, and the Agrarian and Industrialist Group. As a result, Schekochikhin and Ivanenko's parliamentary supporters gathered only 103 votes (against the 226 they required). For some reason, the Russian parliament was not interested in the truth about the September bombings.

The second attempt to table a question, undertaken on March 31, brought Schekochikhin and Ivanenko closer to their goal, but also ended in failure. Voting took place at a plenary session of the Duma, and despite the support of the Communists, the Agrarians and Industrialists and *Yabloko*, as well as part of the faction Our Fatherland Is All Russia, and the Union of Right Forces, the draft question only gathered 197 votes against 137, with one abstention. Not a single deputy from the Unity faction voted in favor.

On March 16, 2000, Zdanovich stated in one of his interviews that according to information in the possession of the FSB, the journalist Nikolai Nikolaev, who presented the "Independent Investigation" series on the NTV television channel, was intending to broadcast an investigation into the exercise in Ryazan from the NTV studio within the next few days, before the presidential elections. The program was scheduled for March 24. It is hardly surprising that only a few days later the news that had been anticipated for many months finally arrived. On March 21, the Federal News Agency announced the results of the analysis of the samples of "sugar" found in Ryazan on September 22, 1999. The information came from the Ryazan Region, from Major-General Sergeiev, the head of the local FSB, who said the analysis had determined that the sacks which had been discovered contained sugar with absolutely no traces of explosive substances. "Following the investigations carried out of the samples of sugar, no traces of TNT, hexogen, nitroglycerine, or other explosive substances were discovered," said the report from the experts. In addition, according to Sergeiev, the analysis had confirmed that the explosive device found together with the sacks of sugar was only a mock-up. The conclusion was: "Consequently we may conclude that this device was not a bomb, since it lacked both a charge of explosive material and the means of detonation."

It gradually became clear that the FSB was attempting to close the criminal case before Nikolaev's TV program and the presidential elections. Following Patrushev's statement about "exercises," the criminal case, initiated by the head of the investigative department of the FSB for the Ryazan Region Lieutenant Colonel Maximov, had been halted. However, on December 2, i.e., more than two months later, the General Public Prosecutor's Office decided that the case had been halted prematurely and set aside the decision taken by the Ryazan FSB on September 27, thereby reinstating the investigation and making it clear that something was not quite right with the FSB's story about "exercises." The completion of the investigation, however, was not entrusted to an independent investigator, but to one of the interested parties, in fact to the FSB, the very organization accused of planning the terrorist act. At least the case had not been closed.

The Ryazan FSB made repeated requests to the FSB laboratory in Moscow for the full text of the report on the analysis of the substance in the sugar sacks and the mechanical device found with them. On March 15, 2000, the FSB finally received from Moscow the long-awaited reply of which its leaders had such great hopes: "It was established that the substance in all the samples was saccharose, the basis of sugar produced from sugar beet and sugar cane. The chemical composition and appearance of the substance investigated correspond to those of sugar as used for food. No explosive substances were discovered in the samples presented. The triggering device could not have been used as a means of detonation, since it lacked a charge of explosive material. Consequently, there was no real threat to the inhabitants [of the building]." This meant, of course, that there were no indications of "terrorism."

"In my view, we have been given sufficiently weighty reasons to halt the investigation in view of the instructional nature of the events which took place on September 22, 1999, in the house on Novosyolov Street," was the opinion expressed on March 21, 2000, by Maximov, the investigator who had initiated the criminal case.

Now the results of the analysis performed by Tkachenko had to be disavowed. This honorable task was discharged by Maximov on March 21: "The analysis was carried out by the head of the engineering and technical section, Yuri Tkachenko. As was subsequently discovered, following a twenty-four-hour period his hands bore traces of plastic explosives, the composition of which includes hexogen. It should be noted that this kind of background pollution in the form of micro-particles can persist on the skin for long periods, up to three months. The analytical procedure to be carried could only have been pure if performed in disposable gloves. Unfortunately, these do not form part of the work kit of an explosives specialist and no funds are available to provide them. We have come to the conclusion that this was the only reason that the 'diagnosis' made by the police officers was the presence of an explosive substance."

No doubt this was precisely what Maximov wrote in the supporting documentation sent to the General Public Prosecutor's Office, when he explained the need to close the case against the FSB under the law on terrorism. We had no right to demand heroism from the investigator. Maximov had a family, just like the rest of us, and it would have been impractical and dangerous to oppose the leadership of the FSB. It should, however, be noted that Maximov's opinion contradicted the view of Tkachenko, who could in no way be suspected of being an interested party in this matter. Tkachenko's principled stance could not bring him anything but problems. And, in fact, after the episode in Ryazan he was sent to Chechnya.

The Ryazan section of explosives specialists headed by Tkachenko was unique not only in Ryazan but in all of the surrounding districts. It included thirteen professional engineers with extensive experience, who had attended several courses of advanced training in Moscow at the Explosive Testing Research and Technical Center and who conducted special examinations every two years. Tkachenko claimed that the equipment in his department was world class. The gas analyzer used to analyze the substance that was discovered—a device which cost about 20,000 dollars—was in perfect working order (as it would have to be, since an engineer's life depends on the condition of his equipment). According to the gas analyzer's technical specifications, it was both highly reliable and highly accurate, so that if the results of an analysis indicated the presence of hexogen fumes in the contents of the sacks, there should be no room for doubt. Consequently, the "imitation" detonator clearly included a live explosive substance, not an instructional substitute. According to Tkachenko, the detonator, which was rendered safe by the explosives specialists, was also professionally constructed, and not a mock-up.

In theory, a mistake could have been made if the apparatus had not been properly serviced and if the gas analyzer had retained traces of material from a previous investigation. Tkachenko's reply to a question about this possibility was as follows: "The gas analyzer is only serviced by a certified specialist according to a strict schedule: there are work plans, and there are prophylactic checks, since the apparatus includes a permanent radiation source." There could also not have been any old "traces," because the identification of hexogen vapor is a rare event in the working life of any laboratory. Tkachenko and his colleagues were unable to recall any cases when they had needed to use the apparatus to identify hexogen.

On March 20, the inhabitants of the house on Novosyolov Street assembled at the NTV studio for the recording of the program "Independent Investigation." Representatives of the FSB also arrived at the television center. The public tele-investigation was broadcast on March 24, with the participation of Alexander Zdanovich, Stanislav Voronov (first deputy head of the FSB's investigative department), Yuri Schekochikhin, Oleg Kalugin, Savostianov, Sergiev, (the head of the Ryazan FSB), investigators and experts from the FSB, independent experts, legal experts, civil rights lawyers, and psychologists.

Performing unmasked and unarmed, the FSB personnel suffered a clear defeat at the hands of the public. The six-month-long analysis of the sugar seemed like a joke. "If you claim that there was sugar in the sacks, then the criminal case based on the charge of terrorism must be halted. But the criminal case has not yet been halted. That means it was not sugar," exclaimed the attorney Pavel Astakhov, unaware that on March 21, the case really would be closed. It was obvious that different sacks had been sent to Moscow for the second analysis, not the ones which were found in Ryazan. But no one could prove this obvious fact.

Raphael Gilmanov, the explosives expert was present in the hall, and he confirmed that it is quite impossible to confuse hexogen with sugar. They are not even similar in appearance. He said that the FSB investigators' claim that the first analysis had been polluted by "traces" from the briefcase of an explosives specialist was unconvincing. Equally unconvincing were the FSB representatives' claims that the engineers called to the scene of the incident had mistaken a mock-up for a genuine explosive device. The FSB officers explained that General Sergeiev, who had reported the presence of the detonating device and was now present in the hall, "is no great specialist in the area of explosive devices," and that on September 22, he had simply made a mistake. For some reason, General Sergeiev did not take offense at being accused of a lack of professionalism, although the public statement he had made about the detonating device on September 22 had been based on the conclusions of experts under his command, concerning whose professional qualifications there was no doubt.

It turned out that the audience in the hall included a lot of military men, who unhesitatingly declared that what had happened in Ryazan bore no resemblance to any kind of exercises, not even those which were made "as close to life" as possible. The preparations for military exercises involved certain compulsory procedures, in particular concerning the possibility of an emergency, the provision of first aid and medication, bandages, and warm clothing. Even the most important of exercises had to be coordinated with local leaders and the government departments concerned. In the Ryazan incident, there had been no preparations and no coordination. That was not the way exercises were conducted, declared one of the inhabitants of the house in Ryazan, a professional soldier.

In general, the FSB officers' arguments were so inept that the response of one of the inhabitants of the house was a curt: "Stop trying to pull the wool over our eyes." Here is a brief extract from the TV debate.

PEOPLE: The FSB's investigative department initiated a criminal investigation. So did it instigate a criminal case against itself?

FSB: The criminal case was instigated on the basis of evidence discovered.

PEOPLE: But if it was an exercise, what was the evidence?

FSB: You haven't been listening. The exercise was conducted in order to check the interaction between various law enforcement agencies. At the moment when the criminal case was initiated, neither the Ryazan police nor the federal agencies knew it was an exercise. . . .

PEOPLE: Then who was the case taken against?

FSB: I repeat the criminal case was instigated on the basis of evidence discovered.

PEOPLE: What evidence? Evidence of an exercise in Ryazan?

FSB: It's not worth even trying to explain to someone who has no idea of criminal law procedure. . .

PEOPLE: What happened to the safety of the citizens who spent the whole night in the street, what about the safety of their physical and psychological health? And a second thing, you are outraged when telephone terrorists phone up and threaten bombings, but how are you any different from them?

FSB: What does guaranteeing the safety of citizens mean? It's the final effect, when there won't be any more explosions. . .

PEOPLE: I'm an ex-soldier. The number of exercises I went through in twenty-eight years, you know, and what these fine respectable people, these generals are telling us about exercises, you know, it's enough to make you sick!

FSB: As a former soldier you probably carried out military exercises. We work in a special service and that service uses special personnel and equipment on the basis of the law on operational and investigative activity. . .

(We interrupt the argument between the people and the FSB to emphasize once again that on the subject of exercises, the law "On operational and investigative activity in the Russian Federation" makes no mention of exercises.)

PEOPLE: If there was someone recording what happened during the exercise, where are those people now?

FSB: If we could only increase our staff ten times over, then of course. . .

PEOPLE: Stop trying to pull the wool over our eyes! The people who saw the hexogen would never confuse it with sugar. . .

FSB: They sprinkled the powder on the lid of a briefcase they've been taking to all their training sessions since 1995. And they even took it to Chechnya. In short, the test papers reacted to the hexogen fumes. . .

PEOPLE: I saw the sacks from only three meters away. In the first place, they were yellowish. In the second place, they were fine granules, like vermicelli.

FSB: Sugar from the Kursk Region. Sugar from the Voronezh Region is different. And the sugar we get from Cuba is altogether yellow!

The Ryazan journalist Alexander Badanov was present in the studio, and the next day his article appeared in a local Ryazan newspaper: "In the television program the people from Ryazan tried to find out what really happened. However, the FSB spokesmen failed to give satisfactory answers to most of the questions. . . . According to Zdanovich, the FSB is now pursuing a criminal investigation based on the September events in Ryazan. Such an absurdity is probably only possible in Russia: the FSB is pursuing a criminal investigation into an exercise conducted by itself! But a case can only be instigated on the assumption that an unlawful act has been committed. What then are we to make of all the previous statements from highly placed members of the secret services that no laws were broken in the course of the exercise? The residents of house number 14 attempted to submit a claim for recompense for moral damage against the FSB to the Ryazan Public Prosecutor's Office. The residents were told that under the procedural rules, they could only present their claim against the particular individual who gave the order to carry out the exercise.

Zdanovich and Sergeiev were asked the same question six times: Who gave the order to hold the exercise in Ryazan? Six times Zdanovich and Sergeiev avoided answering, saying it would prejudice the investigation. . . . The lack of genuine information has given rise to the story that the secret services really did want to blow up a residential building in Ryazan to justify the offensive carried out by federal forces in Chechnya and to rouse the soldiers' fighting spirit. 'I saw the contents of the sacks, and it wasn't anything like sugar,' Alexei Kartofelnikov said in conclusion. 'I am sure that what was in the sacks was not sugar, but genuine hexogen.' The other residents of the house agree with him. It would seem to be in the FSB's own interests to name the person who signed the order to hold the exercise which has undermined the people's trust in the Russian secret services and their prestige."

The practical outcome of the meeting in the studio was that the attorney Astakhov became involved in the old collective complaint submitted by the people from the house. The victims requested the General Public Prosecutor's Office to explain the goals of the operation and also to determine the size and form of compensation for moral damages. This time the reply came back with suspicious speed: "The FSB personnel acted within their competence," said the General Public Prosecutor's Office. The reason for haste is clear enough. Zdanovich had a press conference planned for March 24, at which he intended to "go for" the mass media, and the presidential election was set for March 26.

Following the shameful defeat of Zdanovich and his colleagues in Nikolaev's studio, the leadership of the FSB decided not to take part in more open debates with the public and not to go on NTV any more. It was during these fateful days for the entire country that the FSB also decided to launch the planned annihilation of NTV. On the evening of March 26, the day of the election, in Yevgeny Kiselyov's program *Summing Up*, Boris Nemtsov stated publicly that NTV was in danger of being closed down because it had shown Nikolaev's program "The Ryazan sugar—secret services exercise or failed bombing?"

"I don't know what's going to happen to NTV. After one of the authors, Nikolaev I think his name was, told his version of the bombings in Moscow and other cities. I think there is now a real threat hanging over NTV.... I believe it is my duty to protect NTV if any attempts are made to close it down. And I cannot rule out the existence of such a possibility. At least such attempts have been in relation to a number of journalists, perhaps not coming from Putin, but from his entourage."

Speaking off the record, FSB generals admitted that they had taken the decision to force the leaders of the NTV television channel, Gusinsky, Igor Malashenko, and Kiselyov, out of Russia. Literally the day after Putin came to power, he set about destroying NTV and Gusinsky's media empire Most, and the only one of the three men named above who has been able to remain in Russia is Kiselyov.

By March 24, Zdanovich desperately needed to have in his possession a decision of the General Public Prosecutor's Office of the Russian Federation confirming the legality of the FSB's exercise in Ryazan in September 1999. Zdanovich actually received such a document just before his press conference on March 23. The General Public Prosecutor's Office refused the application made by the citizens of Ryazan for the instigation of criminal proceedings against FSB personnel for holding an "anti-terrorist exercise" in September 1999, on the grounds that "no crime had been committed." The conclusion of the Public Prosecutor's Office was that the actions taken by operatives of the state security agencies to check the efficiency of measures taken by the law enforcement agencies had not breached the limits of competence of the agencies of the FSB of Russia, with regard to "a complex of preventive and prophylactic measures designed to ensure the safety of the public," which had been implemented in the course of the Whirlwind Anti-Terror operation "with reference to the sharp deterioration of the operational situation in the country as a result of a series of terrorist acts." In view of this and also taking into consideration the fact that the actions of the FSB operatives had not resuted in any consequences involving danger to the public and had not involved any violations of citizens' rights or interests, the General Public Prosecutor's Office had decided to reject the application for the instigation of criminal proceedings.

That very evening, the head of the department for monitoring the FSB at the General Public Prosecutor's Office, Vladimir Titov, triumphantly reported this outcome on the five o'clock news bulletin on the state television channel RTR. As retold by RTR and Titov, the familiar tale of what happened in Ryazan had become quite unrecognizable:

RTR: The residents were evacuated. The explosives specialist who arrived at the scene did not find any explosive substance. At first the policemen wanted to declare the whole incident a stupid joke.

TITOV: But then the head of the analysis department, Tkachenko, arrived and checked the sacks with the apparatus he was carrying. The apparatus showed the presence of hexogen.

RTR: A kilogram of the contents was extracted from each sack and taken to the proving ground. But the substance did not detonate. The sacks contained sugar. Two days later the director of the FSB, Nikolai Patrushev, announced that an anti-terrorist exercise had been held in Ryazan. And the experts explained why the apparatus used by Tkachenko had indicated the presence of hexogen.

TITOV: The head of the laboratory was constantly performing analyses and the apparatus reacted to the presence of micro-particles on his hands.

RTR: Today a line has been drawn under the "Ryazan hexogen" case. Copies of the ruling of the General Public Prosecutor's Office are being sent to the Ryazan FSB and for the attention of deputies of the *Yabloko* Duma faction, who drafted a question on the progress of the investigation.

The initial conclusions of experts that the sacks discovered in the basement of the apartment building in Ryazan contained hexogen were overturned in the course of the investigation carried out by the General Public Prosecutor's Office. Repeat analysis proved that the sacks were filled with sugar. However, the press and television carried reports that hexogen had been used in the exercise and that, in conducting the exercise, the FSB had put the public at risk.

TITOV: There is only one conclusion that can be drawn, the self-interest of some correspondents, I would even say dishonesty . . . all they want is to cook up a tall tale, that's all . . . just to increase their circulation.

RTR: The residents of house number 14 to 16 on Novosyolov Street will now finally learn why they had to spend all night out in the street waiting for an explosion.

TITOV: It was a test for the head of the local FSB. They had to see how he would act in an emergency.

RTR: In conclusion the General Public Prosecutor's Office has ruled that the exercise as held did not involve any danger to the public and fell within the limits of competence of the secret services. The official investigation begun by the Ryazan investigators under the law on terrorism last autumn will be closed.

On September 24, now in possession of this remarkable indulgence in which the General Public Prosecutor's Office denied the people of Ryazan the right to proceed legally against the FSB, Zdanovich launched his attack on the journalists. In a highly nervous state, speaking atrocious Russian, he began issuing unconcealed threats:

I would like to draw your attention to the fact that we have not failed and will not fail in the future—I wish to state this officially—to note a single provocation which individual journalists organize against the state service, the institution of the state. . . . That means, to take a concrete example: there is a correspondent from *Novaya Gazeta* who published these articles,

I am not afraid to call him a provocateur, since we have the testimony in full of the soldier who later, so to speak, was used to rehash the story in *Obschaya Gazeta*, too, about the way everything happened, and how those words were, so to speak, dragged out of him, and what he was promised for all of it. It's all proved. Under the current criminal investigation concerning this . . . concerning your publications, perhaps not yours, the proceedings concern some others—it will all be finished in early April. That means your correspondent will be interrogated in the course of the criminal investigation to see why he, so to speak, committed such actions. And under this there are already specific complaints from members of the airborne assault forces, and when it has all been procedurally consolidated, and the minutes are fitted into the criminal case, and it's evaluated in the appropriate manner by the prosecutor's office and members of our Contractual and Legal Department, I wouldn't be at all surprised if we take formal legal action, including through the courts, because no one is allowed to engage in provocation.

Having heard Zdanovich's threats one of the journalists present at the briefing, apparently not too seriously frightened, said: "Well, to be honest I didn't want to ask you a question about Ryazan, the subject doesn't interest me very much, but you launched into the polemic yourself. Can you please explain to me, say I have a private house in the country, can you hold a practice alert there and plant a practice bomb under my house, do you have the legal right?"

Zdanovich's answer demonstrated yet again that although the FSB and Russian society may live in the same state, they speak different languages: "Right, I understand, right then, let me say once again that we acted strictly within the limits of the law on combating terrorism. All of our actions have been investigated by the public prosecutor, and not a single action which violated one or another law has been identified. That's the answer I can give you."

There were too many events crowded into the second half of

March. It was evidently because of the election that the issue of the disgraced *Novaya Gazeta* carrying material on the financing of Putin's election campaign and the FSB never appeared. On March 17, un-identified hackers broke into the newspaper's computer and destroyed the electronic proofs for that issue. Schekochikhin announced that the forced entry of their computer system was only the latest in a series of incidents designed to prevent the newspaper from function-ing normally. In particular, the newspaper's offices had recently been broken into, and the computer containing information on advertisers had been stolen. Over the last two years, the tax police have carried out four checks in the *Novaya Gazeta* offices and the Kremlin has demanded that certain of its sponsors cease financing this uncooper-ative member of the press.

The management of *Novaya Gazeta* attempted to find out why exactly it had found itself in such serious conflict with the FSB. *Novaya Gazeta* journalists actually asked some members of that department to analyze the situation for them. The reply received by the newspaper is nothing if not frank.

> This kind of activity by the state against a publication un-doubtedly indicates that you have entered forbidden territory and stepped on someone's toes. It could be that you were undesirable witnesses to one of the less fortunate episodes in the internal squabbles between the secret services. If this did happen, none of the opposed groups within the system will confirm it. It is in all of their interests to conceal it. They are clearly apprehensive that new living witnesses to the prepara-tion of the Ryazan 'events' may turn up.

By this time, the provincial town of Ryazan had become a place of pilgrimage for foreign journalists. As Pavel Voloshin wittily remarked, Ryazan "will soon have as many foreign journalists per head of popu-lation as Moscow." All the five-star rooms in the local hotels were now occupied by foreign correspondents, and all of them, together with their camera crews, were besieging the local police, the FSB, and even the MCHS. So the FSB and MVD in Ryazan received orders from Moscow to break off contacts with the press. Some officers who had already given interviews hastily took back what they had said. In the Ryazan law enforcement departments, an internal investigation into leaks was begun.

To a man, the residents of the house in Ryazan changed their minds about taking the FSB to court, although no one was convinced the FSB was innocent. Police and FSB officers visited house number 14/16 repeatedly and tried to persuade people not to sue the organizers of the exercise. Even General Sergeiev came, asked them not to complain, and apologized for his colleagues in Moscow. When on September 20, NTV broadcast a report on the imminent first anniversary of the woeful incident, one of the woman said: "That date's coming up soon, and I just feel like leaving home. Because I'm afraid, God forbid, that they'll mark the anniversary with another exercise like the first one. Personally, I have my doubts it was an exercise. I have my doubts." "They treated us like scum," said another woman living in the house. "If only they'd at least told us early in the morning it was an exercise, but it was only two days later. . . . We don't believe it was an exercise." "I don't believe it was an exercise," said Ludmila Kartofelnikov. "How can they mock people like that? On the eighth floor of our house an elderly woman couldn't carry her paralyzed mother out, and she was evacuated on her own. The way she sobbed afterwards in the cinema!" The hero of the events in Ryazan, Alexei Kartofelnikov, also had his doubts: "On that day no one explained to us that it was an exercise. And we don't believe it was. That's the way it is here—if something blew up, it was a terrorist attack. If they disarmed it, it was an exercise."

The residents of the ill-fated Ryazan apartment house were not the only ones who raised doubts: the Russian press did as well. "If the authorities convincingly prove," wrote Versiya, "that it was specifically Chechen terrorists who bombed the buildings with people sleeping inside, then we will-if not approve-then at least understand the cruelty with which our troops came down on the cities and villages of Chechnya. But what if the bombings were not ordered by the

Chechens, by Hattab, by Basaev, by Raduyev? If they did not order them, then who did? It is frightening to imagine. . . . We already understand that we cannot simply declare that the bombings were organized by the Chechens."

Finally, many foreign specialists voiced their doubts as well. Here is what William Odom had to say in response to a question about the causes of the war in Chechnya:

> In my opinion, Russia has fabricated a pretext for this war itself. There exists quite convincing evidence that the police orchestrated some explosions in Moscow. They were caught trying to do the same in Ryazan—and tried to represent their actions as an exercise. I think that the Russian regime has fabricated a whole series of events planned in advance in order to shape Russian public opinion and steer the country in a direction that is unacceptable to most Russians.

Moving beyond the bounds of the law, the FSB based its actions not on the Constitution of the Russian Federation, not even on the Criminal Code and the Code of Criminal Procedure, but on its own political preferences as expressed in formal orders and verbal instructions. The arbitrary lawlessness into which Russia has been plunged has come about above all because the secret services have worked in a planned and deliberate manner to undermine the legislative foundations of Russian statehood in order to create chaos and the conditions which would allow them to seize power. In this war, the secret services' most terrible weapons were the free-lance special operations groups, which they organized and controlled right across the country.

CHAPTER EIGHT

The FSB Sets Up Free-Lance
Special Operations Groups

FREE-LANCE CONSPIRATORIAL military operations groups consisting of former and current members of special armed forces units and the structures of law enforcement began to be set up in Russia in the 1980s. Russia has about thirty state departments of armed law enforcement, and military operations sections were set up within each of them. It is hard to say whether this development was deliberately organized or spontaneous. It is, however, obvious that the FSB tries to have its own people everywhere, and even if it does not always organize the groups in the formal sense of the word, it has controlled their activity to a greater or lesser degree from the very beginning. The story of the establishment in the Maritime Territory of the group headed by the brothers Alexander and Sergei Larionov is an instructive example.

In the late 1980s, Alexander and Sergei Larionov were assigned to work in one of the largest production associations in Vladivostok, named Vostoktransflot. Once there, Sergei Larionov rapidly became the head of the association's Communist Youth Organization. When the privatization of the association began, the Larionov brothers somehow managed to find enough money to buy, either in person or through their representatives, a large block of shares in Vostoktransflot, and then they registered a security service at the company under the name of System SB. This organization became the basis for the most powerful and violent organized criminal group in the history of the Maritime Territory.

The Larionov brothers' men toured the military bases of the Pacific Fleet, approaching the commanders or their deputies for personnel matters and telling them they were hiring men due for transfer to the reserve for work in the special units of System SB, which dealt with the fight against organized crime. So after they were demobilized, ex-members of military sabotage groups went to work for the Larionovs. Their group was structured along the same lines as the GRU, with its own intelligence and counterintelligence sections, its own "cleaners," its own surveillance brigades, explosives specialists and analysts. State-of-the-art equipment was bought in Japan: radio scanners that could intercept pager messages and radio-telephone conversations, "bugs," night-vision devices, and directional microphones concealed in a variety of objects.

The Larionovs' brigade worked very closely with the secret services of the Maritime Territory, primarily with the naval intelligence service of the GRU. Contracts for the elimination of criminal "bosses" came from the local FSB. The Larionovs' own analysts identified seven such bosses who headed groups which controlled businesses in Vladivostok. The brothers decided to "take them out" and take over the businesses for themselves.

The man at the top of the list was a bandit with the underworld name of "Chekhov." Two "liquidators" from the Larionovs' brigade set up an ambush on a road outside the city and raked "Chekhov's" automobile with automatic weapons fire. When the driver leaped out of the car, he was killed by a shot to the head, and the wounded "boss" was taken into the low hills, doused with petrol, and set on fire.

An explosive device of massive power was thrown into the bedroom of another "condemned man." The target escaped unhurt, but the entrance hall of the apartment building collapsed, and four innocent bystanders were killed.

In 1993, conflict arose within the group. One of its leaders, Vadim Goldberg, and his allies kidnapped Alexander Larionov, took him out to the forest, and killed him by stabbing him dozens of times with knives. When he learned his brother was dead, Sergei Larionov went into hiding. Late in 1993, all the members of the group, including Sergei Larionov and Goldberg, were arrested by police detectives. At one of his first interrogations, Larionov declared that he wouldn't say anything yet, but he would tell everything he knew at the trial: everything about System SB and its controllers in the secret services. To prevent this from happening, Larionov was killed. He was being held in the Vladivostok detention center No. 1, in a solitary cell under heavy guard. While Larionov was on his way to another interrogation a prisoner called Yevgeny Demianenko, who had been behind bars for nineteen years, was led into the corridor in the opposite direction. As Demianenko passed Larionov, he pulled out "a point" and killed Larionov with a single blow.

The acts of vengeance against Larionov continued after he was dead. In 1999, unknown persons attempted to blow up his flat with his wife inside it, but she was not hurt. Some time later, a hired killer shot Larionov's lawyer Nadezhda Samikhova. Rumors circulated in Vladivostok that "the secret services are getting rid of witnesses." The public prosecutor's office certainly took a suspiciously long time to bring the case to court. The investigation lasted for several years, and charges were only brought on January 14, 2000. The criminal case against the Larionovs' group amounted to 108 volumes, but there were only nine accused in the dock. Three of them left the court as free men, because the time they had spent in detention was counted against their sentence. The others were given jail sentences of eight to fifteen years (Goldberg himself received a fifteen-year term).

There is good reason to believe that the brigade of the well-known Samara criminal "boss," Alexander Litvinka (known by the underworld nickname of "Nissan"), worked for the FSB. Litvinka lived in Ukraine. In the early 1980s, he arrived in Samara and, following a series of armed robberies, he was sentenced to seven years' imprisonment. He emerged from the penal colonies as a "boss" and was given the nickname of "Nissan" for his love of Japanese automobiles. Having acquired the support of Samara "bosses," such as Dmitry Ruzlyaev ("Big Dima") and Mikhail Besfamilny ("Fiend"). Litvinka set up his own brigade, which consisted of karate experts who were strict teetotalers and obeyed orders unquestioningly.

Litvinka was soon involved in a war for control of the Volga Automobile Plant. In early 1996, a meeting between representatives of two Samara criminal groupings was held at the Dubki Hotel. When the negotiations had been successfully concluded, four unknown persons shot the assembled delegates using Kalashnikovs. Four underworld "bosses" and one "legitimate villain" were killed. Litvinka was identified as one of the assailants, and he was arrested shortly afterwards. A month later he was released from jail, and no charges were brought against him. From that moment on, no one in criminal circles doubted that Litvinka worked for the secret services, and he was declared an outlaw at one of the "thieves' councils." To avoid being killed, Litvinka left the Samara Region and only appeared there on rare occasions, usually to carry out another contract killing of a gangland "boss." It seems clear that Litvinka was responsible for the killing of Ruzlyaev in Samara in 1998, and of the "boss" Konstantin Berkut in 1999.

On the afternoon of September 23, 2000, Alexander Litvinka was killed in Moscow in the vicinity of house number 27 on Krylatskie Kholmy Street. The shooting was carried out by four men. At the crime scene policemen found four pistols abandoned by the killers: two Makarovs with silencers, a Kedr automatic, and an Izh-Baikal. They also found a Makarov belonging to the victim. The assailants left the scene in a white Zhiguli automobile. We can only guess at who it was that eliminated Litvinka, FSB operatives or Samara "bosses." The well-known Kurgan brigade of Alexander Solonik ("Sasha the Macedonian"), consisting mostly of former and current employees of the Russian secret services and military units, was also "run" by the secret services, in particular the SBP and FSB. The Kurgan group appeared in Moscow in the early 1990s and was taken over by the leader of the Orekhov group, Sergei Timofeiev ("Sylvester"). Timofeiev was an agent of the MB-FSK and maintained close contact with a former officer of the Fifth Department of the KGB USSR by the name of Maiorov, who later headed up one of the security organizations in the Toko Bank. Maiorov regularly visited the head of the Operations Department of the Antiterrorist Center, Lieutenant-General Ivan Mironov, the former secretary of the Communist Party organization of the Fifth Department of the KGB USSR, who was now directly responsible for seeking out terrorists.

In the mid-1990s, major changes began taking place within the Orekhov group, when Timofeiev acquired a rival in the person of Sergei Butorin ("Osya"). In September 1994, Timofeiev was blown up in his Mercedes automobile. Then one by one people loyal to Timofeiev disappeared. Butorin created his own group, which included people from the Orekhov, Kurgan, and Medvedkov criminal organizations. His "cleaners" included special operations officers from the GRU, MVD, and VDV. Serving members of various military and law enforcement departments appeared in Butorin's entourage, including one lieutenant colonel from counterintelligence (he was later accused of a number of serious crimes, but the charges were dropped).

In late 1994, three men by the names of Koligov, Neliubin, and Ignatov emerged as the clear leaders of the Kurgan group. The fame of the "Kurgan cleaners" spread throughout Russia. One of the most famous of the hitmen was Alexander Solonik, but the most active and dangerous killer in the group was called Konakhovich.

The Kurgan group fought a bitter war with the Bauman group. According to one of the agents who worked with the Kurgan group, during this war dozens of members of the Bauman brigade were killed, and usually they were first abducted and subjected to extremely cruel torture, including being burned and having their eyes put out before they were eventually finished off. The Kurgan group called the members of the Bauman group "the beasts' brigade" and claimed that it included a number of Dagestanis. One reason the war was fought was to gain control over one of the firms that sold American automobiles. But the real point was that the tires of these automobiles were used to conceal drugs imported from Columbia.

The activities of the Kurgan group were monitored by the 12th Section of the MUR. Operational matters were handled by Oleg Plokhikh. Two members of the Kurgan organization were finally arrested and put away in the Matrosskaya Tishina detention center. In a conversation with his lawyer one of them said that if they used psychotropic drugs on him he might break down and "spill" everything he knew about a dozen major contract killings, including that of the well-known television journalist Listiev. He asked to be transferred to Lefortovo jail and promised to begin cooperating with the investigation if they would give him definite guarantees of his safety, since the Kurgans had been responsible for many killings, including those of several so-called "legitimate villains," which were punishable by death under the unwritten laws of Russian prisons. MUR began preparations to move both the detainees, but they were too late. Information leaked out, and both Kurgans were killed on the same night, even though they were in different cells. It was a contract killing of two suspects, whose testimony would have helped to solve a number of other sensational contract killings.

Solonik was luckier. After his arrest, he was put in a special wing at Matrosskaya Tishina, from where arrangements were made for his flight abroad, to Greece.

The rout of the Kurgans might have been the direct responsibility of the leader of the Koptev criminal organization, Vasily Naumov ("Naum"), who was one of the MVD's secret agents. At one time, the Kurgans had gained the confidence of the Koptev organization, and then, having identified almost all of their rivals' sources of income, they began doing away with the Koptev brigade's leaders. Realizing just who was responsible, Naumov "shopped" the Kurgans to the 12th Section of MUR. Then the FSB became involved in the conflict, because it didn't want the Kurgan group, which it ran, to be destroyed, and because it was afraid of information leaking out and causing a scandal. The FSB quickly figured out that information on the Kurgans was being supplied to the MUR by Naumov, who had close contacts with members of the Kurgan group. They informed the Kurgans of their discovery.

On January 27, 1997, Naumov, accompanied by his armed bodyguards from the police special operations group Saturn, arrived by car for a meeting with the MUR operations officer who was his contact at the MVD building at 38 Petrovka Street. He called the officer on his mobile phone, asked him to join him outside, and waited in the car. While the officer was coming downstairs from his office, a Zhiguli automobile pulled in behind Naumov's car, and the men in it shot Naumov dead with automatic weapons. The Kurgans had made it clear that they knew about Naumov's collaboration with the MUR.

Agent Naumov's activities could not, however, have led to the destruction of the Kurgan group if not for two other circumstances. The first was that Korzhakov was removed from his post as head of the SBP, and the structure was subsequently dismantled. Without Korzhakov's support, the Kurgans were vulnerable. The second was a "paid up" contract issued to the central administration of the MVD for the Kurgan group's destruction. The contract was "paid" by the Bauman bandits, who traditionally had good contacts in the MVD, and after Korzhakov's dismissal they were able to raise the matter of getting rid of the Kurgans in the ministry.

Apart from the MUR, the Kurgans were also being hunted down by Butorin, who gave orders for them to be shot. All of the murders planned by Butorin's group were thoroughly planned and executed at the level of professional secret services, including literally minute-by-minute reporting-in by participants in the operation. The intention was to gather together the core of the Kurgan operatives (Koligov, Neliubin, Ignatov, and Solonik) in Greece and kill them all at the same time.

Butorin's operation for the annihilation of Solonik's group was carried out under the control of the FSB or the GRU. This is probably why there was an information leak, and two weeks of round-the-clock observation of the Greek villa were wasted. Koligov, Neliubin, and Ignatov didn't turn up to see Solonik. Then two people who were loyal to Butorin, "Sasha the Soldier" and "Seriozha," both of whom knew Solonik, arrived at Solonik's house, called him out to the car, and drove off in the direction of Athens. On the way, "Soldier," who was sitting in the rear seat, threw a noose over Solonik's neck and strangled him.

Meanwhile, operatives of the Moscow RUOP had set out to fly to

Greece after receiving information from Butorin that Solonik lived in the small village of Baribobi on the outskirts of Athens. Following the directions Butorin had given them, on February 3, 1997, the RUOP officers discovered Solonik's body. If they had arrived a day earlier, they might have found him alive. But the people who drew up the timetable for their operation knew just who should arrive where and when, and they were late precisely because they were not supposed to find Solonik alive.

That, in general terms, is the official version of events. What actually happened we shall never know. Solonik had left four audiocassettes with his recorded memoirs in a numbered safe in a bank in Cyprus. In January 1997, a few days before he "met his end," he phoned his lawyer Valery Karyshev and asked him to publish the contents of the tapes in case of his death. When Solonik "departed" on February 2, for some reason he took the money from his account with him. Somehow, Solonik's fingerprints disappeared from his case file, and the girl friend who was with him in Baribobi disappeared into thin air.

With typical lawyer's alacrity, Karyshev published Solonik's tapes that same year, and it became clear that the book, which told a lot of stories, but without naming names, was Solonik's special insurance policy: don't come looking for me, or I will name names. Incidentally, Butorin, who was put on the federal wanted list "for committing especially heinous crimes," was never found. They say he became a big businessman. He always had several foreign passports, so he could easily have left Russia altogether.

Another free-lance special group was the organization of GRU Colonel Valery Radchikov, the head of the Russian Fund for Afghan War Invalids. The group was founded in 1991 via the GRU. At the final count thirty-seven people connected with the invalids' fund were killed, and another sixty-two were injured.

In 1994, the fund's first manager, Mikhail Likhodei, was blown up in the entranceway of his apartment block. In October 1995, Radchikov only survived by a miracle when he was seriously wounded by six bullets but managed to evade the killers who attacked him in his car. However, his legal advisor and deputy, Dmitry Mateshev, never recovered consciousness and died following the shoot-out. On November 10, 1996, fourteen people were blown to pieces and twenty-six mutilated by an explosion at the Kotlyakovskoe Cemetery. The dead included Likhodei's widow, Elena Krasnolutskaya, who was financial director at the invalids' fund and Likhodei's friend and successor, Sergei Trakhirov. Radchikov was accused of planning the bombing. On September 3, 1998, when Radchikov was already in jail, another of his assistants, the general director of a new Afghan War fund, Valery Vukolov, was shot dead.

For all these years, money had been embezzled from the fund, which, after all, is the norm in Russia, but the extent of the embezzlement was exceptional. The most conservative estimates put the amount at about 200 million dollars. The case was investigated by the finest men in the public prosecutor's office, led by the investigator for especially important cases, Danilov. He was assisted by four other "bigwigs" and over 100 operatives (making in total a team of over 180). But they were unable to work out where the millions stolen from the Afghan War Invalids had gone. Radchikov himself was accused of stealing only two-and-a half-million.

A few days after Radchikov's arrest, his deputy at the fund, Valery Voschevoz, who monitored all of the fund's cash flows and was one of Yeltsin's agents for the presidential campaign of 1996, was hastily dispatched to the Amur Region as the president's plenipotentiary representative. The trial of Radchikov and his two accomplices, Mikhail Smurov and Andrei Anokhin, lasted ten months. On January 17, 2000, the state prosecutor demanded sentences of thirteen, fifteen, and ten years for the accused.

Radchikov was accused of plotting in 1996 to kill his competitor in the "Afghan movement," the chairman of the invalids' fund, Sergei Trakhirov, and of giving a pistol and at least 50,000 dollars for this purpose to one of his neighbors in the apartment block, the Afghan War veteran Andrei Anokhin. Anokhin, in turn, persuaded Mikhail Smurov to take part in the murder for 10,000 dollars.

Killing Trakhirov was not easy. Everywhere he went he was accompanied by bodyguards from the *Vityaz* unit, which was under the command of S. I. Lysiuk, who worked closely with the FSB. "Hero of Russia" Sergei Lysiuk, the founder and first commander of the *Vityaz* interior forces' special operations unit of the MVD, had been recruited into the ranks of the secret agents of the Special Section of the KGB when he was still a senior lieutenant. The last member of the special service to act as Lysiuk's contact was the head of the military counterintelligence unit, Vladimir Vlasov, who actually removed Lysiuk's name from the listings of the FSB's secret agents (so that he would not be given a new controller) and made him a so-called "archive agent." Lysiuk won his "Hero of Russia" for commanding the *Vityaz* unit in the defense of the Ostankino television center in 1993. He was the one who gave the order to open fire on the supporters of the putsch.

Under the new circumstances, Vlasov was one of Lysiuk's deputies in his commercial firm. Operational information actually indicates that the commercial activities of Lysiuk's firm included training contract killers, including members of Lazovsky's group, but Lysiuk himself might not have known anything about that, even though the Moscow Region criminal investigation department reported frequent sightings of Lazovsky at Lysiuk and Vlasov's base.

So the conspirators decided to blow up Trakhirov at the Kotlyakovskoe Cemetery during the wake for Mikhail Likhodei, the chairman of the Afghan War Invalids' Fund who was killed in 1994. Amazingly enough, just a few days before the bombing, Trakhirov's bodyguards were changed. The new bodyguards were killed in the explosion, but the old ones from *Vityaz* survived. We can assume that Lysiuk might have known about the forthcoming assassination attempt from Vlasov or other people in his entourage.

The court hearings on the case of the bombing concluded on April 18. The accused were offered a final word, and all three of them said they had "nothing at all" to do with the terrorist attack and asked the court to find them innocent. Radchikov's lawyer, P. Yushin, declared that the case had been deliberately fabricated. On January 21, the Moscow District Military Court, under the chairmanship of Colonel of Justice Vladimir Serdiukov, acquitted the accused because "their involvement in the crime committed had not been proved." The court regarded the arguments of the investigation into the case of the explosion at Kotlyakovskoe Cemetery as unconvincing. The acquittal was founded on the results of the court's analysis of the remains of the explosive device, which diverged significantly from the results of the analysis carried out during the investigation. In addition, a female acquaintance of one of the accused, Mikhail Smurov, testified that on the day of the explosion Smurov was at home and could not possibly have set off the explosive device, as the investigators accused him of doing.

Valery Radchikov was also acquitted on the charge of embezzling two-and-a-half million dollars from the fund. All three accused were released directly from the courtroom. On July 25, 2000, the Public Prosecutor's Office lost its appeal to the Supreme Court for the acquittal to be set aside. Radchikov was intending to take the dispute to the European Court. However, at about eight o'clock in the evening on January 31, 2001, he was killed in an automobile accident thirty-nine kilometers along the Minsk Highway on his way back to Moscow in a Moskvich 2141 automobile. That same day the Novosti press agency announced that the law enforcement agencies were of the opinion that Radchikov's death might not have been a simple accident.

Dozens of dead bodies, millions of dollars missing, and not a single criminal caught-taken altogether this is simply a statistical impossibility for the world of crime. You don't need to be Sherlock Holmes to work out who was behind this complicated and highly successful game in which the main player suffered a fatal automobile accident at such a convenient moment.

CHAPTER NINE

The FSB Organizes Contract Killings

In 1993, Lazovsky's brigade included the Uzbek Quartet. All four of the group were Russians who had been born in Uzbekistan. They were also former special operations group officers who, according to the head of the 10th Section of the Moscow RUOP, Vitaly Serdiukov, were supremely skilled in using all forms of firearms and could improvise powerful bombs from items that happened to be at hand. These four criminals specialized in contract killings. Provisional estimates by operational agents made the foursome responsible for about twenty hits carried out in Moscow, St. Petersburg, Lipetsk, Tambov, Arkhangelsk, and other cities. Behind the killers stood a "general contractor," a kind of operations manager who accepted the contracts. With that kind of organization it was effectively impossible to identify the clients who ordered the killings. Tskhai was the first to figure out the "Uzbek system," which always kept the client out of the picture.

The Uzbek Quartet lived in one of the houses on Petrovka Street, close to the Moscow MVD building. The hitmen's victims apparently included several oil and aluminum magnates, bankers, and big businessmen. It is quite possible that the quartet was also responsible for the murder of the vice governor of St. Petersburg, Mikhail Manevich; the general director of Russian Public Television (ORT), Vladislav Listiev; the chairman of the Republican Union of Entrepreneurs, Oleg Zverev, and many others. In any case, the RUOP operatives claimed that the only possible comparison for the quartet in terms of the number of its victims and the "quality" of its work was the Kurgan brigade. The Kurgans, however, killed mostly "legitimate villains" and underworld "bosses."

The Uzbek Quartet and Lazovsky's people were suspected of abducting Felix Lvov, the Russian representative of the American corporation AIOC, from Sheremetevo airport, and later killing him. Lvov's firm was competing for control of the Novosibirsk Electrode Plant, which was the main supplier of electrodes to the Krasnoyarsk Aluminum Plant (KRAZ). In late 1994, the management at KRAZ, headed by the general director Yuri Kolpakov, signed a contract with AIOC, which worked closely in Moscow with the Yugorsky commercial bank. The bank's president, Oleg Kantor, and his deputy, Vadim Yafyasov, were planning to make KRAZ one of the bank's clients and earn big money from restructuring the bank to service the financial requirements of aluminum plants.

The negotiations were proceeding successfully. In March 1995, Yafyasov was appointed deputy general director of KRAZ for foreign trade. Lvov, who already worked with the management at KRAZ, had succeeded in getting the flow of virtually all of KRAZ's goods and raw materials channeled through AIOC, and was working towards getting the American company put in charge of the Achinsk Aluminum Plant, with the subsequent sale to AIOC of twenty percent of the shares. On April 10, 1995, four days before a meeting of the Achinsk Plant's shareholders, which was due to appoint a new general director, Yafyasov was killed in his own car outside the entrance to his home in Moscow.

It is natural that Felix Lvov was frightened by this event. In late May, he testified before a session of the State Duma concerning illegal operations for the purchase of shares in Russian aluminum plants and the involvement in this business of the Uzbek and Russian mafias. But his appeal to public opinion and the authorities did no good. On the afternoon of July 20, the president of the Yugorsky Bank, Oleg Kantor, was stabbed to death on the grounds of a dacha complex outside Moscow, which was guarded twenty-four hours a day. In late July, yet another signal was given when unknown persons abducted a

driver from the firm Forward, which belonged to Lvov, and then
released him after a few days.

On September 6, 1995, Lvov was flying to Alma-Ata from the
Sheremetevo-1 airport. He had already gone through customs when
he was approached by two FSK officers who showed him their identity passes and led him away. Witnesses later identified one of the FSK
officers, a tall, lean man with black hair, from a photograph. He was
"Lyokha," one of Lazovsky's "warriors." There is good reason to
believe that in addition to Lazovsky, Pyotr Suslov was directly
involved in this abduction.

On September 8, Felix Lvov's body was discovered lying on a
heap of rubbish, just five meters from the asphalt surface of a rest
stop, 107 kilometers from Moscow along the Volokolamsk Highway.
He had been shot five times. His pockets contained 205,000 rubles,
Lvov's card as a member of the board of directors of Alpha Bank, and
a Ministry of Foreign Affairs identity card with Lvov's photograph on
it, and a false name (Lvov had nothing to do with the Ministry of
Foreign Affairs).

The killers in the Uzbek Quartet were only caught by chance, when
the leader of the group, who was known as "Ferganets" (i.e., a person
from Fergana) was caught trying to cross the Tajikistan–Kirghizia
border with false documents. A check of the files showed that "Ferganets" was wanted on suspicion of having killed Manevich. Under
questioning he stated that the other members of the group were in
Kirghizia. In mid-July 1998, "Ferganets'" accomplices were arrested,
and all four were taken to Moscow under special security arrangements. Their place of arrest was kept secret.

In fact, the public prosecutor's office of St. Petersburg suspected
another St. Petersburg criminal group, also consisting of special operations personnel, of the murder of Manevich. The group was headed
by forty-year-old former Warrant Officer Vladimir Borisov ("Ensign")
and former tank forces Captain Yuri Biriuchenko ("Biriuk"). Criminal investigation officers managed to identify the group late in the
summer of 1998. On August 21, almost simultaneous attempts were
made on the lives of two brigade leaders in the Sharks criminal

grouping, Razzuvailo and Los, who were also officers in the army's special operations forces. The first was fatally wounded in the hallway of a house on Ligovsky Prospect by a killer with a pistol, who had been disguised as a vagrant by professional make-up artists at Lenfilm film studios. An attempt was made to blow up the second in his BMW automobile on the Sverdlovskaya Embankment of the Neva River, but the bomb was not powerful enough, and Los survived to tell detectives who he thought might have been behind the crimes.

Borisov and Biriuchenko also organized the murder in Pskov in 1998 of yet another brigade leader from the Sharks, Izmorosin. The killings of the two criminal "bosses" and the attempt on a third were combined in a single criminal case, and a special operational investigations group was set up to investigate it under the leadership of senior investigator Vadim Pozdnyak.

For the most part, the members of Yuri Biriuchenko's brigade were former special operations officers, who had learned how to handle weapons in the shooting range of the St. Petersburg garrison and had also, as the investigation later established, been taught the techniques of external surveillance methods and telephone bugging by full-time employees of the GRU and the St. Petersburg FSB. Each of Biriuchenko's fighting men was equipped with cutting-edge technology: an automobile, a pager, a radiotelephone, and equipment for special purposes. Their apartments and cars were registered in other people's names, and the warriors each had several sets of documents, were known by false names, and used a system of digital codes for communicating with each other.

Soon after the unsuccessful attempt on Los's life, operational officers detained Borisov with his closest lieutenant Sergei Kustov (a martial arts trainer) and several rank and file warriors, who were registered as managers with the limited company Petrovsky Auto center. Biriuchenko and the members of his team were hunted across Russia, in Pskov, Vologda and Rostov, and in the villages of the Novgorod Region. Biriuchenko himself hid for a long time in Prague, where he was finally arrested with assistance from Interpol and transported to St. Petersburg under armed guard.

In most of the proven cases, the murders were committed in the hallways of buildings, and the contract killers used a wide range of weapons, from TT pistols and SVD sniper's rifles to homemade explosive devices based on plastic explosives. Normally, a hired killer's "wages" were between 200 and 500 dollars, and for each task completed a bonus of 2,000 dollars was paid.

The investigators accused Borisov, Biriuchenko, and Kustov of four contract murders, banditry, extortion, and other serious crimes. The members of the group were suspected of virtually all the spectacular murders committed in St. Petersburg and the northwest of Russia, beginning in the fall of 1997. In particular, checks were made on their possible involvement in the death of Manevich and the attempt on the life of Nikolai Aulov, the deputy head of RUOP. Several of the operatives who worked on this case are still convinced that they only exposed the tip of the iceberg. According to Vadim Pozdnyak, leader of the operational investigations group, "if we had been released from other current business, we would certainly have uncovered at least another ten crimes committed by this group."

In 1995, Lazovsky set up a group similar to the Uzbek Quartet consisting of veterans from the *Vityaz* and *Vympel* special units: Kirill Borisov, Alexei Sukach (who was awarded a medal "For Bravery" for action in Chechnya, and several MVD interior forces decorations), Armen Shekhoyan, and Pavel Smirnov. Subsequently, the only charge on which they were tried was involvement in contract killings. The group operated for four years, and its "contractor" would appear to have been Marat Vasiliev.

In 1999, Vasiliev was arrested and sentenced to thirteen years of hard labor in a penal colony for the killing in 1993 of a certain Aliev, the owner of a row of stalls at the Liublino market (this was the only crime for which Vasiliev was convicted). In the fall of 2000, Borisov was detained, and after him so were the other special operations men, Shekhoyan, Smirnov, and Sukach. The group's arsenal was discovered in Sukach's apartment: seven submachine guns, ten Makarov pistols, two CZ MOD-83 pistols made in the Czech republic, and a Rohm German revolver. When the trial began in Moscow in April 2001, the accused denied all of the charges that were brought against them. The question of their possible involvement, or Lazovsky's involvement, in terrorist attacks in Moscow in September 1999 was not even raised by the investigators or the public prosecutor's office. Suprunenko kept in mind the sad fate of his predecessor, Vladimir Tskhai, and decided not to give the FSB any reason for getting rid of him.

The *Vympel* operatives were accused of purely criminal offenses. For instance, the public prosecutor's office alleged that on May 21, 1996, Marat Vasiliev suggested that Borisov and Sukach should "sort things out" with the owners of the Usadba cafe and kebab-house located thirty-six kilometers along the Moscow ring road. At three o'clock in the morning, the warriors arrived at the kebab-house, doused it with petrol, and set it on fire. When the owners of the cafe, Gazaryan and Dulian, came running out of the burning building, pistol shots were fired at them (but only over their heads, to scare them).

On September 23, Dmitry Naumov, the head of the Italian firm Dimex was murdered. He sold oil products from Chechnya abroad and had pocketed a large part of the revenue. Naumov, who was known under the nickname "Bender," only rarely made an appearance in Russia. He had dual citizenship and spent most of his time in Italy. In May 1996, however, he came to Moscow on business and stayed at the Balchug-Kempinski Hotel, where Borisov and Sukach saw him for the first time.

On September 23, Naumov turned up in Moscow again and took a room at the Tverskaya Hotel. At about six o'clock in the evening, Sukach, who was on Triumfalnaya Square in front of the Mayakovsky subway station, received two TT pistols with silencers from a go-between and then handed them on to Borisov. The killer was then taken to the hotel in a Zhiguli automobile driven by Pavel Smirnov. Borisov went up to the fourth floor, where he bumped into Naumov in the hall and opened fire from both "rods" at once. All five of the bullets he fired struck his victim in the head. On his way out of the hotel, Borisov told the security guard: "They're shooting people in your hotel and you're asleep." The guard went dashing upstairs and Borisov got into the Zhiguli and drove away. A couple of days later, everyone involved in the murder was in Chechnya.

Lazovsky was arrested but did not give the *Vympel* officers away. The group soon returned to Moscow, and on July 11, 1997, on Marat Vasiliev's orders, they killed the general director of the Harley Enterprises firm, Alexander Bairamov, who imported cigarettes into Russia on privileged terms. The businessman did not want to share the profits from his latest deal, which had earned him eight million dollars. On First Krasnogvardesky Passage, one of the *Vympel* officers' cars cut in front of Bairamov's Mercedes, forcing it to crash into another automobile (with the killers in it). When the drivers involved in the accident got out of their cars, Borisov and Shekhoyan literally shot Bairamov full of holes (Sukach's pistol jammed).

Once again, the group went away to Chechnya for a while, but by May 1998, they were back in Moscow to carry out another contract, for the murder of the general director of the Wind of the Century Company, Alexander Redko, who was an assistant to the Liberal Democrat Party State Duma deputy, Alexei Zuev. On June 18, the killers arrived at the garages on Kravchenko Street and began waiting for their victim. When the businessman pulled out his car and went to close the garage, Borisov and Sukach opened fire. Redko's guards gave chase, but they couldn't catch the former special operations officers. Redko was seriously wounded, but he survived.

On June 25, 1998, the chairman of the town council of Neftiugansk, Petukhov, was killed. Information gathered in the course of an operation with the highly significant title of Predators, led the investigators to conclude that the contract for the murder had been issued by Suslov and carried out by Lazovsky.

On August 23, 1998, Borisov and Sukach killed Dmitry Zaikin, a member of Lazovsky's group, for stealing a large delivery of drugs from Sukach. At one o'clock in the morning, Sukach drove Zaikin to Marino in a Volga automobile and shot him right there in the car. Then Sukach and Borisov drove the body to the wasteland at Verkhnie Polia, dismembered it with a spade, and buried it, throwing the head into the Moscow River.

In 1998, Morev's special group began operations. The way in which it was set up is quite commonplace. Morev served in the armed forces in Chechnya in a separate surveillance battalion of the Eighth Regiment of the special operations forces of the VDV (military unit 3866). Near Argun the unit ran into an ambush, and only three of them were left alive. They were rescued by helicopter. A few days later, the three of them set out for the small village of Svobodny which lay close by. The surveillance officers opened the doors of the houses and tossed grenades inside. The five houses in the village were totally destroyed, and the women, children, and old men inside were killed. Later there was an investigation and the military prosecutor initiated a criminal case. The three soldiers were threatened with a court-martial. At that time, in April 1996, Andrei Morev was recruited by an FSB colonel in the special section to which he had been taken. The colonel offered Morev a simple choice: go to jail or work with us. Morev chose the second option and was given the code name "Yaroslav." He was then transferred to the reserve and set off home to the town of Yaroslavl. For two years, he was forgotten, then in 1998, they summoned him to Moscow.

The special group contained twelve men, all of whom had served in Chechnya and been forgiven certain transgressions in exchange for their collaboration. The group was informed that its main task was to liquidate particularly dangerous criminals and underworld "bosses." The team operated inside and outside Russia. It made working trips to Iraq, Yugoslavia, Ukraine, and Moldavia. Groups of two or three men were always sent on special missions. In Iraq, they liquidated a former intelligence agent from either the SVR or the GRU.

In Ukraine, they liquidated a local businessman by the name of Tischenko. The group flew into Kiev, having been given Tischenko's photograph in Moscow, as well as the address of a secret apartment on Kiev's main street, and the make and number of their victim's car. They obtained a bag containing their weapon from a pigeonhole at the left luggage office of the railroad station, using a number and code also provided in Moscow. The gun was a dismantled SVD sniper's rifle. The apartment in Kiev was empty, and its windows overlooked a road junction with traffic lights. Tischenko always followed exactly the same route, and his car often stopped at this junction, and that was where they shot him, from the window of the apartment. The operation took just one day.

Usually no more than two days were allowed for a liquidation, although the planning and preparation might last as long as a year: the routes followed by the target were checked, and so were his acquaintances, habits, and work schedule. Two days before the deadline, the hired killer was provided with information about his victim, and he arrived at the scene to find everything in place for him to complete the job. For instance, the Yaroslavl underworld "boss," who went by the name of "Perelom" ("Break" or "Fracture," as in a broken arm), was shot down with automatic weapons in the very center of town, as he was driving up to his house. The group worked with gunsights, so that the bandits' girlfriends who were in the car would not be hurt. The automatics were abandoned at the scene, together with the ID of some Chechen (the operation's Moscow controllers thought it would be a good idea to send the investigation off along the "Chechen trail"). The group's final operation to eliminate a target took place on June 2, when they killed a local policeman in Voronezh. They sabotaged the brakes in his car so that the policeman crashed into a specially positioned truck at high speed.

The group gathered for briefings once a week in an apartment at 5 Vagonoremontnaya Street (a woman and her child lived in the apartment). The group met their controller here, an FSB officer by the name of Vyacheslav (he never mentioned his surname even once), and he gave the group their missions. All of the special group's members had "cover documents" with false names. Morev, for instance, had three passports (as Andrei Rastorguev, Mikhail Kozlov, and Alexander Zimin). He also had an external passport in the last name.

The special group was not registered among the staff of any of the law enforcement departments or the Special Forces. In other words, it never officially existed. This free-lance special team worked to a high professional level. In two years of operations, they had only one failure, due to the fact that the target (one of Gennady Zyuganov's assistants) failed to show up at the scene in Moscow. One operation was also called off in Kishinev, when some people in FAPSI had ordered the elimination of the director of a local wine factory, but then canceled the operation at the last moment (by an odd coincidence, warrant officers from FAPSI in Moscow earned some money on the side in their free time as security men in one of the firms shipping wine from Moldavia, and the head of security at FAPSI was informed about this).

On several occasions, the special group brought weapons out of Chechnya. The briefings before these trips did not take place on Vagonoremontnaya Street, but at 38 Petrovka Street, at the MUR. Before they set out, the members of the group were given police uniforms and appropriate identity cards. One of these trips was typical. They made their way via Volgograd to Mozdok in Gazelle vans; while approaching Mozdok, the column was met by an army truck carrying the weapons (submachine guns, SVD sniper's rifles, and TNT). They unpacked it all from the green army crates and soldered it into zinc coffins, as though they were transporting dead bodies. Then the column of Gazelles with "load 200" set off back to Moscow. Since it was escorted by FSB employees, there were no surprises along the way. The cargo was unloaded in Solntsevo, where the special group also gave back their police uniforms and passes and collected their bonuses. The whole excursion lasted two weeks. Depending on the amount of weapons they brought back, each of the participants on such a trip would earn from 700 to 2,000 dollars.

The group's final weapon-smuggling operation took place during the first half of August 2000. At that time, the special team was already having problems. First, several of its members disappeared, then another one drowned in the Volga River. In June, Gennady Chugunov, Mikhail Vasiliev, and Sergei Tarasiev (their real names) were burnt to death in their car. Morev had been traveling with them in the Zhiguli, but he got out earlier since he had a meeting arranged with his cousin. Before the trip, the Zhiguli had stood for a while at number 38 Petrovka Street.

When he heard about his friends' death, Morev first videotaped his testimony as insurance, then left copies of the tape at several different addresses, and got out of Moscow. He was then put on the federal wanted list for ferrying weapons out of Chechnya and attempted murder. Now, Morev wanders around Russia, taking care not to sleep anywhere for more than two nights in a row. But unlike his comrades, he is still alive.

The secret services were also involved in the murder in St. Petersburg on November 20, 1998, of Galina Starovoitova, State Duma deputy and leader of Russia's Democratic Choice movement, and the wounding of her assistant Ruslan Linkov. While the criminals abandoned the Agran-2000 automatic pistol and the Beretta they used to murder Starovoitova, for some reason they took the USP pistol used to wound Linkov in the head away with them. In November 1999, Konstanin Nikulin, a former soldier of the Riga SWAT, was arrested in Latvia. When searched he was found to be carrying a nine-millimeter pistol which forensic examination demonstrated was the one with which Linkov had been wounded.

However, the St. Petersburg FSB refused to accept this. St. Petersburg FSB Press Secretary A. Vostretsov stated that "there is at present no information indicating Nikulin's involvement with this case." The investigative agencies instead put forward a financial explanation for Starovoitova's murder, which essentially claimed that several days before the killing took place, a meeting of sponsors of Russia's Democratic Choice had been held in the organization's Moscow office, and they had allocated 890,000 dollars for elections to the legislative assembly in St. Petersburg. The FSB claimed that the money had been handed over to Starovoitova, and she had written out a receipt, which was put in the safe at the movement's headquarters. Unfortunately, no one had seen this receipt, since a week after the murder, the Russia's Democratic Choice office was burgled, and Starovoitova's receipt disappeared. Russia's Democratic Choice has always rejected the account of the murder as being motivated by theft.

CHAPTER TEN

The Secret Services and Abductions

EVERY TIME WE HEAR about beheadings, we are reminded of the abduction and brutal execution of hostages in Chechnya. Everybody knows that most of the abductions are carried out by Chechen bandits in the hope of extorting ransom. Just how difficult a job it is to get hostages freed can be seen from the well-known case of the abduction of Mahomet Koligov. On September 15, 1998, Koligov, who was born in 1955, was kidnapped in the town of Malgobek by a Chechen organized criminal group from Urus-Martan, headed by Rizvan Varaev. The group's scout in this case and organizer of the crime was Koligov's neighbor, one of the inhabitants of the town of Malgobek. The kidnappers believed that they would not be identified, and they began sending intermediaries to the Koligov family to convey their demands for a ransom of five million dollars. The Koligov's, however, refused to pay up. The scout was rapidly identified and placed under arrest, and all the members of Varaev's group were identified. Varaev then openly admitted that he was holding Mahomet Koligov hostage and demanded the ransom.

The victim's family had resolved not to pay the ransom (they probably didn't have that kind of money anyway). In fact the Koligov family paid for a special state anti-terrorism unit to prepare an operation to capture and eliminate Varaev's band. At 14.00 hours on July 22, 1999, the Koligovs and members of the special unit ambushed members of the gang, who were returning to Urus-Martan from the village of Goiskoe in three automobiles. The column was raked with automatic weapons fire and shelled from grenade-throwers for twenty minutes. Seven members of the gang were killed, and five were wounded. The Koligovs and the members of the special unit then went to Ingushetia, taking with them Aslan Varaev's body and the badly wounded Rizvan Varaev. Rizvan died shortly afterwards, but the Koligovs, nonetheless, announced that the Varaev brothers had only been wounded, and they were willing to exchange them for Mahomet Koligov. In the course of subsequent negotiations with spokesmen for Varaev's gang, the Koligov's were forced to admit that Aslan and Rizvan had been killed, but even so, the bandits agreed to exchange Mahomet Koligov for the bodies of the two brothers. The exchange took place on August 31, 1999, at 17.00 hours on the administrative boundary with the Chechen Republic, close to the village of Aki-Yurt. Mahomet had spent almost a year as a hostage.

The Varaevs were unlucky. Other well-known Chechen kidnappers have been far more fortunate: Arbi Baraev from Alkhankala (Yermolovka), Rezvan Chitigov, Apti Abitaev, Idris Mekhitsov ("Abdul-Malik"), Aslan Gachaev ("Abdulla"), Doku Umarov, and others. In their cases too, the secret services have been accused of involvement in the abduction of people in Chechnya. In the case of Arbi Baraev, there were substantial clues. According to Ruslan Yusupov, a Chechen who served as an officer first in the Soviet and then in the Russian armies, and was recruited by a member of the FSB in Chechnya, Baraev undoubtedly worked for the Russian secret services, and they, in turn, took care of Baraev and his people.

In mid-July 2000, Yusupov was approached by his old schoolmate, Mahomet S., who said he wanted to contact the FSB and give them information on Baraev. Mahomet at least believed that Baraev was responsible for the abduction of dozens of hostages in Chechnya, including members of the FSB, the president's representative in Chechnya, Valentin Vlasov, and journalists from the ORT and NTV television channels. Baraev was also involved in the murder of Red Cross personnel, three British citizens, and a New Zealander.

The FSB agreed with Mahomet that for 25,000 dollars, he would lead the FSB to the exact spot where Baraev was due to meet with his

Chechen field commanders within the next twenty days. Mahomet was told how to contact Yusupov and the deputy head of the district department of the FSB.

Five days later, Mahomet had another meeting with the deputy head of the district department of the FSB. This time, Mahomet brought with him one of Baraev's closest associates, Aslakhanov, under the FSB's guarantee of safety. Aslakhanov was on the Russian federal and Interpol wanted lists for taking part in the execution of an Englishman and a New Zealander, for kidnapping Polish citizens in Dagestan, abducting the photojournalist Jacini, and soldiers' mothers who were trying to find their sons in Chechnya. Aslakhanov moved around Chechnya with the help of a Chechen MVD identity card in the name of Saraliev. In the course of negotiations, the terms of the deal were changed. Mahomet, himself a former guerrilla, and Aslakhanov agreed to hand over Baraev without payment, in exchange for amnesty.

Ten days after that, Aslakhanov passed on information about a forthcoming meeting between Baraev and his field commanders, Tsagaraev and Akhmadov, at a chemicals plant in Grozny. Four hours before the meeting, Yusupov received information confirming this report via the deputy head of the district department of the FSB. The meeting between Baraev, Tsagaraev, and Akhmadov took place as planned, but the FSB did not carry out any operation to arrest them. When Yusupov began trying to find out from the deputy head of the district department of the FSB why the operation had been canceled, the answer he received was: "If I stick my neck out any farther, they'll have my head and yours. We're only pawns in all this, we don't decide anything."

After about another ten days, Aslakhanov reported that he and Mahomet would have to make a run for it, because Baraev's people had found out everything. Yusupov immediately got in touch with the district leadership of the FSB and set up a meeting. When Mahomet and Aslakhanov arrived at the meeting place in the nearby regional center, instead of FSB operatives they were met by guerrillas, who shot them down right there in the street. That same day, unknown persons abducted Yusupov's wife and her sister from a bus stop, and took them to the office of the republican SWAT where they told the policemen that "these trollops' men are working for the Russians." The women cried and tried to explain that they were married, but no one would stand up for them. Their abductors took them away to some deserted yard, beat them until they were barely alive, and raped them.

Yusupov contacted the criminal investigation department of the Leninsky District of Grozny and asked them to find the owners of the white Zhiguli automobile used by the abductors. The detectives told Yusupov that these people did not live in Grozny, and no one knew them. Shortly after that, Yusupov discovered that the abductors were members of Baraev's brigade, former members of the Chechen SWAT, who came from Achkha-Martan, and they had committed a long list of crimes, but since they were Baraev's people, no one was trying to find them.

A week later, two Chechens from the republican FSB and a Russian member of the GRU turned up to see Yusupov. They told Yusupov that Aslakhanov had been killed because of him, and then beat him up in front of his wife and children, and took him away to a private house in the next city district. An hour later, two of Baraev's guerrillas arrived at the house. From the questions which they put to Yusupov, it was clear that everyone present knew all about Yusupov's work for the FSB. When Yusupov denied collaborating with the FSB, he was beaten again, and the beating was actually administered by Chechens from the FSB. The following day, Yusupov was taken to Grozny and dumped in the rubble. Two days later, he and his family left Grozny.

The Chechens had a humorous saying at this time: "In Chechnya there are three-and-a-half armored personnel carriers, ten secret services, and one Chechen per square meter." They also used to say: "Take away the GRU, FSB, and MVD secret agents, and peace will dawn." It was hard to tell just who was working for which Russian special service. There were persistent rumors that, in addition to Arbi Baraev, the Akhmadov brothers from Urus-Martan worked for the Russians. Local residents said that until just recently, the Akhmadov brothers and Arbi Baraev had been living in their own houses. During the second Chechen War, Baraev twice held boisterous weddings in his house in Alkhankala. The Akhmadovs and Baraev traveled around the republic quite openly in their own automobiles without encountering any problems when their documents were checked at roadblocks. Privates on guard at the roadblocks saluted Baraev as he passed. In the summer of 2000, it became known that the Akhmadov brothers carried FSB identity cards. The FSB agent for the Urus-Martan district, Yunus Magomadov, may well have been fired for leaking information and exposing the identities of secret agents.

Baraev was involved in the FSB's work on printing counterfeit dollars in Chechnya. From the very beginning of the Chechen campaign, the printing of counterfeit dollars had been transferred to the Chechen territory, so that if the printing works were exposed or discovered, the blame for the crime would fall on the Chechen leadership. One of Baraev's printing works was discovered in April 2000 (the house in which it was located belonged to Baraev's relatives). The dollars were shipped to the central regions of Russia via Ingushetia and exchanged at a rate of thirty to thirty-five cents.

The counterfeit notes were very high quality; it was virtually impossible to identify them using the detectors in operation in the ordinary treasury bureaus, specialized equipment that only banks possessed was required. A large proportion of the profits earned were used to pay fighters their "salaries" or buy weapons and ammunition. The counterfeit dollars also circulated outside Russia. It is believed that in the last few years up to ten billion counterfeit dollars might have been put into circulation, i.e., about 10,000 dollars for every Chechen. It makes no sense to assume that Baraev alone was responsible. It is more likely that Baraev was simply used as a cover for the business of producing counterfeit notes, which was organized by the FSB.

Diplomatic, but entirely unambiguous, hints at Baraev's collaboration with the FSB were given by the President of Ingushetia, Ruslan Aushev, at a press conference held on July 6, 2000. When asked who was responsible for the recent attack on a military column in Ingushetia, Aushev replied:

The column in Ingushetia was attacked by Arbi Baraev's detachment. There is, by the way, one thing which I do not understand: Arbi Baraev is based in the village of Yermolovka, and any of you who have been to Grozny know that is almost a suburb. That's where he is; I think he has married for the fifth time. So fine, there he is, and everybody knows where he is. It seems to me that the joint forces group needs to take rather more decisive action, especially as Baraev is attacking army columns. . . . I know that Arbi Baraev, according to my information, is located in Yermolovka, which . . . you know it's not really a problem to resolve this. I was saying recently he got married yet again. . . . And our Federal Security Service office knows that. Everybody knows it.

The well-known civil rights activist and Duma deputy Sergei Kovalyov was more frank:

Let us take one of the most important dealers in human beings, a young scoundrel, probably quite an audacious one. Let us forget that absolutely everyone in the Northern Caucasus says: "Arbi Baraev? But he's a KGB agent!" All right, so these are confident claims, but they can't be verified. But there are a few riddles here. A few months ago, everybody knew that he was living not far from Grozny in the village of Yermolovka. He got married there for the nth time, as permitted by Islam, and was living with his young wife. The commander of the federal forces was asked: "Why don't you take Baraev?" He replied with a true soldier's naiveté: "if they tell us, we'll take him." So why don't they tell him? We had meetings with Chechen members of parliament. One of them, a very reliable and well-respected man, told us that one of his relatives, who had recently come down from the mountains, arrived in Yermolovka. And then a so-called "clean-up" started. His documents weren't in order—what was he to do? Well-wishers told him:

"Go to Baraev's house, no one will touch you there." He went
to Baraev's, and the clean-up just passed him by.

It was apparently through the GRU or MUR that information was
leaked to the press to show that the Akhmadovs and Baraev had pro-
tectors in very high places. A number of Moscow newspapers published material stating that Baraev was in Moscow in August 2000,
and stayed in a house on Kutuzovsky Prospekt. It had been ascer-
tained that Baraev met with highly placed Russian officials and
apparently the cars, which had pulled up at the entrance to Baraev's
apartment, included one bearing the number of head of the president's office, Alexander Voloshin.

Possibly President Aushev's statement and the scandalous articles
about Baraev's stay in Moscow provided the decisive argument in
support of those who wished to eliminate Baraev. The details of his
death remain unclear to this day. Supposedly he was killed in his
home village of Alkhankala some time between June 22 and 24,
2001, in the course of an operation, which some sources claim was
carried out by a division of MVD and FSB forces, while according to
other sources it was a GRU special detachment consisting of Chechen
nationals. According to information provided by State Duma deputy,
MVD General Aslanbek Aslakhanov from Chechnya, Baraev was
killed in a blood feud by people whose relatives he had himself killed.

If Baraev had lived, his testimony could have been highly damaging to a number of highly placed officials, as well as members of the
secret services and the military. There was nobody who wanted
Baraev alive and capable of telling tales which would cast light on so
many murky dealings. A dead Baraev could be blamed for any number of things....

If Baraev was the most famous of the kidnappers, Andrei Babitsky, a journalist from the American Radio Liberty, was one of the
most unusual victims. Despite the obvious difference between Babitsky's case and other cases of abduction, it provided new proof of the
Russian secret services' involvement in abduction.

After the start of the second Chechen War, the military authorities in Mozdok refused to give Babitsky accreditation. The requirement for administrative accreditation was unlawful, since a state of emergency had not been declared in Chechnya, and no zone of "anti-terrorist" operations had ever been declared. According to a decision of the Constitutional Court of the Russian Federation, unpublished enactments of the Russian government or the military departments of state, which infringe on the rights and freedoms of the citizen, are to be regarded as null and void. On the basis of this understanding of Russian law, Radio Liberty correspondent and Russian citizen, Andrei Babitsky, traveled to Chechnya in defiance of the administrative prohibition. In late December 1999, he came back from Grozny to Moscow for a few days, bringing with him video footage which was later shown on the program *Itogi* on NTV. On December 27, he returned to Grozny, and on January 15, 2000, he was preparing to travel back to Moscow.

On his way out of Grozny on January 16, close to the Urus-Martan intersection on the Rostov–Baku highway, Babitsky and his Chechen assistant were detained at a roadblock manned by the Penza SWAT. The statement made by the investigator of the Public Prosecutor's Office claimed that it was a member of the FSB who searched Babitsky and confiscated his belongings. This provided documentary proof that Babitsky was arrested by the FSB. He was later handed over to the Chechen SWAT, where one of the SWAT commanders, Lom-Ali, personally beat him up, after which he handed Babitsky over to Fomin, the head of the FSB department in Urus-Martan.

Babitsky was officially arrested under a decree on vagrancy, and he was sent to the detention camp at Chernokozovo "in order to establish his identity." There, Babitsky was beaten again and forced to "sing" for hours under torture. In video footage shown on television on February 5, the traces of the beatings were clearly visible. In contravention of the Criminal Law Procedural Code, no report was drawn up of Babitsky's arrest in Chernokozovo. He was denied the right to see his relatives or have a meeting with his lawyer (as stipulated in article 96, part 6 of the Criminal Procedural Code). The

General Public Prosecutor's Office of the Russian Federation did not bother to answer queries from lawyers, including those from the famous lawyer, Genri Reznik. Nor was any reply forthcoming to a inquiry about Babitsky from Duma deputy Sergei Yushenkov.

Babitsky's colleagues began looking for him on January 20, but since the Russian authorities denied that he had been detained, it was a week before anything became clear. On January 27, the authorities announced that Babitsky had been arrested, because he was regarded as a suspect and had been detained for ten days (ending on January 26). The Public Prosecutor's Office was planning to accuse Babitsky of an offense under article 208 of the Criminal Code of the Russian Federation ("Organizing an illegal armed formation or participating in such a formation"). "If our guys have got your friend, and I think they have, then that's it, curtains, you won't be seeing him again. Nobody will. Sorry to be so blunt," Alexander Yevtushenko, a correspondent of the newspaper *Komsomolskaya Pravda*, was told by an old acquaintance who was an FSB officer.

On February 2 at Chernokozovo, a package was accepted for prisoner Babitsky. However, the investigator, Yuri Cherniavsky, would not permit a meeting with Babitsky, hinting that he would be released in four days. The journalist's release was demanded by Radio Liberty, the Council of Europe, the U.S. State Department, the Union of Journalists, and civil rights activists (including Andrei Sakharov's widow, Elena Bonner). In negotiations with U.S. Secretary of State Albright, Russian Minister of Foreign Affairs Igor Ivanov stated that acting President Putin personally had the situation "under control."

At 4 P.M. on February 2, the prosecutor of the Naur District of Chechnya, Vitaly Tkachyov, announced that Babitsky's preventive detention had been replaced by a signed undertaking not to leave Moscow, where he was on the point of being sent from Gudermes. Later, the press secretary of the Public Prosecutor's Office of the Russian Federation, Sergei Prokopov, announced that Babitsky had been released on February 2. (Only later did it emerge that Babitsky was not released, and he spent the night of February 2 in a motorized cell, a truck used for transporting detainees. At three o'clock the following afternoon, with barely a sign of embarrassment, Yastrzhemb-sky declared that after being "freed," Babitsky had been exchanged for three prisoners of war. Then he corrected himself and said it was for two.)

Since Babitsky was wearing a shirt that had been sent to Cher-no-kozovo on February 2, the obvious conclusion was that he had been handed over on February 3. No one in Chechnya knew the "Chechen field commanders," to whom Moscow claimed Babitsky had been handed over in exchange for "captive Russian military personnel." President of Chechnya Maskhadov declared that he did not know where Babitsky was. And no one had seen the "exchanged" Russian soldiers.

In actual fact, apart from Babitsky all the individuals involved in the exchange were members of the FSB. One of them, a Chechen working for the FSB, had helped to hoodwink Babitsky, and when Babitsky realized what was going on, it was too late. In an interview on NTV on the evening of February 8, Russian Minister of the Interior announced that he had made the decision to exchange Babitsky. But another official tried to convince journalists that the "exchange" had been a local initiative, and the Kremlin was looking into who was responsible for what had happened, because the "Babitsky affair" was working against Putin.

Official government spokesmen claimed that Babitsky was alive, and that a video recording which confirmed this would arrive in Moscow the next day. In fact, the videotape was handed over to Radio Liberty by unknown persons on the evening of February 8, sooner than promised. One of the "Chechens" who had supposedly traveled from Chechnya to hand over the tape was wearing an MVD uniform. The video footage showed Babitsky in an exhausted condition.

Journalists who analyzed the tape said that the way Babitsky was taken by the arms was typical of the police, but that Chechens did not handle people that way. In fact, not even the members of the FSB who were involved in the "exchange" made any real effort to conceal the falsification. When an FSB department was celebrating the anniversary of the withdrawal of Soviet forces from Afghanistan, one of them confessed to Alexander Yevtushenko: "You saw the warriors in masks. And the one who grabbed hold of Babitsky. They showed it on television. Well, that was me."

The area where the "exchange" took place was not far from Shali, which was entirely under the control of federal forces and not far from the village of Nesker-Yurt, also under federal control, where there were federal soldiers and fortified roadblocks and armored personnel carriers. The people in masks drove off with Babitsky and took him, as it turned out later, to the Chechen village of Avtury. Although this village was not yet occupied by federal forces, the journalist did not by any means end up among resistance fighters. He became a prisoner in the house of relatives of Adam Deniev, well known for his collaboration with the Moscow authorities (his religious and pro-imperial organization "Adamalla" had an office in Moscow). In this house Babitsky was detained for three weeks, without being permitted to make contact with the outside world.

On February 23, the kidnappers led Babitsky out of the house, ordered him to lie down inside the trunk of a Volga, and drove him to Dagestan. On this day—the anniversary of the deportation of the Chechens—the number of soldiers at federal checkpoints was greatly increased and the residents of Chechnya preferred not to leave their homes any more than was necessary, but the kidnappers' cars—the Volga and the Zhiguli that accompanied it—were never stopped: at each checkpoint, the drivers merely slowed down in order to show some kind of document.

In this way, Babitsky was brought to Mahachkala. Here he was given a passport with someone else's name, but with a professionally attached photograph of himself (as it turned out later, a blank passport with this number had been issued, perfectly legally, by one of the passport offices of the MVD). The kidnappers demanded that Babitsky should cross the border into Azerbaijan with this passport. But Babitsky managed to escape. After returning to Mahachkala, he called his friends from his hotel (where he had been compelled to use the false passport) and the world finally found out that the journalist was alive. Then he gave himself over to the Dagestan police.

Despite the fact that the policemen later received medals for rescuing Babitsky, he was accused by the authorities of using a false passport, held for several days in a jail in Mahachkala, and later tried, sentenced to a heavy fine, and then pardoned. . . .

For some reason the General Public Prosecutor's Office was not interested in the fact that Babitsky had been abducted, beaten, and tortured, but for the half-dead victim to be using someone else's passport was clearly a serious crime. The passport became the basis for the main charge in Babitsky's case.

Throughout all of this, of course, the structures of coercion and the officials involved in the Babitsky affair were confident that they could act with absolute impunity, and this confidence was based on the fact that Babitsky's suppression had been sanctioned by the leadership of the FSB.

Almost all of the participants in this incident are known. We have already mentioned Deniev's group. The person who arranged Babitsky's "exchange" has also been identified as FSB Colonel Igor Petelin (recognized in the television footage by Novaya Gazeta's military correspondent Vyacheslav Izmailov). And Babitsky himself later saw a photograph of one of his kidnappers in the newspaper—as one of the bodyguards of the President of Chechnya Akhmad Kadyrov.

In the war in Chechnya, the secret services carried out reprisals against their enemies without the slightest regard for the law. The strange story of the kidnapping of Kenneth Gluck, the representative of an american medical charity, on January 9, 2001, close to the Chechen village of Starye Atagi, led many people to suspect that Gluck had been abducted by Russian Special Forces. At a press conference in St. Petersburg on April, 18 2001, Zdanovich made it clear in Patrushev's presence that the FSB had no interest in Gluck's work in Chechnya: "the FSB, to put it mildly, has grave doubts about whether Kenneth Gluck was really a representative of a humanitarian organization." After this, Zdanovich claimed that the well-known field commander and trader in hostages, Rezvan Chitigov, worked for the CIA in Chechnya.

It became clear that the FSB regarded Gluck as a CIA agent

involved in spying for the United States. This was apparently the reason the FSB had decided to exclude him from the Chechen republic.
First, Gluck was kidnapped and then on February 4, his liberation
was stage-managed "without any conditions or ransom as a result of
a special operation carried out by FSB agents."

It was absolutely clear to everyone that no special operation had
been carried out to free Gluck, and he had simply been set free by his
abductors, who had decided not to kill him. After the Babitsky case,
the FSB no longer bothered to use conspiratorial methods, having
come to believe in its own absolute impunity. The reality of the Gluck
case was no less obvious. Everybody could tell that Gluck had been
abducted by the FSB. "That's why the whole business of Gluck's capture and release was so strange," Zdanovich declared at one of the
press conferences. It would be hard to disagree with him. When one
and the same organization kidnaps someone and then liberates him,
it really does look rather strange.

Against this background, the story of the kidnapping by GRU
operatives of former chairman of the Chechen parliament, Ruslan
Alikhadjiev, seems almost natural and lawful. Having been a successful field commander during the first Chechen war, Alikhadjiev did
not take part in the military operations of 1999–2000. In mid-May
2000, he was detained in his own house in Shali. According to local
people, the arrest was carried out by agents of the General Staff GRU,
who took the former speaker of parliament to Argun, where his trail
went cold.

After May 15, not even Alikhadjiev's lawyer, Abdulla Khamzaev,
ever saw him again. Khamzaev said that he made repeated inquiries
at various levels concerning the fate of his client, but was never able
to meet with him. Information emerged from the Public Prosecutor's
Office that a criminal investigation had been initiated into Alikhadjiev's
disappearance under article 126 of the Criminal Code (abduction).
The Prosecutor's Office had not initiated criminal proceedings against
Alikhadjiev and, consequently, had not sanctioned his detention. The
MVD knew nothing about what had happened to Alikhadjiev. On
June 8, 2000, Khamzaev was notified by the FSB that Alikhadjiev

was not in the FSB's Lefortovo detention center. Khamzaev did not receive an answer to his inquiry from the General Public Prosecutor's Office. Finally on September 3, the radio station *Ekho Moskvy* reported that Alikhadjiev had died of a heart attack in Lefortovo, and his family had already been officially notified of his death.

The abductions of Chechens in Chechnya by federal agencies of coercion in order to punish them, extort ransom, or kill them were almost heroic exploits that went uninvestigated and unpunished. The police of the October Temporary Department of Internal Affairs in Grozny, led by Colonel Sukhov and Major V. V. Ivanovsky, was suspected by journalists and public figures of abducting and killing about 120 inhabitants of Grozny and other regions of Chechnya. The corpses were presumed to have been dumped in the basement of a building on territory which was guarded by the October Temporary Department of Internal Affairs. The policemen later blew up this building in order to cover up their crimes.

The organization of security sweeps in order to abduct Chechens and extort ransom for the release of hostages, became an everyday event, a part of life in wartime. Cases are even known of Russian officers selling Russian soldiers to Chechen bandits as slaves, and then declaring them deserters.

The war in Chechnya has made human life cheap in Russia. Brutal killings and trade in slaves and hostages have become the norm. Tens of thousands of young people have gone through the war. They will not be able to return to civilian life.

Chechnya is the FSB's workshop, the training ground for the future personnel of the Russian secret services and freelance brigades of mercenary killers. The longer this war goes on, the more irreversible its consequences become. The most frightening of them is hatred. Chechen hatred of Russians. Russian hatred of Chechens. This conflict was created artificially by the coercive agencies of Russia, mainly the Federal Security Service.

CHAPTER ELEVEN

The FSB: Reform or Dissolution?

All according to plan!
Youth slogan invented by Putin's PR-team

Why blame us, you who know everything?
For evil, all is according to plan, even a clean conscience.
Vladimir Vysotsky

FOR THE SAKE of objectivity, we should point out that attempts to reform the FSB from within have been made by isolated individuals in the system, but they have not been successful. On the contrary, efforts made by individual FSB officers to maintain the honor of the ranks of the special agencies and the crushing defeat suffered by heroic individuals in this war have only served to demonstrate, yet again, that reform of the FSB is impossible, and this agency of the state must be abolished. One of the many documents which make this clear is a letter addressed to Russian President Yeltsin on May 5, 1997, long before the bombings of the apartment buildings. Since in the first edition of this book we published this letter without its author's knowledge or consent, we felt we had no right to give his name. However, by the time of the second edition a significant change has taken place in his life: he has been arrested. For this reason we have made the decision to publish his name. The author of the letter to Yeltsin was former FSB colonel and lawyer Mikhail Trepashkin. Trepashkin was arrested in Moscow in 2003 on the fabricated charge of illegal weapons possession and divulging state secrets (espionage). He is still in prison.

ON THE UNLAWFUL ACTIVITIES OF
A NUMBER OF OFFICIALS OF THE FSB

Dear Boris Nikolayevich,

Circumstances oblige me to appeal to you personally in view of the fact that the director of the Federal Security Service Colonel-General N.D. Kovalyov, and other leaders of the FSB are taking no measures to deal with the problems of state security in Russia raised by myself in reports and statements, which I have forwarded to them beginning in 1996.

In recent years, organized criminal groups have been attempting to infiltrate the FSB by any possible means. Initially, the most common approach was to establish relations with individual members of the FSB and engage in criminal activity under their protection ("roof"). And then these groups moved on to delegating their members to join the ranks of the FSB. They are accepted for service via acquaintances working in the personnel departments or as section leaders.

The infiltration of members of criminal groups into the ranks of the FSB was particularly intensive under M. I. Barsukov and N. D. Kovalyov. Under these leaders, a number of members of the Solntsevo, Podolsk, and other criminal groups were taken into the service. . . . In order to ensure their safety the "right people" were promoted to key posts. At the same time, a number of professionals with extensive operational experience were dismissed without due cause. All of this took place with the connivance of former personnel section officer N. P. Patrushev.

The actions of FSB leaders, Barsukov, Kovalyov, and Patrushev, are intended to force professionals out of the structures of the FSB in favor of criminal elements. For instance, when Patrushev was appointed to the post of head of the Internal Security Department of the FSB, instead of combating criminal groupings, he began to persecute members of the FSB, professionals with long experience of the fight against crime, and forced them to resign from the security agencies. As a result, the department ceased pursuing cases against armed criminal groups.

At the present time, former head of the Internal Security Department of the FSB Patrushev has been transferred to the post of head of the Administration and Inspection Department of the FSB, and Kovalyov has replaced him with Zotov, concerning whose connections with criminal organizations much information has been supplied to the FSB. Prior to this appointment, Zotov supervised the anti-terrorist center, which had almost no successful operational activities to its name, while at the same time terrorist acts were being committed and continue to be committed on all sides. In Moscow alone, large amounts of illegal weapons and munitions are in circulation. It was Zotov who, in December 1995, made special efforts to block the progress of a case dealing with a Chechen organized criminal group. According to operational sources, Zotov was given a present of a foreign-made jeep-style automobile by one of the groups, which he sold after his appointment to a general's post in order to conceal the fact.

Kovalyov has appointed a number of officers to general's posts without regard for professional ability or services in the field, but on the basis of acquaintance and loyalty to the director. For instance, in August 1996, a Long-Term Programs Department was established within the FSB. This department, directly subordinate to FSB director Kovalyov, absorbed a considerable number of professional personnel from other sections. However, no one in the FSB knows why Kovalyov maintains this department, since its aims and objectives and the functional responsibilities of its personnel have yet to be defined. In effect, the Long-Term Programs Department of the FSB does nothing to combat crime, but guarantees the safety of non-state organizations (such as the Stealth Company and others). Nonetheless, friends of Kovalyov-Khokholkov, Stepanov, and Ovchinnikov—have been appointed to general's posts in the Long-Term Programs Department. The first two have already also received their general's epaulettes. Khokholkov and Ovchinnikov had both previously been investigated by the Internal Security Department of the FSB. The first maintained close relations with bandits and accepted monetary remuneration from them, so that he could afford to lose as much as 25,000 U.S. dollars in a single night at a casino. . . .

The bandit Stalmakhov, who is well known to the RUOP MVD of the city of Moscow, stated in conversation with one of our sources that since 1993, the members of his group, which included a number of former employees of the KGB, had engaged in smuggling activities. Their criminal activities were covered up in exchange for monetary remuneration by highly placed members of the FSB, including generals of the Economic Department of the FSB, Poryadin and Kononov, Moscow Region FSB General Trofimov, and director of the FSB, N. D. Kovalyov. In February 1994, in my capacity as senior investigator for especially important cases of the Investigative Department of the MB, I detained nine automobiles ('wagons') containing contraband goods with a value of more than three million U.S. dollars. Due to measures taken by the officials named above, the contraband was released and stored at the factory Hammer and Sickle, from where it was subsequently illegally sold. A number of trumped-up claims were made that I was involved in extortion, which made it impossible for me to work on locating the contraband goods.

Likewise alarming are the leaks of operational information from the FSB to criminal organizations.

Head of the FSB N. Kovalyov (and before him, M. Barsukov), and department heads Patrushev and Zotov, are thwarting efforts to curtail the criminal activity of organized groups guilty of committing serious crimes, in particular efforts to curtail the criminal activity of Chechens in the city of Moscow. . . . An operation that relied on available materials led to the arrest of members of a Chechen organized crime group involved in the extortion of 1.5 billion rubles and approximately 30,000 U.S. dollars at the commercial bank Soldi. Those arrested included V. D. Novikov; L. M. Bakaev; and also K. N. Azizbekian, head of the security agency Kobra-9; Colonel G. U. Golubovsky, group leader in the general staff of the Russian Army; Senior Police Lieutenant V. V. Uglanov, an operative of the MVD.

Individuals who were arrested while assisting the extortionists to enter the bank included organized crime group members B. B. Khanshev and S. A. Aytupaev, as well as three agents of the Moscow police—Senior Operative and Police Major G. F. Dmitriev, Department Chief and Police Major V. I. Pavlov (both armed), and Junior Police Officer I. A. Kolesnikov.

In the course of the interrogation it was established that this organized crime group received substantial assistance in resolving issues of a criminal nature from the consultant of the General Staff Academy of the Russian Federation, Major General Yu. I. Tarasenko, who was paid 5,000–10,000 U.S. dollars monthly by V. D. Novikov. After being interrogated, Tarasenko acknowledged that he had received financial compensation from V. D. Novikov and K. N. Azizbekian, and admitted that he directed officers of the army general staff and police agents to assist the Chechen organized crime group.

On December 1, 1995, the investigative division of the City of Moscow filed criminal charge No. 055277 in accordance with statute 148, article 5, of the criminal code of the Russian Federation.

In the course of the initial investigative, operational, and search measures, it was established that, in addition to extortion, the members of the above-named criminal group had committed murders in Moscow and in Chechnya, had stored weapons and munitions at an illegal depot outside Moscow, and had moved weapons and munitions from the military depots in the town of Elcktrogorsk to areas of military operations in Chechnya.

Since I was one of the leaders of the operation, I played an important role in uncovering the criminal activity of the Chechen organized crime group. However, already at the beginning of December 1995, I was removed from the case in connection with a work-related background examination, and the weapon I had been issued was recalled. The causes and grounds of the background examination remain unknown to me to this day.

Upon completion of the "background examination," an order was issued on February 8, 1996, (No. 034) concerning my punishment for supposedly undermining the operation, although the materials of criminal case No. 055277, the letters of the Moscow RUOP MVD office and the Tver general prosecutor's office, state precisely the opposite.

The members of the commissions, referring to "aforementioned" indications, reached a fabricated conclusion and determined that in arresting dangerous criminals I had exceeded my legitimate authority. These circumstances served as grounds for my dismissal from work related to uncovering the activities of criminal groups.

According to operational data in my possession, the members of the aforementioned criminal group allocated 100,000 U.S. dollars to blocking the work on the case and declared that they had enough funds "to buy the FSB and the MVD and the Ministry of Defense."

A brief comment on the outcome of the opposition offered by Trepashkin at the time of the first edition of this book in 2002. Following his letter to Yeltsin, Trepashkin was dismissed from service. Zdanovich slandered him in the media, accusing him of being a common criminal. The dismissed officer took the leadership of the FSB to court. During the court hearings, which lasted for more than a year, the leadership of the FSB planned and carried out two attempts on the lieutenant colonel's life. However, somehow he managed to survive and win his case, in which one of the respondents was Patrushev.

Unfortunately, the new director of the FSB (who was Putin) refused to implement the court's decision, even though it carried the force of law, thereby demonstrating, yet again, the impossibility of reforming the FSB or of combating it on the basis of the existing legislation. In 2003, after the former FSB officer became the lawyer of the sisters Tatiana and Alyona Morozov (whose mother died in an apartment-house bombing in Moscow in September 1999), and offered to represent their family's interests in a case involving the investigation of the terrorist attacks committed by Russian security agencies, Trepashkin was finally arrested.

There is nothing surprising about the idea of dissolving the FSB. In December 1999, perhaps under the influence of the bombings in Russia, the newspapers carried information concerning a planned dissolution of the FSB. This is what one of the Moscow papers printed:

> According to well-informed sources, in the next few days. A new armed law enforcement agency may be set up on similar lines to the FBI in the USA. It is presumed that the job of heading up the new structure will be given to an officer with the rank of First Deputy Prime Minister. According to our information, it is planning to appoint the present minister of the interior Rushailo. . . . It is intending to endow the new department with the function of supervising all of the law enforcement agencies, including FAPSI, the MVD, the FSB, the Ministry of Defense, and so on. The new department will be based primarily on the structures of the MVD. At the initial stage, it will take from the FSB the departments for combating terrorism and political extremism and economic counterintelligence. And if in the future the new department should also absorb the counterintelligence functions, the FSB will effectively cease to exist.

However, gently dissolving the FSB in the MVD is not enough. The Supreme Court of the Russian Federation must initiate a full-scale investigation into all of the sensational terrorist attacks, first and foremost into the September bombings, whether they succeeded or were foiled, including the incident in Ryazan, this investigation must be transferred from an FSB due to be disbanded to a specially created agency at the MVD, and the individuals involved in organizing terrorist attacks in Russia must be punished as the law requires.

The State Duma must draft and approve as a matter of urgency a law of inspection and promulgation, which prohibits former and current members of state security agencies from occupying elected positions or state posts for the next twenty-five years, and obliging all former and current members of the state security agencies to retire by a certain date, in conjunction with a commission established specifically for this purpose. This decree of the State Duma must also extend to the current President of Russia and former head of the KGB Vladimir Putin.

In Place of a Conclusion
The FSB in Power

THE FEDERAL SECURITY SERVICE has now succeeded in getting its own candidate elected president. When Putin spoke on the anniversary of the founding of the All-Russian Extraordinary Commission in 2000, he began his address to his colleagues by saying that the FSB's assignment had been completed—he had become the Prime Minister of Russia.

The restoration of the memorial plaque to Andropov on the Bolshaya Lubyanka building which houses the FSB, a toast to the health of Stalin with the leader of the Russian communists Zyuganov, bombings in residential buildings and a new war in Chechnya, the passing of a law making it legal once again to investigate individuals on the basis of anonymous denunciations, the promotion to positions of power of FSB generals and army officers; and finally, the total destruction of the foundations of a constitutional society built on the admittedly frail but, nonetheless, democratic values of a market economy, the strangling of the freedom of speech—these are only a few of the achievements of Prime Minister and President Putin during the initial months of his rule.

To this must be added the militarization of the Russian economy; the beginning of a new arms race; an increase in the smuggling and sale of Russian weapons and military technologies to governments hostile to the developed nations of the world; the use of FSB channels for the smuggling of narcotics under the control and protection of the FSB from Central and Southeast Asia to Russia and onwards to the West.

Future historians will have to answer the question of who was responsible for the brilliant succession of precisely planned moves which brought Putin to power, and who it was that proposed Putin as a potential candidate to the first president's intimate entourage, which in turn presented the former head of the KGB to Yeltsin as his successor. But perhaps even more astonishing is the fact that Stepashin and Primakov, the two candidates for the role of successor who preceded Putin, also came from the structures of coercion. Yeltsin was amazingly stubborn in his efforts to hand over his post to someone from the agencies of state security.

In the year 2000 elections, the Russian voters were faced with a delightful list of candidates: the old KGB-man Primakov, who confidently boasted that if he came to power he would put 90,000 businessmen (i.e., the entire business elite of Russia) in jail; the young KGB-man Putin, who before he was elected emphasized the need to continue Yeltsin's policies; and the communist Zyuganov, whose future actions could easily be predicted.

In order to jail 90,000 businessmen, Primakov would have had to arrest sixty people every day, including weekends and holidays, throughout his four-year term as president. The young KGB-man Putin promised to be less bloodthirsty. Perhaps the election campaign was deliberately scripted by someone on the principle of good cop/ bad cop? The bad cop Primakov voluntarily withdrew his candidacy, following a crushing defeat in the elections to the State Duma. That only left the young KGB-man and the communist. It was the same kind of black-and-white choice as in 1996, and Putin won. He has not entirely disappointed the people's trust. At least he appears not to be working at a rate of sixty people a day, unless you count the whirlwind of terror and anti-terror and the war in Chechnya. But Putin undoubtedly deserves the title of tyrant, since he deliberately destroyed the initial shoots of self-government in Russia with his very first decrees, and he now exercises that transparent form of arbitrary rule, which the Russian people know as *bespredel* (literally—"without limits"). He is perfectly described by the definition of a "tyrant" given by the *Soviet Encyclopedic Dictionary* of 1989: "a ruler whose power is founded on arbitrary decision and violence."

Russia, however, is an unpredictable country—this is the only thing which we know for certain about it. And it may prove to be a source of strength more powerful than the clenched fist of the secret services.

Epilogue

An organization is considered to be a terrorist organization if at least one of its structural components participates in terrorist activities with the consent of at least one of the governing organs of this organization. . . .

The organization is considered to be a terrorist organization and is subject to liquidation on the basis of a court decision.

Upon the liquidation of any organization determined to be a terrorist organization, the property belonging to it is confiscated and appropriated by the government.

The Federal Law of the Russian Federation

on combating terrorism

Enacted by the State Duma on July 3, 1998.

Approved by the Council of the Federation on July 9, 1998.

Signed by President B. N. Yeltsin on July 25, 1998.

AT MIDNIGHT ON September . . . of the year 20. . . , the Federal Security Service (FSB) of Russia was disbanded by Decree of the President of the Russian Federation in a truly historical decision which marked the beginning of a new era in the development of democratic institutions in Russia. In view of this Decree's obvious importance, we have decided to present the full text of the Decree to our readers.

DECREE OF THE PRESIDENT
OF THE RUSSIAN FEDERATION

On the dissolution of the following agencies of state security: the Federal Security Service, the External Intelligence Service, The Federal Secret Police Service, the Federal Agency for Governmental Communications and Information.

1. The activities of the agencies of state security of the USSR and Russia from December 1917 to the present are hereby declared to be in contradiction of the laws of the Russian Federation as promulgated in the Constitution of the Russian Federation and contrary to the interests of the people.

2. The following agencies of state security are hereby disbanded: the Federal Security Service, the External Intelligence Service, the Federal Secret Police Service, the Federal Agency for Governmental Communications and Information.

3. The legal instruments governing the activities of these agencies are declared null and void as of the date of publication of this Decree.

4. Within thirty days from the publication of this Decree, a Public Commission shall be established to investigate the crimes committed by agencies of state security against the state's own citizens both within Russia and beyond its borders. The membership of this commission shall include prominent public figures, civil rights activists, lawyers, deputies of the State Duma, and representatives of the mass media. The chairman of the Public Commission shall be appointed by the President of the Russian Federation and shall be accountable to him.

5. All restrictions on access to archives of the agencies of state security are hereby removed. The Public Commission for the investigation of crimes committed by agencies of state security against the state's own citizens is hereby instructed to devise and implement a program for the publication of documents of particular public interest.

6. The records of operations carried out by agencies of state security in relation to persons of Russian or foreign nationality shall be made available to such persons or, if they are no longer alive, to their surviving relatives.

7. Should individuals who have been the subject of operations conducted by agencies of state security consider that the agencies of state security have violated their civil rights and thereby caused them moral and material harm, they shall be entitled under the terms of currently effective legislation to make application to the judiciary of Russia or their country of residence for legal action to be taken against specific members of the agencies of state security.

8. As of midnight January 1, 2002, the agencies of the Ministry of the Interior shall stand guard over all offices of the agencies of state security and continue to guard them until further notice.

9. The Ministry of the Interior shall appoint a commandant (from the staff of the Ministry) to be responsible for guarding the offices of the agencies of state security throughout Russia. Agents of the Ministry of the Interior shall rigorously suppress any acts of insubordination by members of the agencies of state security.

10. Within a period of ninety days from the promulgation of the present Decree, the Public Commission for the investigation of crimes committed by agencies of state security against the state's own citizens and the Ministry of the Interior of the Russian Federation shall jointly define the terms for the transfer of a number of the functions of the abolished agencies of state security to the competence of the Ministry of the Interior.

11. The Office of the President shall draft a law of inspection and promulgation applicable to present and former members of the agencies of state security and their agents and shall, within a period of ten days from the publication of the present Decree, forward the draft bill to the State Duma for consideration. Special attention shall be paid in this matter to those members of the organs of state security, whose activities were connected the so-called struggle against dissent.

12. All present and former members of the agencies of state security shall within a period of one month furnish the tax office of the relevant territorial unit of the Russian Federation with a formal declaration of property owned by themselves and their close relatives (including parents, brothers and sisters, and close relatives of husbands and wives, both present and past), the said declaration to include the following: real estate, vehicles, accounts in Russian and foreign banks, shares and securities issued by Russian and foreign companies, together with a detailed statement of the sources of income which was used to acquire such property. In the course of the year 2002, the tax authorities of the Russian Federation shall take appropriate measures to verify these declarations and decide upon appropriate action in accordance with procedures specified under the terms of Russian tax legislation.

As from the date of signing and publication of the present Decree until such time as the tax investigations have been completed, all individuals and organizations are prohibited from performing any transactions for the purchase, sale, gift, alienation, or mortgaging of real estate, vehicles, shares and securities, or the transfer of money from accounts belonging to present or former members of the agencies of state security or their relatives. All such transactions performed during the period specified to which present or former members of the agencies of state security or their relatives are party shall be declared null and void.

13. Until such time as they are discharged to the reserves of the Armed Forces of the Russian Federation, all military personnel of the agencies of state security shall be bound by the following terms:

a) they shall remain at their places of residence;

b) within seven days of the publication of the present Decree, they shall register temporarily with the Office of the Interior for the area in which they are registered as resident, for which purpose commissioners shall be appointed from among the officer corps of the Ministry of the Interior;

c) within twenty-four hours of the publication of the present Decree, they shall surrender the official personal weapons of their rank, official identity cards, undercover identity papers, keys and seals to the commissioner at the Office of the Interior, together with a detailed account of their workplace and official functions, the titles of their departments and sections, and individual positions;

d) until such time as they are discharged to the reserves, military personnel of the agencies of state security must report in person to the commissioner at the Office of the Interior for the area in which they are registered as resident as follows: generals and admirals once every three days; senior and junior officers once every five days; warrant officers, first sergeants, sergeants, and privates once every seven days. The commissioners at the Offices of the Interior shall establish special records for this purpose;

e) for violations of these instructions, the officers commanding Offices of the Interior shall impose upon the guilty parties penalties up to and including garrison arrest. Failure to sign in as required shall be regarded as failure to report for duty;

f) financial allowances shall be paid via the financial agencies of the aforementioned Offices of the Interior at the rates set for supernumerary military personnel, until such time as a decision is taken to discharge the persons concerned.

14. Within seven days of the publication of the present Decree, members of the agencies of state security shall draw up a detailed account of their work in the agencies of state security from the day of their enrollment to the date of publication of the Decree on the dissolution of the said agencies, which shall include the following:

a) specific mention of their involvement in particular operations and the titles of such operations, concerning whom and on whose instructions the operations were carried out, and, in addition, everything known to them about operations carried out by other members of their agency and other agencies;

b) a statement of the complete identification data of resident agents, other agents, owners of apartments used for secret meetings and clandestine or conspiratorial purposes, the names and addresses of contacts; the locations at which their private and professional files are kept; their operational names, together with the identification data of the subjects of relevant operations and the locations of their files;

c) Senior staff members of the agencies of state security must indicate the full titles of their units and the identification data and places of residence of their subordinates;

d) the accounts specified above must be submitted to the commissioners at the Offices of the Interior, logged in the register of individual statements, and forwarded directly to the chairman of the Public Commission;

e) individual members of the agencies of state security who have permitted the deliberate destruction of operational records without authorization shall be subject to the provisions of criminal law.

15. Persons who have previously served in the agencies of state security of the USSR and Russia and continue at the present time to serve in the state institutions of the Russian Federation must be withdrawn from active service within five days and shall remain at the disposal of such departments until such time as the law of inspection and promulgation applicable to present and former members of the agencies of state security of the USSR and Russia shall come into effect.

16. The provisions of the present Decree shall apply to all present or former members of the agencies of state security

and also to all persons who have at any time served in or been members of the secret service staff of the agencies of state security of the USSR and Russia.

1 7 .   The present Decree shall be regarded by all military personnel of the agencies of state security as a written order from their Commander in Chief. Those who disobey this order shall be held criminally responsible.

1 8 .   This Decree comes into force on the day when it is signed and published in the mass media.

President of the Russian Federation
Commander in Chief

Anticipating the future is always a risky business, and attempting to anticipate political developments in Russia is even more so. Nonetheless, we would maintain that the only inaccuracy in the "presidential decree" which serves as the epilogue to this book is its precise date. We are absolutely convinced that this decree will be promulgated at some time in the near future. If not, then what would be the point of our writing this book?

APPENDICES

---

*Documents Collected
by the Authors*

STATEMENT OF THE
PRESIDENT OF THE CHECHEN REPUBLIC OF ICHKERIA,
FEBRUARY 11, 2002

NOXIÇIYN RESPUBLIKA   CHECHEN REPUBLIC
NOXÇIYNÇÖ   OF ICHKERIA

PREZIDENT

No. 10-718   February 11, 2002

Statement of the President

The Russian occupation of the Chechen republic is now in its third brutal year. As the civilized world grapples with the menace of international terrorism, the state terror perpetrated by the Kremlin in the Caucasus is all but ignored by the same community of nations pledged to defend democracy and human rights in the face of extreme aggression.

The silence over Chechnya is the price of coalition-building: the Western rapprochement with Moscow, vital to allied operations in Central Asia, hinges on the diplomacy of expediency and amnesia, and the daily suffering, hunger, horror, fear, violence and death visited upon the Chechen people can be forgotten so long as Russian President Vladimir Putin endorses the war on terror.

Russia cites the spate of bombings that struck its cities in September 1999 as the *causus belli* for its invasion of Chechnya, the effort it now happily cites as another battle in the common global struggle against terror of radicalized Islam.

Chechens were held responsible and Moscow's tanks and fighter planes were soon wreaking destruction on my nation. Meanwhile,

Putin won his presidential bid on a wave of delirious nationalist sentiment that numbed awareness of Russia's chronic socio-economic problems with the intoxication of military adventurism.

Yet Chechen responsibility for the bombings was never proven, a credible investigation and cast-iron prosecution of suspects never carried out. Worse, a team of Russian Federal Security agents was later caught planting explosives and detonators in the basement of an apartment building in the City of Ryazan, southeast of Moscow. The official response was that the agents had engaged in a counter-terror readiness exercise. It was a dubious explanation then and it still is now.

Some conscientious Russian parliament members moved for an in-depth probe of the affair, especially concerned over possible security service complicity, but the Duma quashed the inquiry in March of 2000. As the Russian military campaign escalated, a top Russian cabinet member revealed after his resignation that the Russian invasion of Chechnya had been planned many months in advance of the bombings. The attacks on Russia's cities in 1999 remain a mystery, but the inconsistencies of the Kremlin's rationale for its war cited here are not an esoteric hypothesis but documented fact repeatedly published in leading Western newspapers.

An often circulated lie however sadly gains currency. The criminally irresponsible fallacy circulated by Russian intelligence and parroted by the media that legions of Chechen fighters were present in Afghanistan had at least been proven false. Yet again, Russian Defense Minister Sergei Ivanov and Federal Security Service boss Nikolai Patrushev are still touting the myth that Chechens were behind the terror bombings that sparked Moscow's genocidal war.

In exile in London, Boris Berezovsky, the Russian kingmaker fallen from grace, promises to reveal the opposite. If Berezovsky, once a privileged member of Putin's inner circle, is brave enough to come forward and genuinely has proof of the Kremlin's skullduggery at the outset of the war, the West would do well to heed any future evidence offered by him.

In any case, once more the Chechen republic unequivocally refutes any moral or material complicity in the 1999 bombings and asks such bodies of the international community as are willing to launch a transparent and non-partisan investigation into their origin without hindrance.

We further ask that those honorable members of the Duma who pursued the cause renew their efforts and seek to obtain the evidence that will definitively remove hostilities and open the path to negotiated peace. We also urge in good faith that the United States, the European Union, the OSCE, the UN and Interpol aid such an effort by contributing independent observers and investigators. We also ask that the findings of such an inquiry be submitted before an international court of law for final judgment and that all the actors found guilty of their role in the conspiracy be submitted to international justice.

The Chechen Republic is not a rogue dictatorship, a medieval theocracy or a pariah terrorist organization: it is a legally and democratically constituted government, freely elected by its citizens without prejudice or coercion under the protection of international law and abiding by the standards of the OSCE, which monitored our landmark elections following our war of independence.

The Chechnya that Putin describes is one we could never recognize. The hateful narrow creed that terrorists bent on destruction claim as their guide, we reject as the apostasy of fanaticism. We are only ourselves and we simply ask that the truth of our tragedy be known and that we be allowed to live in peace and freedom.

Aslan Maskhadov   President,
                                     The Chechen Republic
                                         of Ichkeria

APPENDIX 2

TESTIMONY OF
SENIOR LIEUTENANT ALEXEI GALKIN,
NOVEMBER 18, 1999

Senior Lieutenant A. V. Galkin is giving an interview to a group of foreign journalists, including one from America and one from Turkey. The questions are asked in English and translated into Russian. The printout gives the Russian translations of the questions as spoken by the interpreter and Galkin's replies.

JOURNALIST/INTERPRETER: Can you introduce yourself, please?
GALKIN: Assistant head of sector, Senior Lieutenant Alexei Galkin, employee...

(The foreign journalists point out that Galkin is badly seated and the camera light is not falling on him. They seat Galkin a bit further to the right.)

JOURNALIST: You can move this way a bit closer to the light. Say it again into the camera, please.
GALKIN: Assistant head of sector Senior Lieutenant Alexei Galkin, employee of the GRU of the Russian Federation.
JOURNALIST: Can I ask you, please, how you came to be here?
GALKIN: Together with Major Ivanov and Senior Lieutenant Pokhomov, I was arrested on October 3 in the Chechen Republic of Ichkeria during an attempt to drive from Mozdok to the settlement of Bino-Yurt in order to carry out a special assignment.
JOURNALIST: And during the attempted border crossing, all these documents here-this here is your identity pass, this here—did you have it on you?

(Shows the identity pass.)

GALKIN: I had this pass on me, and these documents here were in our personal belongings.

JOURNALIST: And what exactly is the purpose of this information here, that there is in this little book, what kind of information is in it?

GALKIN: In here there is a verbal exchange table (He shows it) for working with communications equipment, that is a table of coded messages for transmitting information via open channels of communication such as ultra-short wave radio sets like Motorola, Kenwood and radio telephones.

JOURNALIST: What is the purpose of the information in this little book here?

(*Shows the book.*)

GALKIN: It is a notebook with mathematical formulas for setting off explosions at construction sites, structures, buildings and various other facilities.

JOURNALIST: Are these your notes, your handwriting?

GALKIN: Yes, that is my handwriting.

JOURNALIST: What were you intending to do with this information, with this information?

GALKIN: Our task was to mine the highways in order to destroy the vehicles of refugees and the general public, and also to mine and destroy buildings where the general public lived.

JOURNALIST: Did you take part in the bombing of buildings in Moscow and Dagestan?

GALKIN: I personally did not take part in the bombing of the buildings in Moscow and Dagestan, but I know who blew them up, who is behind the bombing of the buildings in Moscow and who blew up the buildings in Buinaksk.

JOURNALIST: Can you tell us?

GALKIN: The Russian special services are responsible for blowing up the buildings in Moscow and in Volgodonsk, the FSB together with the GRU. The bombing of the buildings in Buinaksk was the work of members of our group, which at the time was on a mission in Dagestan.

JOURNALIST: And as far as I know, here you have been recorded on tape, you confessed to all this, apparently you were filmed with a video camera. And when ... when you, during the filming were you speaking of your own free will?

VOICE OFF CAMERA OF THE HEAD OF THE CHECHEN SECURITY SERVICE ABU MOVSAEV: That ... Don't answer that question.

JOURNALIST: How have you been treated here?

GALKIN: I've been treated well. As I prisoner of war I have not been beaten, they have fed me three times a day and when necessary given me medical assistance.

JOURNALIST: Here is the statement made by you. Do you confirm that you made it voluntarily without any pressure on the part of anyone?

GALKIN: This statement is printed from my words, I wrote this statement by hand [*holds the piece of paper in front of his face*], with my personal signature.

JOURNALIST: Now, at this moment, as you are speaking with us, are you afraid of anything?

GALKIN: No, it is simply that this is the first time I have faced journalists ... journalists from western television companies, so I am a bit nervous.

ABU MOVSAEV'S VOICE OFF CAMERA: Their departments are not allowed to appear on ...

GALKIN: It is quite simply that due to the nature of our work we have to ... we are not supposed to show ourselves in front of television cameras. (*Smiles tensely.*)

JOURNALIST: Thank you.

VOICE OFF CAMERA: Ah, yes, now questions, only in Turkish.... Come over here...

JOURNALIST: They're the same questions, only in Turkish, they will ask and that is all ...

(*Questions are asked in Turkish, then translated into Russian.*)

JOURNALIST: Do you confirm that all these documents belong to you? This identity pass here, this statement, it all belongs to you.

(*Galkin shows the identity pass in an open position.*)

GALKIN: Yes, all these documents belong to me.

JOURNALIST: With what aim did you arrive in the region of Dagestan and afterwards in Chechnya?

GALKIN: We went to Dagestan and Chechnya to carry out terrorist acts in Dagestan and in the Chechen Republic of Ichkeria.

JOURNALIST: And against whom were these, were they directed? Were you supposed to carry out explosions against peaceful civilians or somebody else?

GALKIN: These bombings were directed against peaceful civilians.

JOURNALIST: And who ... Who was it that sent you on this mission?

GALKIN: We were appointed and sent on our mission by order of the GRU of the armed forces of the Russian Federation.

JOURNALIST: Can you name the actual man who sent you?

GALKIN: It was Colonel General Korabelnikov, head of the GRU and head of the 14th section of the GRU Lieutenant General Kostechko.

JOURNALIST: Did you personally and did your unit have anything to do with the explosions in Moscow?

GALKIN: Personally our unit had nothing to do with the explosions in Moscow, since at that time we were in Dagestan. The members of our unit, the members of our unit of 12 men, who were then in Dagestan, carried out the bombing of the house in Buinaksk.

APPENDIX 3

ABU MOVSAEV'S DISCUSSION WITH
A GROUP OF FOREIGN JOURNALISTS
ON THE TESTIMONY OF
SENIOR LIEUTENANT A. GALKIN

ABU MOVSAEV: At the present time we have with us a member of the GRU, their leader Colonel Ivanov, the same individual who supervised the blowing up of the house. The GRU ... At this time you can photograph the Senior Lieutenant (*Shows identity pass*) Senior Lieutenant Alexei Galkin, who was redeployed to the territory of the Chechen Republic of Ichkeria from Dagestan. Is that it, have you photographed him? (*They take photographs*) More? In Volgodonsk members of the special services carried out the explosions. And so today when they call us terrorists it proves the opposite. (*Shows something*) These are their coded messages, that is, the coded messages are here. It's a book for working with explosives—detailing which explosives to use and how to use them. We have these all completely—the conclusive evidence and all their ... It all (*He demonstrates something*) all this proves it (*They take photographs*) ... That's all. Now, next, the next point ...

QUESTION: (*Questions are usually asked in English and then translated into Russian by the interpreter, not always accurately and correctly.*) On whom exactly, on whom did you find this book?

ABU MOVSAEV'S ANSWER: Their group, the GRU, was arrested here. That is, that was, so that today you'll understand—that's the GRU of the Russian Federation, the 14th Department.

QUESTION: On exactly what date did you find this book?

ANSWER: We arrested them, this group, on October 3–4 1999.

QUESTION: When did they find this man?

INTERPRETER'S ANSWER: On the same day, the fourth, October 4.

ANSWER: The Fourteenth Department of the GRU. The GRU of the

Russian Federation primarily handles killings of political leaders and sabotage. Here's the statement made by Senior Lieutenant Galkin. (*Shows it.*)

QUESTION: Did he make a voluntary statement?

ANSWER: Yes. There's his signature.

QUESTION: Why didn't he make a statement immediately on October 4?

ANSWER: Ah, no . . . well at first we worked on him, worked on him for a long time, then he turned, we sent the cassette to Istanbul to the November 18 summit, where it specifically . . . . they pointed out why they . . . After that, listen to this, after that the Russian leadership, the GRY, made a statement, supposedly they thought that we'd shot them. Since we'd spread the rumor.

QUESTION: His motivation for confessing? What motivated him?

ANSWER: What motivated him was when he saw that the Chechen people were being totally wiped out, indiscriminately. We showed him videos of children being murdered, women and old men being murdered. Since I'm a special services instructor I'm familiar with their Department, with what they do, and when we gave him legal proof he confessed.

QUESTION: And he accepted responsibility for one explosion, is that right?

ANSWER: No . . . The explosion—at that time in Buinaksk. The explosions in Buinaksk were supervised by Colonel Ivanov, who is his superior and was deployed to Chechnya with him. He named Ivanov and other employees, yes, no . . . but he didn't take part.

QUESTION: On the basis of this confession alone you draw the conclusion that the other explosions in Moscow were also the work of the Russian government? You only think . . .

ANSWER: Eh, no . . . We don't "think," we have proof. The first proof, the first proof is that any group that they deploy in the rear of the enemy, they already know, their leader announces that we're going into the territory of the Chechen Republic since we set off the explosions in Moscow, Volgodonsk and Buinaksk. That is, not specifically their group, in all of them, that is in the eyes of the peaceful community we made terrorists out of them, killers in the abduction of people, today we have to prove that these people are . . . they have to be wiped out, that is the Chechen people. At the political briefings. Until now . . . the second point where we have proof is what I repeated before this and I repeat now: hexogen was used. There is no hexogen on the territory of Chechnya. Hexogen marked "top secret" in red is only held by the special services of the Russian Federation, and without the consent of the leaders of the GRU and the FSB no one has the right to take a single gram of this hexogen. And afterwards GRU employees arrested by us explained that on the last raid their Colonel Ivanov explained to them at the political briefing that these explosions were carried out by our employees together with the FSB. Yes, yes, and another thing, they all talked about it. . .

QUESTION: Do you accuse, place the guilt for these explosions on the government of Russia, the GRU, the FSB or one individual in particular?

ANSWER: I'll tell you who specifically. Vladimir Putin, as chairman, developed the plot. Specifically the heads of the special services of the Russian Federation, former intelligence agents who were appointed by Putin. These are the people that Putin currently trusts the most. There is a second point: the fact that today, in the political arena, Putin will stop at nothing to become President of the Russian Federation, even murder. (*The light goes out, they stop recording. Abu Movsaev lights a cigarette.*) When I'm smoking, please, don't film me. (*They switch on the light, recording is resumed.*)

ANSWER: Another thing, I am not trying to prove to you today that we are angels, I am not trying to convince you that we are good people. We only want to prove one thing: that Russia is a terrorist state. Nothing else. All that we do today . . . that we are trying to do, we are doing for the sake of Allah—if the West interferes it won't interfere on our behalf, if, honestly speaking, we are sure today that the West, the leadership of the West, will not at least intervene in the murder of the Chechen people, everything else, you know, all the wars end through negotiations. I believe that we

won the last war, I think . . . this war, we'll win this war. So that
you have some concrete information, today we were informed
that the Russians have taken Argun. Right now bitter fighting is
taking place in Argun and the Russian forces are pulling back.
Right, any more questions for me? Afterwards . . . And I have just
one request: translate for them . . . too many questions . . . I won't
let them ask the GRU officer too many questions. You can . . . You
can ask him . . . ask why he was redeployed in Chechnya, as far as
Dagestan, where they worked before that, and . . . well, and now
the statement (*Shows it*)—did we force him or not. We did not force
a statement . . . when our men fall into their hands they kill them
straight away. Although we can't dress and feed him the way we
should-the Russians themselves are to blame, because we're completely blockaded. Another thing: international law provides for
members of special services who have crossed a border to set off
explosions, to assasinate political leaders, by judicial . . . they hold
a judicial inquiry and have them shot. We could have shot them
before this. (*Shows the GRU man's book, shows the code notebook of
the other prisoner.*)

QUESTION: Is the signature actually this officer's or someone else's?
ANSWER: It belongs to the second member of the GRU, it's . . . Ah,
   it's his own, his . . . These are the second member's coded messages,
   coded messages and coded signal messages, that they gave them,
   these codes are prepared in advance, this is all that they were
   given, these are their routes where . . . yes, these are their coded
   messages, the signalman and the demolition man . . . These are
   theirs, yes . . . these . . . they're code names, satellite links . . .
   There . . . There look . . . There's a verbal exchange table for a
   satellite communications radio location for managing radio traffic. It's . . .

QUESTION: It's stupid for an intelligence officer to carry papers like
   that on his person.
ANSWER: They didn't think . . . They were being transported by
   Chechens in a secret vehicle, since sometimes we don't check
   Chechen vehicles, with a beard, especially. Their way of thinking

. . . They were relying on it. There's data—it's what, look, the enemy's designated—the page (*Shows and talks about designations from the code notebook*). If they saw an enemy, that is, us. They . . . Code names . . .

INTERPRETER: A beetle is an armed personnel carrier, a spider is an automobile, a string is a plane.

QUESTION: Well, in general, what is it? That is, what else?

ANSWER: It's when they come across, for example, one of our population centers, when they have to make strikes, they transmitted code names when we're in there, so we wouldn't understand. There, for example, Berlin, they call a town Berlin, on Chechen territory there's Bratskoe, Nadterechny district. Bar, the word Bar, that's the Nadterechny district too. These are the population centers where they worked initially and made the strikes.

QUESTION: Did all the planned explosions take place or were several explosions prevented? Were other explosions supposed to take place?

ANSWER: Naturally. They, according to my operational information, in Penza they wouldn't have been, in Ryazan that is they wouldn't have been caught by employees of the MVD accidentally, then there were supposed to be detonations in Volgograd, in the Stavropol Region, in the Saratov Region, well, that is, basically, where mostly Chechens live (*Repeats this.*) Saratov . . . Well, basically, where compact. . .

QUESTION: What is your position?

ANSWER: Head of the President's Special Department. At that time I gave proof of the murder . . . the Red Cross killing. At that time I was in charge of a special missions detachment, that the Red Cross killing was committed by Deniev's people, who are currently in Moscow. Look, and everywhere there. . .

INTERPRETER: Adam Deniev. . .

ANSWER: He is an employee, an agent of the special services. He has a GRU identity pass, he has all the identity passes . . . When we signed the agreement between the FSB of the Russian Federation and the National Security Service, we applied officially to Nikolai

Kovalyov, the head, then the head of the FSB, with proof, for them to hand over Deniev to us, to which Kovalyov answered that he couldn't hand over Deniev to me since they were very interested in him continuing his work. And our Public Prosecutor of the Chechen Republic of Ichkeria repeatedly made official demands to the Public Prosecutor's Office of the Russian Federation to hand over Deniev specifically for the Red Cross killing, but we couldn't get hold of him.

QUESTION: Why did Deniev kill the Red Cross people?

ANSWER: The material . . . when I resigned . . . I left it with our branch, the special services and with the prosecutor's office, our prosecutor's office.

QUESTION: Do you know who killed Fred Koening?

ANSWER: I do know. He was at my house in the period before the war, back then and just before he left for the last time, he stayed at my house that night. He had proof of what was going on in the Russian Republic's filtration camps. After he disappeared without a trace, Djokhar Dudaev, the president, the first President of the Chechen Republic, set up a brigade to search for and locate Koening. As the head of the special services I was a member of the brigade, that is we established that he was last seen on the crossroads at Chechen-U, where the Russian forces were located. With certainty . . . If today in the Russian Federation . . . Then the rumor spread that in the Great Martanov district (*Inaudible*) we still haven't found, I'm sure, that if the Russian forces enter the Martanov district, if they seize it, they'll definitely find the burial site, that is they're the only ones who know where the burial site is. In 1996 we were contacted by an officer of the Russian Federation saying he could show us the burial site, but he wanted 100,000 dollars. Since we didn't have that kind of money (*Inaudible*). They said to me that he would actually sell us the medallion that was on his body.

QUESTION: What do you know about the murder of the employees of the British television company?

ANSWER: I know. (*Inaudible*). One of them was actually abducted.

The last time American and German journalists came I (*Inaudible*) we gave them specifically, but to remember everything in my head. From this document a criminal case could be (*Inaudible*). That, you understand, today I can (*Inaudible*) there were loads of abducted people were within the borders of Dagestan, Ingushetia and Northern Ossetia. And they also kept them there. Here the organized criminal groups of all the republics and of our state even had between them some kind of (*Inaudible*). Our criminal groups informed the relatives of this or that person and supposedly accepted responsibility. Specifically I can, for instance Arbi Baraev, who everyone thought was a villain, that he'd carried out all the kidnappings. If you remember, four Frenchmen were abducted in Makhachkala. Remember? Well that was the Dagestanis who contacted Baraev and asked him to say that these Frenchmen were in Chechnya. For that phone call Baraev received $200,000. Since Baraev at that time (*Inaudible*). On the border of Chechnya and Dagestan, in Gerzel, Baraev received $3,000,000. He kept $200,000, gave $2,800,000 to the Dagestanis, and the Frenchmen were handed over in Dagestan. There are many similar cases. Really? That's the first time I'd heard of that. I heard that he had supposedly disappeared on the border of Georgia and Chechnya. There weren't any cases on the territory of Chechnya, it didn't happen that . . . There was one attempt in August, in September there was one attempt, we immediately arrested those people and in accordance with sharia legal procedure we handed them over for a sharia trial.

APPENDIX 4

TRANSCRIPT OF THE HEARINGS OF
THE PUBLIC COMMISSION FOR
THE INVESTIGATION OF EVENTS SURROUNDING
THE APARTMENT-HOUSE BOMBINGS
IN MOSCOW AND VOLGODONSK AND THE RYAZAN
TRAINING EXERCISE IN SEPTEMBER 1999

Teleconference: Moscow–London, July 25, 2002

From Moscow:
Commission Chairman Sergei Kovalyov, Deputy Chairman Sergei
Yushenkov, Secretary General Lev Levinson, Commission Members
Leonid Batkin, Valeriy Borschev, Alexander Daniel, Gennadiy
Zhavoronkov, Otto Latsis, Karina Moskalenko, Lev Ponomarev,
Yuri Prosvirin, Yuri Samodurov, Alexander Tkachenko, *and possibly
other members of the Public Commission for the investigation of events
surrounding the apartment-house bombings in the cities of Moscow and
Volgodonsk and the training exercise in the city of Ryazan in September
1999;* reporters.

From London:
Alexander Litvinenko, Tatiana Morozova, and Yuri Felshtinsky.

KOVALYOV: Ladies and Gentlemen, allow me to open today's . . .
I don't even know what to call it. Well, let's say, meeting. This
meeting is fundamentally different from the working methods that
the Public Commission has employed until now, different from its
working sessions. The difference is clear: this is the first session
before such a broad public audience.

We can't say that we're pleased by this. The materials we
received today are of great interest for our work. And it just

turned out that today publicity not only couldn't be avoided, but happened to be necessary.

We weren't acquainted in advance—we received the main contents of the materials that were sent to our Commission only this morning. We haven't analyzed them, we haven't evaluated them. All that remains to be done. We will probably have additional questions, and we hope that our partners abroad will agree to other sessions like this one, so that those questions might be answered.

I want to say just a few words about our Commission's basic working principles and about what it has worked on thus far and what it will continue working on. I will be very brief. And there are serious reasons why I will be brief.

First. We give no preference to any one account of the barbaric bombings that were perpetrated in September 1999. Our aim is to remain absolutely impartial—tediously impartial, I would say—painstaking in our analysis and conclusions. We have not reached any conclusions, not even tentative ones.

The different accounts of the bombings. There exist two extreme interpretations of these events—the so-called Chechen Trail interpretation, and the interpretation that views the events as a crime by the Moscow security services. I repeat: these are two extreme interpretations. Both of them have their pros, and both of them have their substantial cons. We, I repeat, will remain absolutely impartial.

But these are extreme interpretations, and it is quite likely that neither of them will turn out to be correct. Because other accounts of the events are possible—I'd call them intermediate accounts. We will act in strict accordance with the demands that it is reasonable to make of any investigation, and that are made of investigations everywhere in the world: no account of the events can remain unchecked.

Now a couple of words about what we do in our daily work, so to speak. We meet with various people, talk to them, and keep a record of our conversations. We still hope that sooner or later we'll be given the opportunity to meet with official representatives of government agencies and to ask them questions that are very vital for us. We make wide use of official inquiry requests—because the Commission's members include several Duma deputies, and an official inquiry request by a deputy has a certain special legal status—and we are building a "collection" of the answers to these inquiries. I'd prefer not to describe this official correspondence right now. We get various kinds of responses. In exceptionally rare cases, they contain quite substantive and detailed answers to all our questions. But the average response consists of either—pardon my language—mooing, or of something devoid of content.

Nonetheless, I for one am counting on government agencies to change their attitude toward our work and to become our active partners. What are the grounds for this hope? The charges being leveled against the government truly are frightening. The only way to refute them is through a thorough and open investigation, with full disclosure of all the details, all the results, to an anxious public. This is what we are hoping for.

Now let's proceed to the main part of our meeting. We will listen to our partners in London, and then we will both have a chance to ask questions. In addition, let me repeat that I hope this will not be the last time that we are in contact, and that we will have the opportunity for more detailed discussions in due course. Thank you for your attention.

YUSHENKOV: Let me introduce our London partners. From left to right: Alexander Litvinenko, Tatiana Morozova, Yuri Felshtinsky.

FELSHTINSKY: Hello.

YUSHENKOV: Who will be. . . ? Alexander Litvinenko, you, yes?

FELSHTINSKY: I'd like to let Tanya Morozova speak first—for a couple of minutes.

MOROZOVA: Let me express my gratitude to the entire Commission for gathering in Moscow, and to all the reporters for being here to discuss and to listen to what is happening. We have a lot of news here. You will be able to present some of these findings to [the world]. I personally have no interest in political discussions. What am I interested in? I'm interested in the truth. That's why I'm here.

Now Mr. Kovalyov, I know that you met with Mikhail Trepashkin. I would very much like you to consider him our representative—mine and my sister's.

FELSHTINSKY: I'd like to add, also directed to Sergei Kovalyov, that we're actually grateful that this is a public discussion, because the only thing that's truly important in this whole matter is that our discussion, our analysis, is completely open. In essence, the only thing that could undermine this investigation is if attempts are made to make these meetings private and closed. Because the reality is—as many people have repeated, and as the slogan on the website says, I believe—we want to know the truth. And it's very important for us that our side—at least our side—should act publicly and openly. Because, unfortunately, the other side—let's call it the government, let's call it the FSB—is doing everything it can to prevent our discussions from being public, to prevent our facts and conclusions from reaching a wider public, in order to prevent anyone from knowing the truth about who is ultimately responsible for the terrorist attacks of September 1999. Therefore, I'd like to express my gratitude to you one more time for the fact that this meeting, this discussion, is open and public. And I am hopeful that all other meetings of the Public Commission will be public as well, because this is the only opportunity that the Russian public has to receive news about this issue.

Thank you. I can probably yield the floor to Alexander now.

LITVINENKO: Hello. Thank you very, very much for inviting us to this meeting. Yuri Felshtinsky and I have decided to provide these materials specifically to you. Why? Because you're working publicly and openly.

I want to add the following to what Felshtinsky has said. I'd like you to question the people whom we're going to name as witnesses just as publicly and openly, with reporters present. This will protect all of us from various fabrications, machinations, insinuations, and charges to the effect that someone somewhere is trying to fabricate something or to give this whole matter a political spin. In other words, for us to find the truth and for people to believe that it really is the truth, we must do this openly. That's my position. And that's why we are turning specifically to you.

FELSHTINSKY: We're probably ready now to yield the floor to Moscow, and to answer any questions that may come up or have already come up.

YUSHENKOV: Yuri, I still think that Alexander should very briefly go over the contents of the documents that he sent us, to give the members of the press a chance to see the heart of the matter.

LITVINENKO: Yes, of course. Here's what I want to say about the materials.

Yuri Felshtinsky and I managed to contact Achemez Gochiyaev, who, according to the FSB account, is the leader of the terrorist group that organized the bombing of the apartment buildings in the city of Moscow in September 1999. I believe that the materials which Gochiyaev sent us are highly relevant for establishing the truth.

I want to stress that Achemez Gochiyaev came to us on his own initiative, and as far as I know, these materials, this declaration which he sent us, were given freely and voluntarily.

In his declaration, Achemez Gochiyaev provided quite detailed autobiographical information, which you, respected members of the Commission, should have no trouble verifying,

In addition, Achemez Gochiyaev stated that he did, in fact, rent the spaces where the bombings took place. But that he did so at the request of his acquaintance.

In my view, the most important statement contained in this declaration is that Achemez Gochiyaev, after the second bombing took place—on September 13, on Kashirskoye Highway—that he himself, according to his own declaration, notified the police, the emergency medical service, and the 911 emergency service, that other bombings might take place at other addresses that he had rented, including the ones on Borisovskie Prudy and in Kopotnya.

I want to note the following: A stockpile of explosives was indeed discovered at the address on Borisovskie Prudy, with six timers, ready to be used. And this is where I, as a former intelligence operative, have a very serious question for the law enforcement agencies. If you really went to this address and discovered six timers and a stockpile of explosives, then why didn't you set up an ambush, as an operative would say, and arrest the criminals when they came to get these explosives, instead of announcing everything on TV? In other words, warning the criminals that the police knew the location of the explosives and timers.

Next. Achemez Gochiyaev gives [. . .] information about the person at whose request he rented these storage facilities. I think this person won't be that hard to track down simply using the means available to any lawyer. I believe that the law enforcement agencies should also provide assistance with this task.

In addition, Achemez Gochiyaev makes the very serious claim that his sister was subjected to unlawful methods of investigation (she was tortured to make her denounce her brother). He also states that his brother, who works as a policeman in Karachaevo-Cherkessia, warned him that there were orders not to arrest him, but to eliminate him.

These facts can also be verified, and I'd like you to verify them publicly and openly. You could call these people in for the Commission's next meeting, in front of reporters, in front of the public, and let them testify or explain why they don't want to testify.

These are the statements that I consider most important. If they're verified, they will help us get to the truth of the matter. That's all.

YUSHENKOV: Alexander, could you show the videos and photographs now? And second: when was the last time you had contact with Gochiyaev? Are you sure that he's still alive, etc.?

LITVINENKO: Let's begin with his statement. Here is his handwritten declaration on six pages.

YUSHENKOV: We received it, we have it. We haven't received the photographs and videos.

LITVINENKO: I think that a comparison of his handwriting will make it simple to determine whether or not he wrote it.

Second. Here are the photographs of himself that he sent us. Here are the magnified photographs. First photograph. . .

YUSHENKOV: Can we get more focus? Is there a cameraman there? . . . Maybe, closer to the camera, Yuri? No?

FELSHTINSKY: These photos will be delivered to you in electronic format. They're already up—I'm just now being told—on the website Grani.ru. That's why we didn't send them. It'll be easier to look at them on the Internet.

LITVINENKO: Here's a photo, here's a second photo of him. Here's another personal photo, another one.

YUSHENKOV: Thank you. If they're up on the website, there's no need.

LITVINENKO: In order to establish whether or not this person is Gochiyaev, we consulted an expert and gave this expert all of these photographs together with the official photographs from the FSB website—the photograph from the "Wanted" section on their website. This is that photo, the photo from the "Wanted" section. Here's that photo and two photos in which he's pictured together with Hattab. Supposedly.

The expert's conclusion was that, based on the photographs that were sent us by Gochiyaev and on the photographs that are posted on the "Wanted" site, he could make a positive identification of Gochiyaev. In other words, this and this is the same person. The expert also said that this photograph, where Gochiyaev appears with Hattab—on this photograph, a positive identification cannot be made. This photograph cannot be used as evidence in court, and there may also be traces of digital manipulation. In other words, in normal language, this photograph is a fake, which cannot be a document.

And so the next question immediately comes up: what reasons does law enforcement have to show the public a fake?

Mr. Yushenkov, could you repeat the questions?

YUSHENKOV: When was the last time you were in contact with Gochiyaev? You had no direct contact with him, right? Only through intermediaries?

LITVINENKO: In terms of establishing a connection with Gochi-yaev, establishing a contact with him—I'd like Yuri Felshtinsky to clarify this issue, because all contacts . . . Well, first he had contact with the intermediary, then I did. And you know, the situation here is like this: we're now trying not to lose this connection, this contact, because the agreement with the intermediary is that after these materials are verified . . . Gochiyaev writes, in fact, that "this is a brief description, we'll talk about the details later."

My hope is that Gochiyaev himself will learn about what's happening, and if we have some other additional questions, I think he will give us answers. But I'd ask Yuri Felshtinsky to talk about these contacts in greater detail.

FELSHTINSKY: I believe some information has already been given to you. The members of the Commission have it in printed form. But I want to say right from the start, before the reporters start asking questions about this topic, that our contacts are a one-sided affair. Gochiyaev, the people around Gochiyaev, Gochiyaev's intermediaries, Gochiyaev's messengers—however you want to put it—can contact us, but we cannot contact them.

Nevertheless, this dialogue is perfectly real. The possibility of reaching Gochiyaev, of talking to Gochiyaev, undoubtedly exists. It's possible to get answers to certain questions. And in this sense, I think our work is more effective than that of certain government agencies. I think it's clear why this is so. For the same exact reason that it's clear to absolutely everyone, even to Gochiyaev, that what we're interested in is the truth, while the Federal Security Service is interested in completely different issues. That's the short answer to this question.

There was a question as to when the first contact was made. We've described this episode, too. Gochiyaev gave his testimony in several installments on April 24, if I'm not mistaken.

I'd like to add a few words about the photographs. Here are the photographs that our independent expert in London has concluded are not very convincing or inauthentic and has even called a photomontage. They are the only connection that exists between

Hattab and Gochiyaev. In fact, it must be said that these photographs are currently the only connection between Hattab, Chechnya, and the September 1999 bombings. In other words, after many, many months of painstaking work by the Federal Security Service, they have no evidence and no indications that the September 1999 operations in Moscow were carried out by Chechens or by Chechen field commanders, including Hattab.

Moreover, we all know that some time ago the Federal Security Service arrested Adam Dekkushev and brought him to Moscow, and that Dekkushev, according to the FSB's statement, testified that the bombings in Moscow had been perpetrated by this same Hattab, by these same Chechens.

In connection with this, I want to announce that we have in our possession the written testimony of two other participants—according to the FSB account—of the bombings in Moscow in September 1999, Krymshamkhalov and Batchaev. They've already given us their testimony. And according to this testimony (which we have in written form, as well as on videotape), neither Hattab, nor any Chechen field commanders, nor any Chechens at all, had anything to do with the September 1999 bombings in Moscow. I make this announcement in connection with the fact that the Federal Security Service is currently involved in a serious hunt for these people, that it is entirely possible that sooner or later these people might meet the same fate as Dekkushev, and that we don't know what testimony they'll give once they're in the hands of the FSB.

Moreover, if the FSB is interested in the participants of bombings at the "lowest" level—people such as Dekkushev, Batchaev, and Krymshamkhalov, all of whom the FSB claims were participants in the bombings—then we, in contrast to the FSB, are interested not only in the individuals who physically blew up the buildings, but also in those people who issued the orders that these buildings should be blown up, and also in those who handled this operation at the middle level.

Therefore, I must announce, again publicly and openly, that

according to Krymshamkhalov's and Batchaev's testimony, the leaders of the operation to blow up the buildings in Moscow in September 1999 are the Federal Security Service of the Russian Federation. In this same written testimony, the head of this operation is named as FSB Director Nikolai Patrushev. According to this same written testimony, the individual in charge of its execution was Major General and Director of the Department for the Defense of Constitutional Order German Ugriumov, who died in unclear circumstances on May 31, 2001 (there is justifiable reason to believe that he was killed by the Federal Security Service).

Also, we are now checking the possibility that one of the real leaders of this operation at the ground level was the well-known security agent Max Lazovsky. As you know, it was more or less legally established that he had a connection to the terrorist attacks in Moscow in 1994, and most likely to the terrorist attacks in Moscow in 1996.

We are now checking all of this information. This information supplements the information from Gochiyaev, which we relayed to you earlier.

YUSHENKOV: Thank you. Is there a representative of the FSB here? Who would like to ask a question, I mean. (*Audience laughter*) No, yes? Mr. Kovalyov, then how did we decide? First Commission members ask questions about specifics, and then reporters, yes?

BORSCHEV: Alexander, could you be more specific: Gochiyaev personally called to warn about possible bombings on Borisovskie Prudy and in Kopotnya? And do we know the name of the person who received this information from him?

LITVINENKO: According to Gochiyaev's statement, on the morning of the 13th he personally called the police, the emergency medical service, and 911. As a former law enforcement agent, I know for a fact that all such communications are tape-recorded. Therefore, I think that if the Commission requests and obtains from law enforcement the tape-recordings of the phone calls to 911, to the police, and to the emergency medical service, and if it listens to them at a meeting—publicly, openly—then all of this information can be verified.

In addition, the mobile phone number that Gochiyaev used can be established, and the records can be checked: which phone calls came from this number on the morning of the 13th. You can take a specific stretch of time and obtain this information. This is a task for specialists. I think that Trepashkin and other lawyers are in a position to arrange it. They can write the official inquiry requests, obtain the records, submit them to experts, give them a legal, juridical evaluation, and present these materials in their entirety before the Commission and before the Russian public.

YUSHENKOV: Thank you. Leonid Batkin.

BATKIN: Hello. Here is my question.

Gochiyaev's testimony is very specific and in this respect it inspires trust, seems sincere. Except for one point, which is, moreover, a crucial point in my view, and which greatly puzzled me. I quote: "A certain man came to my firm, whom I've known very well ever since my school days. . ." and so on. This "certain man" instructed Gochiyaev to rent the spaces in the buildings that were blown up or that were later indicated by Gochiyaev as the sites of possible future bombings. Gochiyaev himself asserts that he has known this man very well—"since his school days." This whole story is connected specifically to him, and he appears to be the actual organizer (at the middle level, as you put it) of the bombings in Moscow. But why is he not named? Why is nothing concrete said about him? Who is he? Why is he always "a certain man," although he is at the center of the incidents? What does Gochiyaev have to hide? And why didn't you ask him this question?

LITVINENKO: I understand your question. First, I'd like to correct you slightly. This person didn't instruct Gochiyaev to rent the space, but suggested that he do so. In other words, Gochiyaev was not taking orders from him.

Second, Gochiyaev indicates certain facts about this person. He indicates that he's been acquainted with him since school. In other words, this person is a fellow countryman. But for this reason, he doesn't give his name.

We asked the intermediary this question: Why doesn't Gochiyaev give this person's name? The intermediary pointed to his final statement: "This is a brief description of everything that happened, we will talk about later." I understood this to mean that this was the first installment of Gochiyaev's testimony. Gochiyaev doesn't know us, he doesn't completely trust us. After his sister was tortured, after orders were issued "not to take him alive," he's naturally afraid to name this important witness.

But I will tell you as an agent why I think he's afraid to give the name . . . We asked the intermediary and the intermediary said: he's afraid to give the name. I believe that Gochiyaev is being foolish in this respect, but I can't force him, can I?

Even with the information we have, it's not difficult to find this person. Question the people who worked with Gochiyaev at his firm during this period. Identify all of his countrymen who approached him and whom he supplied with mineral water. In other words, it's not that big of a problem.

And if we obtain the phone call records—these phone calls can be used to find this person, who, as it says here, called him on the 9th at five in the morning. You see, yes? It looks like Gochiyaev isn't giving us his name, it looks like he's trying to protect the witness, but by doing so he has completely exposed him to us. Any agent will tell you that. To identify this person and to track him down—well, I'll tell you, for a good operative it's a two- or three-day job.

YUSHENKOV: Yuri Samodurov. And then—Gennady Zhavoronkov.

SAMODUROV: Alexander, Gochiyaev's declaration, which you sent us, contains the following sentence: "Now I am almost convinced that this man, with whom I worked, is an agent of the FSB. I will provide information about him later." These are Gochiyaev's words. If Gochiyaev gets in touch with you, can you ask him to provide the Public Commission with information about this man?

He himself can decide how he wants to present this information—
publicly or privately.

LITVINENKO: I will try to contact Gochiyaev after our meeting and
ask him a series of questions. Why didn't I do this before our meeting? I wanted Gochiyaev to become convinced personally,
through the media, that we didn't hide his declaration, didn't
stamp it "confidential," as this is done by certain individuals in
the Russian Federation, didn't start using this declaration behind
the scenes, didn't sell it to someone. Because there are people
who are trying to buy and sell this information-you understand
this, right? There are many different kinds of crooks. I want
Gochiyaev to see that our investigation took place in the open.
And I still hope that . . . Even right here on this TV Bridge—I think
that he will see this—I would turn to him and tell him that all the
materials he sends us will be given to your Commission. Publicly
and openly.

You must understand that I'm not trying to accuse or acquit
Gochiyaev. I can't confirm that Gochiyaev is innocent. I can only
say one thing: that Gochiyaev sent this declaration, that it contains statements that deserve the most serious attention, and that
they must be carefully and objectively examined and publicized.

I will do what you ask and, if we have further contact with
Gochiyaev, I will ask him to name this person who, in his opinion,
is an FSB agent. But I think that Trepashkin and other lawyers . . .
If the law enforcement agencies provide complete and objective
replies to all their inquiries and don't interfere, they will be able to
find this person sooner, establish his identity sooner than
Gochiyaev.

In other words, there's the question of whether the law
enforcement agencies will or won't interfere. Will they or won't
they exert pressure on the witnesses. That's the question.

And here I'd like to put a request to the Commission. A
request that is extremely serious and extremely important.

We have direct proof of the FSB's involvement in the bombing of the building in Ryazan. (That was no training exercise, it was the bombing of a building, and we have direct proof of this. I don't want to say too much about it now, because I think that we'll present this proof at our next meeting.) I would like the Commission to present the Director of the FSB Patrushev with an official request to declassify the Ryazan file and to make it available for our next meeting, so that we can objectively verify the materials in this file and compare them with the materials in our possession. That's my request.

ZHAVORONKOV: Alexander, what makes you so convinced—what is your conviction based on—that Gochiyaev's messenger is not an FSB agent? The KGB has played various games in the past. I don't need to tell you about the Savinkov case, how he was lured to Russia and then thrown down a stairwell.

LITVINENKO: I haven't said anything anywhere about the messenger being or not being an FSB agent. I never said anything like this in any form. I'm saying one thing: we received a written handwritten document that states that Gochiyaev wrote it, and we received photographs of him. Everything that I was able to verify in London, I verified. I consulted experts and the experts concluded that the photographs were in fact photographs of Gochiyaev. In other words, the official website has a picture of him in the "Wanted" section. In other words, this is that man. But the rest—verifying Gochiyaev's handwriting—is up to the lawyers, who are in Moscow.

And as for this messenger, I can't characterize him in any way. You see what I mean, yes? If this is, let's suppose, a plot by the FSB, some special operation . . . Listen, but why would the FSB need all this? I mean, if this comes out, then it will just confirm once again that the FSB, instead of trying to establish the truth, is, excuse me, wasting the taxpayers' means and resources in order to keep up some kind of petty intrigue around me, which they've been doing now for the past five years. This is what we're talking about.

TKACHENKO: Alexander, hello. This is Alexander Tkachenko. My question to you is this. You said that Gochiyaev personally warned the authorities about possible future bombings in Kopotnya and on Borisovskie Prudy, yes? Do you think that there are records, police records, EMS records, showing that he was the one who really gave the warning?

LITVINENKO: First of all, you have to establish the unit that came out to Borisovskie Prudy, to establish the head of this unit, and to establish the origin of the signal. But if they start talking about "agents, secrets"—at this late stage, that kind of thing no longer works.

Next. If I were a director and an officer conducting a search for a criminal responsible for terrorist attacks, what are the first steps I would take? I would send an official request to the Ministry of Internal Affairs—to all of those agencies, emergency services—requesting that they save the tapes for that day and for that entire period, put them in envelopes, and hand them over to the investigation. And I'd study all these documents, these records, very meticulously. I'd identify the people making these phone calls, and I'd question all these people as witnesses. Not just on this day, not just on the 13th, but for the entire time, all of September. If the law enforcement agencies haven't done this, then we need to find out why they haven't done this: either this is a lack of professionalism, or it's deliberate. And if they have done this, then I think they should provide you with these tape recordings.

In addition, if, let's suppose, Gochiyaev isn't on these tapes, then you have to look at the mobile phone—was there a call made from the mobile phone? And this is also an important question. It can be checked.

YUSHENKOV: The members of the Commission, I believe, have no further questions? Or do you have one, Mr. Batkin?

BATKIN: Yes, I have one more question of a completely different nature. The FSB's statement mentions certain Wahhabis. I must say, in general, that this whole new FSB account completely contradicts their assertions about a Chechen trail, which, in spite of the complete lack of evidence, carried a certain weight for two-and-a-half years. Now we're forced to talk about a Daghestani trail. That means we must explain the motives and circumstances which could have somehow compelled people from Dagestan to decide to blow up buildings in Moscow. Apart from the mention of Hattab (the Arab trail, so to speak) on the basis of a false photograph, no evidence exists. But where are these Wahhabis? The city where Gochiyaev was born—Karachaevsk—are there Wahhabis there now? Were there any then? Who was their leader? Can we find out anything about this group, which the bombers in Moscow supposedly came from?

And one last thing. Going back to this mysterious "certain man," I want to say, as a warning, that I personally don't believe that he'll be found. Because this is a central figure. If Gochiyaev is telling the truth, and we have certain grounds for believing that he is, then this man must either be safely hidden, isolated—or else he is dead, or else he is long gone. Because he's the link between all the threads in this picture (if, I repeat, Gochiyaev has told the truth). And it's impossible to refute what Gochiyaev has stated, because there's certainly are a significant number of documents and facts connected with his firm and his business. He can't lie about that.

LITVINENKO: In answer to your question, I want to say the following. Concerning the motive. I wouldn't want to be accused again of ... Unfortunately ... I sometimes give interviews, try to explain, and there are cases when, for instance, a phrase is taken out of context and given a completely different meaning from what was said. Therefore, I now want to give a [relatively simple] explanation. Concerning the motive.

I'm not defending anyone. We're being told that Hattab placed an order with Gochiyaev, and that Hattab's motive was revenge for their defeat in Dagestan. (This was a declaration made by Lieutenant General Mironov, director of the operational investigative agency that conducts searches—a department in the FSB.) In other words, the motive is the defeat in Dagestan. That's it, completely straightforward.

Now let's take a closer look. If a person has a motive. . . Let's take person X. If person X has a motive to commit a crime as revenge for being defeated somewhere, and if he was defeated in August, then he will plan this crime after August. Right? First he was defeated, then he had a motive, and then he starts planning it. But if person X was defeated in August—between the 7th and the 26th of August—then he can't start planning his crime in July. You see how absurd that is?

Premeditated crimes cannot be without a motive. A crime can't be planned before a motive exists. Any lawyer will tell you that—go ahead and ask, you have respected lawyers there, and they will explain to you that a crime cannot be planned before there is a motive. Everyone understands this. You have to establish the motive. If we're accusing a person of committing a crime, the first thing we must do is to establish a motive: why did he do it? And only then do we start sorting out what he did in order to realize his intentions.

About the Wahhabis. I'm not a specialist in the Koran, in Islam. I didn't serve in the units that deal with fighting dissent, political parties, and various religious movements. I served in a unit that dealt with fighting terrorism and organized crime. By the way, my last position was director of a sub-unit that searched for people who were on the international wanted list. So I can't answer this question in detail. But if you're interested, I can study the documents connected with Wahhabism, and at our next meeting I can give you more. . . Or to invite specialists who understand what Wahhabism is as a religion, what this religion is, what it's founded on, and what motivates the people who join one or another religious group.

MOSKALENKO: Hello. I have a question—or rather a recommendation. It's possible (you assume that it's possible) that Gochiyaev will want to collaborate with the Commission. In that case, I would like to provide him with our recommendations—if, of course, he can hear us now.

One of our colleagues has just now told us that it's impossible to refute Gochiyaev's statements. For the moment, I'd like to say that it's just as impossible to refute them as it is to corroborate them. If he has any, I would call them, permanent traces—in other words, facts that cannot be erased and are easy to identify, easy to establish—he must tell us about these facts, and we'll be able to check them, up to a point. That is the recommendation I would make.

Otherwise, we will study your documents, materials, and the members of the Commission will have other questions for you.

LITVINENKO: Fine, I will certainly convey your request. But I'd like to say that the materials that Gochiyaev sent contain his address, his place of residence at that time, his autobiographical data, which can be checked. Also, people who saw him at different times can be questioned. We also have the location where, according to the official account, he went through training in terrorist camps in Chechnya. By looking at the times, you can determine where and how long he stayed.

But again, what is it I want to tell you? I want to turn to the law enforcement agents, to the people with whom I worked side by side for twenty years. I want to ask these people to help you. Because it will be extremely difficult for lawyers to do this on their own. Or at least, not to interfere, do you understand?

LATSIS: You know, if the Commission has no objections, we will give the floor to the reporters? I'm afraid that we're not leaving them much time.

KOVALYOV: You anticipated my suggestion. And I would like to say that the Commission will prepare its questions and submit them to you soon. There are many questions. But now, we should probably give the press an opportunity.

I would like to make one brief comment. Your words, my respected London colleagues, have one recurring theme: All the steps in the investigation must be transparent from the very beginning. Allow me to disagree with you. I will explain what I mean.

The Commission will undoubtedly publish a vast and detailed report about its work—when it considers it feasible and useful to do so, when this work nears its completion. To make all the intermediate steps public? You know, I'm somewhat surprised. After

all, Mr. Litvinenko has participated in similar investigations. And
I don't have to be a mind reader to see that you're firmly committed to one specific account of the events (by the way, I note again
that the Commission has no single account and is not examining
any single account—it's examining different accounts, as an investigative commission ought to do). You're committed to one, quite
specific account. That is your right. But by making all the steps
transparent from the very beginning—all the intermediate, technical steps—you give the people whom you suspect the opportunity
to see your next step.

You often cite your professionalism in investigative work. Personally, I find this rigid insistence on the absolute transparency of
all technical and intermediate steps very surprising. We in the
Commission have an opportunity to discuss our working principles. My colleagues can correct me, but I believe that most of the
members of the Commission are inclined to hold many working
sessions in private, and consider this expedient, and that the only
thing that can be open, absolutely transparent and absolutely
detailed, concealing no details, is the final conclusion.

I considered it necessary to make this remark specifically
because you, Alexander, and you, Yuri, are constantly insisting on
the opposite. I urge you to give this some thought.

ASHOT NASIBOV: In the press release for reporters that we have
received here it says that Gochiyaev was given a video camera,
through the intermediary, for recording his answers, and that he
sent back a video recording and several photographs. We've been
shown the photographs. Why not show the video to the reporters?

FELSHTINSKY: You know, for purely technical reasons, we don't
quite understand how to do this. Yes, we are certainly ready to place
the videotape at the disposal of the reporters. This is a very short-
term issue, connected with the technical transfer, with the practical transfer of this information into the hands of the reporters.

LITVINENKO: We'll be glad to give you a copy.

FELSHTINSKY: Unfortunately, we cannot now come to Moscow.

ZOYA ORYAKHOVA (*Prima* news agency): I have two questions.

Yesterday in Paris the Spokesman for the Chechen Democratic Association, Borzali Izmailov, held a press conference. He stated that Gochiyaev's statement was in the hands of the Chechen public commission for the investigation of the bombings. He made this document public and said that, in his opinion, you had obtained it through an American reporter. Do you have a comment on this statement?

Second question. In his declaration Gochiyaev states that he is prepared to make a public declaration before the press, but he thinks the guarantees for his safety in a third country will not be any better. Could you help Gochiyaev make a public appearance in a third country?

LITVINENKO: About the possibility of Gochiyaev meeting with reporters and making a statement before the press: we will definitely ask this question, only I don't know how he will arrange it. Frankly, that's his problem—how to organize it. I cannot travel to a third country. I'm not a law enforcement agent. Nor can we undertake a secret operation, you understand. The transfer of a person to another country is a secret operation that we have no means or authority to organize.

FELSHTINSKY: About the publication of Gochiyaev's materials in the Chechen media (on the Internet, as I understand it): this is just another indication of their authenticity, proving that the Chechen side also accepts their authenticity. We received these materials directly, without any tricky maneuvering. I don't know what they mean when they say that we obtained them through an American reporter.

YUSHENKOV: These materials are authentic—*Prima* news agency?

LITVINENKO: We now have an opportunity to check: we can look at Gochiyaev's handwriting. I think the passport office will have a sample. We can ask his wife, his sister. She will bring us his letters, notebooks, records, and we can check: is the handwriting his or not his? That's not a problem. It's easily done.

EZHENEDELNY ZHURNAL: From what it says in the press release that we received, your contacts with Gochiyaev's representative took place in March–April. Why is this information being made public only now, four months later? What have you been doing for these four months?

LITVINENKO: First, we were verifying the materials, verifying everything we could. Second, we were getting in touch with members of the Commission and asking them to make these materials public. We made our request to make these materials public, I think, about one or one-and-a-half months ago, after additionally verifying them, and the 25th was set as a date. We saw no need, when we received the materials, to run somewhere with them that very day. They had to be verified. We also had to establish a contact—to let them know that we were going to publish them, that we were going to make them public-and to wait for an answer. So that, for instance, the contact wouldn't disappear in case there were any additional questions. There's a certain question of correctness here.

FELSHTINSKY: Also, two other considerations. First of all, it took some time before the information from Gochiyaev produced concrete results. And also, as has already been said, we were getting expert opinions about the photographs.

KOMMERSANT NEWSPAPER: Could you give us the name of the lab of the expert who considers the photo of Hattab with Gochiyaev a fake?

LITVINENKO: This is his business card, his name—

KOMMERSANT: That's all in the press release. Name the lab where he works.

LITVINENKO: ... This person is an official expert. He gives testimony in British and international courts. I know that yesterday he got phone calls from reporters. He was giving expert testimony in a British court. He has a license. Here, for example, is a notarized confirmation of his findings.

KOMMERSANT: Why don't you show the videotape you received?

FELSHTINSKY: That's a question for those who arranged the technical transfer of the documents. I don't know much about this side of things. But I know that the photographs were delivered, but . . . You yourself can come or ask someone—we'll give it to you. We'll make multiple copies. That's not a problem. Currently, there are only two or three copies of the tape. Also, we didn't know up until the last moment what format the photographs and texts were going to be delivered. . . . The texts and photographs were sent to us only, I think, either today, or late yesterday. That's basically it. I repeat, this is just a question of time.

KOMMERSANT: A question for Mr. Felshtinsky. You mentioned some additional testimony from a certain Batchaev, who claims that Hattab has no relation to the bombings in Moscow, and that Gochiyaev doesn't either. Who are the people making these claims?

FELSHTINSKY: These are very well-known people. These are the people who are accused by the Federal Security Service of organizing the bombings in Moscow and Volgodonsk. These are the people who are currently being rather actively pursued by the FSB in Georgia. These are the people about whom the FSB declares (such a declaration was made, I believe, two days ago to one of the wire news services) that the question of their arrest is only a matter of time, a short period of time. I readily believe that the question of their arrest may indeed be only a matter of a short period of time.

Precisely because experience shows that people who wind up in the FSB's interrogation rooms for some reason give testimony that is advantageous exclusively for the FSB, and moreover that even this testimony, in contrast to the testimony that we receive in written form and that we make public, is not shown to the public . . . In order to prevent the same thing from happening—when these people end up in the FSB's hands and then start testifying that they got the order to blow up the buildings from Hattab or from some Chechen field commanders—I wanted to make use of this opportunity and to get it down on record that we already have written testimony from Batchaev and from Krymshamkhalov.

And this written testimony, I repeat, does not confirm the FSB's account. Rather, it indicates that neither Hattab, nor any of the Chechen field commanders, nor anyone from the Chechen leadership, was behind the September 1999 bombings or paid money for the organization of the September 1999 bombings, and that completely different people are behind these bombings, namely, I repeat, the Federal Security Service, under the leadership of specific individuals—Patrushev and German Ugriumov.

KOMMERSANT: What is the basis of. . .

LITVINENKO: I want to add to what Felshtinsky has said. When the FSB gives us, for example, Dekkushev's testimony, they give us nothing except the testimony. You know: "Dekkushev said. . ."— and that's it. But [. . .] Gochiyaev has made this declaration, but if the FSB catches Gochiyaev, the FSB will say: "Gochiyaev said this. . ." In other words, besides the testimony, there's nothing else. That's the first thing.

And second, you understand that the FSB is an interested party. In Ryazan, there's direct evidence of an attempt to blow up an apartment building. For two–three years now, Patrushev has been accused of terrorism. This is not just something I am saying. This is something reported by the media. They state openly that Patrushev organized these bombings. And there hasn't been a single coherent response! You see what's going on? Not a single FSB agent came to this meeting . . . They went to the British security services. Why the security services? Because these services are secret. That's why they go to them. They're hoping that I'll pass these materials to the British security services, and that from these security services these materials will secretly pass to Mr. Patrushev, and that we'll never hear anything about them.

That's why I will say one more time: I'm only prepared to answer questions from the security services in public.

FELSHTINSKY: Still, I am afraid that we cut you off and you didn't finish your question—from Russia.

QUESTION: A question from Russia—here, please! Question from Russia!

(*Audience noise.*)

QUESTION: Mr. Felshtinsky, tell us, please, what is this testimony based on? What does Patrushev have to do with it, what does Hattab have to do with it? Nothing is clear.

FELSHTINSKY: The point is that these people are, according to the FSB and in our opinion, the main witnesses in the case of the September 1999 bombings. The General Prosecutor of the Russian Federation has issued an official warrant for their arrest. I repeat: according to the FSB and in our opinion, they are at the very least the principal witnesses (together with Dekkushev, perhaps) in the September 1999 bombings. These are very valuable, very important witnesses. And tomorrow something is going happen to them. If tomorrow, for example, they're accidentally killed while being taken into custody in Georgia, we risk never finding out what they know about the September 1999 bombings in Moscow.

I have the written testimony of both participants (or suspected participants) of these events, stating that they know everything about the events of September 1999 and are ready talk.

SERGEI KUZNETSOV: I have a question from Russia. Sergei Kuznetsov, Radio Liberty, Ekaterinburg edition. A question for Alexander Felshtinsky. Exactly what you were just . . . Excuse me, for Alexander Litvinenko.

September 2 (going back to the book) is the anniversary of the possible signing of the decree that's published in your book: to dissolve the FSB. Don't you think that such a decree would be remarkably appropriate right now? This would give the Commission the best opportunity to work effectively. Has your attitude to this decree changed at all? And, at the very least, would you not recommend that our president immediately remove Mr. Patrushev-at least for the duration of this Commission's investigation?

LITVINENKO: Recommend to Putin to remove someone from their post? I consider this inappropriate. He is a grown man, occupies a high position, and must decide for himself whom to appoint and whom to remove. He is personally responsible for his subordinates.

Regarding the decree. There is a law about terrorism, about the fight against terrorism in the Russian Federation. This law clearly states that any organization which contains elements that are engaged in terrorism must be declared a terrorist organization and dissolved.

But we already have instances when agents of the Federal Security Service committed terrorist attacks: Captain Schelenkov, 1994, the bombing of the railroad; Lieutenant Colonel Vorobyov, the bombing of the bus, before the start of the first war in Chechnya. Based on these facts alone we can already pose a question in terms of the law about fighting terrorism: in general, does the FSB of the Russian Federation—under the current conditions in Russia, within the framework of the current laws and Constitution—does it operate within the bounds of what is acceptable in the country, or doesn't it? If we bring up these facts. . . (*Audience noise*)

YUSHENKOV: Alexander, I understand. Yuri and Alexander, you still haven't answered the question from Kommersant: where did you get the testimony of these new parties about this matter? And on what basis, in general, did they supply you with this evidence, and so on? And what support is there—does the testimony that you obtained have any objective support?

FELSHTINSKY: We were contacted more or less the same way as with Gochiyaev. Yes, people got in touch with us and told us that they wanted to tell the truth, again, about what happened in September 1999. We are now in active contact with these people. Naturally, as always, this contact isn't direct but through their intermediaries. I don't even know how to answer this question more precisely. These people, I repeat, are either participants or at least witnesses. They claim that they know everything [. . .]—everything about what happened in Moscow in September 1999.

Alexander asked them questions, many questions, to which they gave extensive answers. And from their answers to these questions (absolutely specific, so to speak, concrete questions, that we asked) a very clear picture emerges.

I repeat: this picture is that no Chechens, on any level, not even the hired Hattabs and so on, had anything to do with ordering the bombings in Moscow and Volgodonsk (and in Dagestan, by the way) in 1999, that this whole bombing campaign was organized by the Federal Security Service. I repeat: specific people are named.

YUSHENKOV: Yuri, when will you send us these materials, this testimony?

FELSHTINSKY: You must understand, and I hope that the reporters will understand this also, that Alexander and I are both private citizens, we don't have ID's in our pockets, we don't have gun holsters on our belts, we don't have Russian or foreign law enforcement behind us. The work we're engaged in, which is actually quite difficult, exhausting, and even dangerous, is directed against a very powerful apparatus, which is called the Federal Security Service, that has tens of thousands of people working for it. While we strive to be as open as possible—going back to the question of openness—and to make public each new bit of evidence in this independent investigation of ours as quickly as possible—we (I hope you'll understand) must devote some attention to the safety of our work. And at this stage, right now, I don't want to give you the pieces of information that we already have, simply because, I repeat, these are people with whom—in contrast to Gochiyaev, with whom we're not currently in active contact—we are in active contact with Krymshamkhalov and Batchaev, and we're constantly receiving small installments of new information and new. . .

YUSHENKOV: Yuri, that's fine. Since the topic for today is only Gochiyaev, let's [not] go into the topic of. . .

LITVINENKO: Sergei, I would also like to say, to point out, that we ourselves are constantly being watched. For example, Russian intelligence agents recently tried to enter my apartment. My wife didn't let them in. It was shown in court that they were not diplomats but Russian intelligence agents. Their documents [are in court], I can show them to you. You see what's going on? My relatives are being pressured. My close relatives, who come to visit me here, are detained and searched in Sheremetevo, strip-searched, you understand? My 65-year-old mother-in-law was strip-searched in

Sheremetyevo-2. There are constant threats. Over there is Mr. Trepashkin, the lawyer. He'll confirm that they threatened me, that I'll be killed, thrown under a train, if I don't stop. You see what's happening?

YUSHENKOV: No, we understand your position. . .

LITVINENKO: These facts I'll also present to your Commission. I'll give you these facts.

YUSHENKOV: Fine, fine.

LITVINENKO: Why are they doing this? Because they're not interested in being objective.

YUSHENKOV: Please, next question.

ROSBIZNESKONSALTING INFORMATION AGENCY: I have a question for Tatiana Morozova. If I'm not mistaken, earlier you announced your intention to file a lawsuit against Russia in connection with the inadequate investigation of these bombings, in which your mother died. Tell us, please, have you acted on your intention, have you brought charges?

MOROZOVA: Yes, we filed a lawsuit and now the lawyers are handling it. The lawsuit was filed at the Lublin Municipal Court on March 4 of this year, right before the press conference on March 5.

I'm very grateful to you, respected reporters and members of the press, for coming to this studio. I hope that my plea, my appeal, will reach all the people who answered those phone calls that Alexander spoke about, at the 03 emergency service, and the 911 emergency service. I hope that these people will respond and get in contact with the Moscow Commission that is investigating this tragedy. I truly hope that people will respond. I think that their hearts have not yet become frozen and that help will definitely come to us. Please, convey my appeal.

YUSHENKOV: Yes. . . Thank you. Who has questions? Raise your hand, so we can see.

LEV MOSKOVKIN: I have a more ideological question. At the present time the position of the security services in the public consciousness is remarkably firm, in contrast to ago. Even if we take your side and accept your arguments—how should we understand them? What are you hoping to accomplish, what are you trying?

YUSHENKOV: I think we've all said that we're investigating facts and want to determine the truth. *El País*, please.

LEV MOSKOVKIN: That's probably a question for everyone, both for the Commission and for you. . . Well, you haven't answered. . . Alexander, the question is to you.

LITVINENKO: I want to say the following. These bombings that happened—they affected every Russian family. How? Some people died under the rubble of these buildings. Some people are now fighting in Chechnya—the President of Russia has said explicitly that these bombings were the *causus belli*. Some people are now fighting in Chechnya, dying, killing. As for the majority of Russia's citizens, they have exchanged their freedom in return for safety. In other words, the people of Russia have given the law enforcement agencies permission, in return for their own safety, to search the trunks of their cars, to enter their apartments. They are forced to patrol the doorways of their buildings, and cannot walk twenty meters away from their apartment without a passport in their pocket, a residence permit, some type of registration. That's what we're talking about, you see.

And that's why I think that everyone must now define his own civic stance. And every Russian citizen must take an interest in discovering the truth. I want to find this truth, you understand? And to use, among other things, the experience that I have of twenty years in law enforcement. I'm not the most experienced agent. Nor am I an inexperienced agent. I have served for twenty years, and I would like to devote the knowledge that I have to finding the criminals responsible for these bombings. That's my position.

YUSHENKOV: *El País*, Spain.

EL PAÍS: I have a very specific question. Gochiyaev's testimony from April 24 shows that a certain man paid him a visit at his firm, a man whom he knew very well, and from the text it follows that this is the man who set him up. So the question is: why isn't this man named?

YUSHENKOV: This question has already been asked.

EL PAÍS: Already been asked? I'm sorry. But is this man from the FSB or not? (*Audience laughter*)

FELSHTINSKY: The last time Alexander Litvinenko answered, so I'll answer now. You see, what we've shown you, what we've received, is, I repeat, the first and so far the only written testimony of Gochiyaev's that we possess. I repeat: the assumption was—for Gochiyaev evidently, and for us of course—that this contact would continue.

On what grounds did Gochiyaev choose not to reveal the man's name (which we were very interested in, and believe me, this question was posed repeatedly and insistently)—I cannot now say. But as Alexander explained, to determine this man's name is a couple of days' work for any investigator.

NEZAVISIMAYA GAZETA: I have a question for the members of the Commission. Mr. Kovalyov, you said that you're making use of official inquiry requests—sending letters to various agencies, government offices. I'd like to know concretely: to what agencies, and how are they reacting? Are they receptive? Who is ignoring you?

KOVALYOV: You see, I deliberately said that today there won't be any details about this issue. There probably won't be any details for quite a while. Why? I'll tell you. We're not limiting ourselves to isolated inquiry requests. We're engaged in an active correspondence. I have some experience from the 60s–80s, if you like. Not every response. . . You make a report about the correspondence only once you clearly understand that the correspondence is over, that everyone's position has been established and will not change. Then you can present it before the public.

YUSHENKOV: Some people have given very detailed answers.

KOVALYOV: The most substantive and detailed answer came from the Minister of Education, Mr. Filippov.

YUSHENKOV: Simply about hexogen. About that research institute.

As I understand it, there are no more questions. Our thanks to the reporters. Thank you. We'll conclude this part of the meeting for today, yes? Do the members of the Commission have any questions? When will we have our next meeting? Yes, fine. Respected reporters, thank you. Maybe we'll call a break and then meet in here? All right, so we'll call a break for the Commission members. Goodbye.

AN OPEN LETTER TO THE COMMISSION
FOR THE INVESTIGATION OF THE
APARTMENT-HOUSE BOMBINGS
IN MOSCOW AND VOLGODONSK
BY KRYMSHAMKHALOV AND BATCHAEV

Esteemed Commission!

By force of circumstances we have found ourselves accomplices in a crime that took the lives of almost three hundred people. We are referring to the terrorist acts of September 1999 in Moscow and Volgodonsk.

Since then we have been declared wanted criminals at the federal and international levels and been obliged to hide from the law enforcement agencies of the Russian Federation.

Since September 1999, the special services of Russia have undertaken repeated attempts to arrest us or eliminate us. As a result of the statement made recently by Gochiyaev and ourselves in recent times these attempts have become more determined. It seems that in the near future our fate will indeed be arrest or death.

These are the reasons why we wish precisely at this time to address you in an open letter.

1. We confess to being accomplices in the terrorist acts that took place in Moscow and Volgodonsk in September 1999.

We declare that neither Hattab, nor Basaev, nor any of the Chechen field commanders had any connection whatsoever with the terrorist acts of September 1999.

We met Hattab and certain field commanders for the first time only after we had fled to Chechnya to evade pursuit by the Russian law enforcement agencies following the terrorist acts.

2. We are accomplices in the terrorist acts, but at the very lowest level. We had no involvement at all with the actual explosions. We were

only involved in transporting sacks, which we believed to contain explosives, for temporary storage and for subsequent use to blow up administrative buildings of the special services and military buildings, not apartment-houses.

We did not expect that the explosions would take place where the sacks were stored, in the basements of apartment-houses. We did not know when the terrorist acts were to be carried out.

Having learned of the explosions we fled to Chechnya.

3. Not being Chechens by nationality, we were sincere supporters of the Chechen people's struggle for independence. It is precisely these views which allowed the people who were really behind the organization and execution of the terrorist acts in Moscow and Volgodonsk in September 1999 to recruit us to take part in the terrorist acts. Today we understand that they pulled the wool over our eyes and that in 1999 we did not understand who our commanders actually were and for whom we were working.

Today we understand and we know. It has taken almost three years to come to terms with what happened, to gather the information and the proof of who actually was behind the explosions.

Many of those who took part in the September 1999 operations in Moscow, Volgodonsk, Ryazan and Dagestan are no longer alive. As long as we are alive, we want everyone to know what is most important. According to the information we have gathered, received from various participants in the operation at various levels, the instigator of the bombing operation in Russia in September 1999 was the Federal Security Service (FSB) of the Russian Federation. In connection with this, the name of the director of the FSB, Nikolai Patrushev, was mentioned repeatedly.

The curator of the entire bombing program was German Ugriumov, who was subsequently eliminated, according to our information, by the FSB. According to our information the total number of members of the group was over thirty. We know only two of them as mid-level managers: 1) a lieutenant colonel, a Tatar by nationality, with the nickname Abubakar; 2) a colonel, a Russian by nationality, with the nickname Abulgafur. We assume that Abulgafur and the well-known Russian special services agent Max Lazovsky are one and the same person.

4. We have been implicated in this tragedy for the Chechen and Russian peoples. We beg forgiveness from those to whom we brought grief in September 1999. We also beg forgiveness from the Chechen people for being used by the FSB, which led to the second Chechen war. We do not ask leniency for ourselves and we shall dedicate the remainder of our lives to the Chechen people's struggle for independence.

Yusuf Krymshamkhalov, Karachaevan,
born November 16, 1966   [signature]

Timur Batchaev, Karachaevan,
born June 27, 1978   [signature]

July 28, 2002

APPENDIX 6

A. LITVINENKO, Y. FELSHTINSKY:
LETTER TO S. KOVALYOV ABOUT
A. GOCHIYAEV'S STATEMENT

To the Chairman of the Public Commission for the
investigation of the bombing of apartment blocks in Moscow,
Deputy of the State Duma of the Russian Federation
S. A. Kovalyov, Moscow

London, July 25, 2002

Dear Sergei Kovalyov!

We are forwarding to you materials on the testimony of ACHEMEZ
GOCHIYAEV for consideration at a session of your Commission.

Yours truly,

Alexander Litvinenko   *Yuri Felshtinsky*

THE TESTIMONY OF ACHEMEZ GOCHIYAEV

Materials for a session of the Public Commission for the
investigation of the bombings of apartment blocks in Moscow
Prepared by Alexander Litvinenko and Yuri Felshtinsky
July 25, 2002

1. *The circumstances of contacts with Gochiyaev*

In late March 2002 an unknown individual phoned Yuri Felshtinsky
and offered information concerning Gochiyaev.

We did not make a decision immediately. The second telephone
call from the unknown individual was received in mid-April. Agreement was reached for a meeting in one of the European countries.

In late April 2002, a meeting took place between Felshtinsky and Litvinenko and a messenger. The messenger was given a list of questions for Gochiyaev concerning (1) the authenticity of Gochiyaev's identity and (2) the circumstances of the terrorist acts in Moscow in September 1999, and also a video camera for recording Gochiyaev's answers.

Several days later in a different European country a meeting took place with a certain intermediary. We were given a video recording and several photographs establishing Gochiyaev's identity and also his written testimony.

The materials were received without payment, no money or valuables were handed over for them (with the exception of the video camera, which was not returned due to the difficulty of sending technical equipment across national borders).

2. *The authenticity of Gochiyaev's identity*

Having studied the photos, the video materials and Gochiyaev's testimony, in which he stated that he was not connected with Hattab and Basaev, in one of our conversations with an intermediary we asked him to obtain from Gochiyaev a reply to a question concerning the authenticity of a photograph showing him with Hattab that was published on the official site FSB.ru. Several days later the intermediary informed us that it was not Gochiyaev in the photograph, but some other man.

In order to verify this claim we contacted an independent expert, Geoffrey John Oxley.

The independent expert was provided with eight photographs. Nos. 1 and 2 were displayed on the internet site FSB.RU, in the "Wanted" section; four photographs (Nos. 3, 4, 5, and 6 were received from Gochiyaev, and also two photographs including Hattab that were displayed on FSB.RU (Nos. 7 and 8).

The conclusion of the expert was that photos Nos. 1–6 show Gochiyaev. From this it follows that photos Nos. 4–6, which we received from Gochiyaev, really do show Gochiyaev. As for photos Nos. 7 and 8, which the FSB claims show Hattab together with

Gochiyaev, expert analysis established that the photos were not originals and appeared to have been subjected to digital processing (in other words photomontage).

In answer to the question of whether the man shown in photos Nos. 1–6 and photos Nos. 7–8 are one and the same person, the expert said that photos Nos. 7 and 8 are not criminalistically reliable and cannot be used as proof.

3. The essence of Gochiyaev's testimony

Gochiyaev provided rather detailed biographical information about himself (schooling, army service, place of employment). In addition he indicated that beginning in 1996 he lived in Moscow at the following address: Apartment 188, House 6, Marshal Katukov Street, where he was officially registered. From 1997 he was the head of the firm Kapstroi–2000.

Gochiyaev claims that in June 1999 he rented space for commercial purposes in the basements of the buildings that were subsequently blown up, and also in two other buildings where explosions were averted: in Kopotnya and at Borisovye Prudy Street. He claims that he was used "blind" to rent these spaces by a man whom he had known "from his school days" and who in his opinion is a FSB agent.

It was precisely this man who on the morning of September 9 informed Gochiyaev that there had been a small fire at his storage facility on Guryanov Street and asked Gochiyaev to come to the site of the incident immediately.

After the second explosion on September 13, Gochiyaev realized that the storage facilities he had rented were being blown up and immediately informed the duty offices of the police, the emergency medical services, and the 911 rescue services of the possibility of further explosions at Borisovskye Prudy Street and Kopotnya.

This is the most important part of Gochiyaev's testimony. He was the individual who warned the authorities about the two other storage spaces in Kopotnya and at Borisovskye Prudy Street (where afterwards stockpiles of material with explosives and six timers were discovered), thereby averting further terrorist attacks.

Gochiyaev also denies that he is connected with Basaev and Hattab, that he underwent training at a camp at Urus-Martan, and that he was rewarded financially for the explosions.

Gochiyaev claims that there is an FSB order "not to take him alive," referring to information from his relative who works in the police in the town of Karachaevsk.

According to Gochiyaev, his sister was beaten by the FSB in order to make her give knowingly false testimony against him.

4. Recommendations

- Confirm Gochiyaev's biographical details as indicated in his statement (schooling, military service, residence and employment in Moscow).
- Hold an exhaustive investigation into the episode of the discovery of explosive devices in Kopotnya and at Borisovskye Prudy Street. In particular, determine who reported these addresses and under what circumstances. Requisition and listen to the tape recordings of messages received on September 13, 1999, in the duty offices of the Ministry of the Interior (MVD), the emergency medical services, and the rescue services.
- Ascertain which subunits of the law enforcement agencies responded to these emergency calls. Determine the reasons for which, following the discovery of the explosives and six functioning timers at Borisovskie Prudy Street and in Kopotnya, no ambush was set to detain the terrorists. And determine why this information was instead given to the media.
- Verify Gochiyaev's mobile telephone number and obtain a printout of calls for September 1999. Determine who phoned Gochiyaev at about five A.M. on September 9, 1999.
- Question Gochiyaev's acquaintances in Moscow to establish his whereabouts from September 8 to September 13, and his psychological condition at the time of the terrorist acts.
- Verify whether Gochiyaev's firm Kapstroi–2000 was registered in Moscow. Study Gochiyaev's business operations in Moscow beginning in June 1999. In particular check the mineral water

deal which according to Gochiyaev he conducted with the man whom he regards as "an FSB agent" and who used him, Gochiyaev, as a patsy.

• Question Gochiyaev's acquaintances, relatives and employees in order to establish the identity of the man who he says proposed the renting of the basements.

• Request that the law enforcement agencies of other countries-in case they should arrest Gochiyaev—not hand him over to the FSB, which in numerous cases is proven to have concealed information, destroyed evidence, intimated witnesses, falsified evidence, and employed prohibited methods of investigation. Gochiyaev, who is an important witness to terrorist acts, must be questioned by independent and impartial investigators.

APPENDIX 7

WRITTEN STATEMENT BY A. GOCHIYAEV, APRIL 24, 2002

Below we publish the written testimony of A. Gochiyaev, as given to us on April 24, 2002, in full, with the author's spelling and punctuation retained.

April 24, 2002

My name is Achemez Gochiyaev. I was born on September 28, 1970 in the city of Karachaevsk in the Karachaevo-Cherkessia Republic, formerly the Stavropol Region.

Till the age of 16 I lived in Karachaevsk and graduated from secondary school No. 3. I lived at apartment 34, 14 Kurdzhiev Street. On graduation from school I went to Moscow to study, there I entered Technical Training College No. 67 to study, which was at the Pervomaisky station. A year later I graduated from the college and was drafted into the army. Then I underwent training in the Strategic Rocket Forces in Belarus for half a year and served the rest in Siberia, the Altai Territory, and the Pervomaisky village. After the army for about two years I was at home, then I went back to Moscow and worked, tried to do business. In 1996 I got married, got a residence permit and I am registered at apartment 188, 6 Marshal Katukov Street, Strogino. I started my own firm building cottages and trading. The firm was called "Kapstroi 2000."

As for the FSB's claims that I am the organizer of the explosions in Moscow, that I have links with Basaev and Hattab and that they paid me 500,000 US dollars for these explosions, that I underwent training at a camp at Urus-Martan, all these claims are absolute lies.

I never had anything to do with the FSB or any other analogous law enforcement authorities.

As I have written earlier, I lived and worked in Moscow. In June 1999 a man came to my firm—a man I knew very well from the school years. He offered me to do business with him; he said that he has good opportunities for food retail. At first he ordered mineral water. I delivered it to him; he sold it and paid me on time. Then he said that he needs storage space in Moscow's southeast, where he supposedly has retail stores. I helped him rent these sites on Guryanov Street, Kashirka, Borisovskie Prudy and Kopotnya.

On September 9 I was at a friend's house, and at 5 A.M. this man called me on my mobile and told me there was a small fire in the basement storage on Guryanov Street and that I must go there right away. I said that I would come and began to get ready. I turned on the television and saw what had really happened and I decided not to go anywhere and wait it over.

On September 13 when the apartment building on Kashirskoye Highway exploded, I definitively realized that I've been set up. I immediately called the police, the emergency medical service and even the "911" rescue service, and told them about the basements at Borisovskie Prudy and Kopotnya, where they were subsequently able to avert the explosions.

I was declared a suspect, then an organizer of the explosions, and since then I have been forced to go into hiding.

Having analyzed all these events, I come to the conclusion that this entire monstrous plan was developed and executed by the people who profited from it at the time. But there was something that went wrong in their plan: the fact that I was able to escape from them. I think that the fact that I wasn't at home but at a friend's house on September 9 has played an important role.

Now I am almost positive that the man with whom I worked (I will supply information on him later) is an agent of the FSB.

Internal affairs employees of the city of Karachaevsk, following Moscow's request, pointed out in the documents they prepared for me that I am a native of Chechnya, in order to somehow tie me to Chechnya. In truth, I have never lived in Chechnya.

From my brother Boris Gochiyaev, who works in the district division of the police, I found out that they had an order not to take me alive. Then I realized that the publicity the FSB had given me announcing that I was a terrorist, the organizer of the explosions, a inveterate criminal etc., that all that was done deliberately; they were hoping to eliminate me and trumpet to the entire country and the whole world that the "super-terrorist" had been exterminated who had blown up houses in Moscow and so close this terrible business.

Regarding my sister, I know that she was frequently questioned; first they offered her money, then they intimated her, threatened her, beat her and tried to force her to testify against me, so that she would publicly admit that I executed these blasts. After that, they put her husband Taukan Frantsuzov in prison, accusing him of involvement in the Moscow blasts. Later the accusations, as everyone knows, were found to be insufficient, but he was still convicted of being a part of some criminal group and sentenced to 13.5 years in prison. I consider this to be revenge against me. (Should it become necessary I will be able to provide witness testimony of my sister, only I will need some time.)

As far as Ryazan is concerned, I've never even been there and I don't know that city.

To answer the question of whether I am ready to come to a third country in order to make a public statement . . . In the situation in which I have found myself, no guarantees regarding my safety exist; regarding a public statement, I am ready to meet with a journalist (or journalists) and answer all their questions.

This is a brief description of all the events that have taken place (we will talk about the details later).

APPENDIX 8

PRINTOUT OF THE INTERVIEW
WITH A. GOCHIYAEV

August 20, 2002

The interview was given to someone he "knew well" and recorded with a video camera. As proof of the tape's existence we were sent the first minute of the video interview. The handwritten transcription was sent to us on January 18, 2003. The text has been noted down from the videotape with many inaccuracies. A precise printout of the first minute of the videotape is given below. However, to judge from this first minute of the video interview, there are no substantial distortions of meaning. In the text of the handwritten transcription, on the initiative of the owners of the tape the names of two people, (K.) and (Kh.), have been omitted, as we were warned that they would be. The people who control Gochiyaev and own the tape were expecting to get from us money precisely for these names.

Text of the first minute of the interview, checked against the tape:

QUESTION: Tell us about yourself, where were you born?

ANSWER: My name is Achemez Gochiyaev. I am a native of Karachaevo-Cherkessia. Until 1988 I lived in the republic. In 1988, after graduating from secondary school, I went to study in Moscow, was drafted into the army, then went back and lived in Moscow again. Until September 1999 I lived in Moscow. I lived in Moscow in the Strogino Region, on Marshal Katukov Street.

QUESTION: How did it happen that precisely your name began to be linked with the blowing up of houses in Moscow? The special services of Russia accuse you directly of organizing these explosions. (*Recording breaks off*).

PRINTOUT OF THE HANDWRITTEN TRANSCRIPTION
OF A. GOCHIYAEV'S VIDEO INTERVIEW,
AUGUST 20, 2002

The spelling and punctuation of the original document have been retained.
   In this interview a great deal is left unspoken. The first and last names
of currently active fsb employees involved in these events are known. To this
day they are living peacefully in their homes and occupy high positions.
   This is the only interview. The correspondent is a person he knows well.

QUESTION: Can you introduce yourself please?

ANSWER: I am Achemez Gochiyaev. I was born in the Karachaevo-
   Cherkessia Republic. Until 1988 I lived in the Karachaevo-
   Cherkessia Republic. After graduating from school in 1988 I
   went to Moscow, to study. From there I was drafted into the army.
   I went back and lived in Moscow again. Until September 1999, I
   lived in Moscow on Marshal Katukov Street.

QUESTION: How did it happen that precisely your name began to
   be linked with the blowing up of houses in Moscow? The special
   services of Russia accuse precisely you of organizing these explosions. Why is it you they blame?

ANSWER: How did I come to find myself in this situation. In 1997
   I set up a firm for building cottages. I did building work. In the
   summer of 1999 an old acquaintance whom I had known from
   the school days came to the firm to see me. He is called (K.). He
   invited me to go into business with him. He said that he had outlets for selling goods, i.e., food products, and that I should help
   him. I would supply him with various food products, then he
   would sell them and pay me. One time he ordered mineral water
   from me, I delivered it to him and he paid me. Then he asked me
   to help him rent storage space in the south of Moscow, he said he
   had good retail space there. I found four storage facilities, showed
   them to him, and assisted him in renting them. Immediately after
   this the explosion at 9 Guryanov Street took place. That day I was
   not at home, I was at a friend's place. (K.) phoned me on my

mobile and said that there had been some kind of fire at the storage facility and that I had to go there right away. I said, "All right" and started getting ready. It was already almost morning. I phoned for a taxi and switched on the television. On the morning news I saw that there was almost nothing left of the house. That put me on my guard and I waited. And when, a few days later, there was a second explosion on Kashirskoye Highway, I finally realized that I had been set up. I immediately phoned the police and the rescue services and informed them of the other two storage facilities; at Borisovskie Prudy Street, in the Kopotnya district, and another space in a prefabricated garage. After that I had to leave Moscow. I went back to the republic and lived there for a while. Now what can I say. I know that this man (K.) no longer hides the fact that he is an FSB employee, and that he works in the FSB in the city of Cherkessk. I didn't know that before, when I helped him.

QUESTION: Do you think it was precisely (K.) who set you up?

ANSWER: Yes, of course. I'm sure of it, he was the one who did it. Who was with him, how it was done I don't know for sure, or these people either. The only thing I can tell you is that once on my way home I decided to drop in to visit him-he wasn't expecting me. When I walked into his place, there was another man there with him. After I'd said hello, that man left immediately. By following the press and searching the Internet just recently I found out who that man was. He was (Kh.)...!!

QUESTION: Are you sure that is definitely the man you saw?

ANSWER: Yes, I recognized him from a photograph!... Apart from that, in late August and early September (K.) made several trips to Ryazan and asked me to help him there. Supposedly he had outlets for selling goods there as well, but since he had no firm of his own, as he explained to me, he asked me to register the storage facilities with my firm. Before I could do that he found another firm that helped him rent the space. I know for certain that (K.) made a trip to Ryazan at the beginning of September.

QUESTION: Why did he choose precisely you and not someone else to rent these storage facilities?

ANSWER: I think that the point is that I worked in Moscow.

QUESTION: When did you work there?

ANSWER: I was working there in 1997, building cottages.

QUESTION: Was the firm registered?

ANSWER: Yes the firm was called KAPSTROI–2000. My construction office was near the Barikadnoye metro station. There's a two-story building beside the metro.

QUESTION: The press has often presented you as a Chechen, that the terrorist attacks in Moscow were organized by Hattab, and that you were a member of Hattab's group. There's a photograph published on the Internet where you and Hattab are in the same shot. How genuine are these photographs?

ANSWER: I can tell you the following. If you mean the photograph on the Internet where I am supposed to be in a beard and a cap beside Hattab-I've seen that photograph. That man is not me, he doesn't even look that much like me, and it has already been proved that it is a photomontage! Although the Russian FSB claims to this day that it is me. Now we can see and understand why it was done. They needed a Chechen connection. Even in my documents as a wanted man I was described as a Chechen, although my identity documents were issued by the Karachaevsk District Department of the Interior and consequently at the FSB they knew that I am a Karachaevan. They needed to link me with Chechnya. This was why it was done. I never knew Hattab or his group and I had nothing to do with them. But it is now obvious why they did this.

QUESTION: You say that you are innocent. Then why are you hiding?

ANSWER: The reason is that the special services are searching for me. After the explosions in Moscow I went back to my own country, and realizing that they had set me up I knew that I had to go into hiding. I lived for a while in my own country-that was after the events in Moscow in 1999. My own brother was working as the head of the Criminal Investigation Division of the district and he warned me through relatives that they had a secret order not to take me alive, i.e., to eliminate me. He warned me to be careful. He was fired from his position. I also know that the Russian FSB is offering big money to have me eliminated.

QUESTION: But why do they need to have you eliminated?

ANSWER: Because I possess information, I know certain facts, the names of these "people," the employees-the real perpetrators of what happened. It's not hard to check. To this day they are still active employees of the FSB who often visit Moscow.

QUESTION: Why shouldn't you contact the Russian embassy and tell them the way things really were?

ANSWER: There is no point. This system, KGB, FSB-is all one system. The name changes, but the essence, the working methods and the goals are the same. They have a rich pedigree, and there is no sense at all in trusting them. I know it would not do me any good. I am talking now so that the world can know the truth, how it all happened. That is what I am hoping for.

QUESTION: Do you feel any guilt for not trying earlier to tell the world about these events in Moscow? After all, these bombings were one of Russia's motives for the invasion of Chechnya. Why did you not speak out about this sooner?

ANSWER: Only now have people appeared who are willing to listen, interested in the truth being made public. Earlier nobody wanted that. I made attempts, but it went nowhere-people were afraid to expose themselves

QUESTION: Afraid precisely of the Russian authorities?

ANSWER: Yes. They are afraid now, and very afraid.

QUESTION: What else would you like to say? Are there facts that are more convincing?

ANSWER: I've already mentioned certain facts. There are others, a great deal has been left unsaid.

QUESTION: What was it that finally led you to go into hiding from the authorities? When did you realize that it was precisely you they wanted to set up? When did you come to believe this?

ANSWER: Immediately after the second explosion I realized that I had been set up. I had no idea after the first explosion. One thing that put me on my guard was that (K.) didn't tell me what had really happened there. He phoned my mobile and said, "Come over, there's been a little fire," although it was clear from the television report that something terrible had happened. Later on I stopped by there to take a look-it was a horrible sight. I didn't meet with (K.). I came, looked, and left. All those false documents that I supposedly used were prepared by him in advance so their operation would be a success and nothing would go wrong along the way. They didn't expect to not find me at home, or I wouldn't be talking to you now, or to anybody else.

QUESTION: After what happened did anyone get in touch with you?

ANSWER: No. After the 13th I left Moscow. I know that afterwards there were Moscow FSB employees working in our republic. They tried to break down my relatives, frightened them very badly. I heard they first offered my sister money. When she refused the threats began and the demands for her to give an interview saying that I was capable of the acts. First bribery, then threats. I know they took her out to the cemetery with her little child, who wasn't even three yet, so that she would give testimony discrediting me, otherwise they would have killed her and her child. Those are the FSB's methods.

QUESTION: What do your friends and acquaintances think about this?

ANSWER: As for my friends and acquaintances: no one who knows me believes that I could have done it.

QUESTION: There is testimony against you from several prisoners?

ANSWER: I know that there are several people who are supposedly also accused of terrorist acts, and these prisoners are giving testimony against me. But knowing the system of the KGB and FSB, there are 150 million people living in Russia and with that system it's always possible to manufacture witnesses for a specific case. This is not a problem for the FSB. And there is another point, too: when they say how it all happened there, the thing that amazes me most of all is the naiveté of our Russian citizens. How can they think that it is possible to bring, as they say, ten tons of explosives into Moscow and carry out an explosion-it isn't possible. Nobody apart from the special services could get away with this. This naiveté of our citizens surprises me greatly.

QUESTION: The mass media are saying that in Western Georgia, in Adjaria, one of the men suspected of involvement in the terrorist attacks in Russia has been arrested and supposedly he is now giving testimony that satisfies the Russian special services. Do you not think it possible that he can give testimony against you? And in general, are you acquainted with this man?

ANSWER: All I know is that a certain Adam Dekkushev has been arrested and he is giving some kind of testimony. I do not doubt in the least that he is giving precisely the testimony that is in the FSB's interests. And that is not surprising, knowing the system. Let us recall one example from history, the arrest of Beria. On the second day after his arrest Beria confessed that he worked for 10 foreign intelligence services. Consequently, everyone who falls into the hands of the FSB says what suits the FSB.

QUESTION: Does it follow from this that all of these testimonies are fabricated and beaten out of the suspects under investigation by force?

ANSWER: Of course. This is no secret to anyone who has fallen into their hands even once, or come up against the system.

QUESTION: Are you not afraid for your life? Are you not afraid of falling into the hands of the special services?

ANSWER: Of course, I do not rule it out. I know that the special services are offering big money to have me eliminated.

QUESTION: Is it a question of elimination?

ANSWER: In the special services it is only a question of elimination. That is, it is not in their interest to take me alive, because I will talk. But it is not ruled out that the same thing could happen to me as to this man. And I will say what they want to hear from me, even if I am signing my own death sentence with my words. The *truth* is what I am saying now, while I am free. Not in their hands.

QUESTION: So you do not offer any guarantee for your own self, that if you are caught you will not give false testimony against yourself?

ANSWER: Of course not. If I end up in their hands, in the hands of the FSB, I will not be saying what I am saying now, I will be saying what they want.

QUESTION: Well if Beria was unable to resist these tortures I think there are probably not many who could stand up against the FSB. And they have a lot of ways of beating information out of you.

ANSWER: Of course.

CORRESPONDENT: Thank you for agreeing to give us an interview. Thank you very much. And we hope that this interview of yours will cast light on the true perpetrators and the instigator of this crime.

ANSWER: I very much hope so too.

WRITTEN STATEMENT BY A. GOCHIYAEV,
FEBRUARY 2005

The General Prosecutor's Office of Russia accuses me of organizing the Moscow apartment-house bombings in the autumn of 1999. I consider myself innocent and accuse the state security services, and specifically the FSB, of perpetrating and carrying out these monstrous bombings.

My name is Achemez Gochiyaev. I want to tell the truth and to make the hidden reality of these events known to everyone. By analyzing all the events that took place prior to these bombings, and the events that took place after them, I have come to the conclusion that this was a premeditated and well-prepared operation of the state security services.

When these events took place, I was living and working in Moscow. I worked in construction. My firm was called K–2000. It was located near the metro station Barikadnaya. In early summer of 1999, an old friend from school-whom I hadn't seen practically since school-called on me at my place of work. His name is Dyshekov Ramazan. He told me that he was living and working in Moscow and that his line of work was food and produce distribution. After that, he visited me a few more times, and one time he made me an offer to go into the mineral water business with him, and asked me to find him suppliers of mineral water. I had someone from my hometown working in my firm—his name was Chinchikov Raul. I gave this job to Raul and he handled all further work between my firm and Ramazan. Our work went well. Ramazan paid on time, there were no problems. After a while, Ramazan asked me to help him rent some warehouse space in southern Moscow and in the city of Ryazan. He told me that he had good points of distribution in these locations. I asked Raul to find some facilities. He found many different options and offered them to Ramazan.

Ramazan, in turn, picked out the ones that suited him. I gave them money to rent these facilities and the two of them together went to rent them. Ramazan rented these facilities in person.

When the bombing in the building on Guryanov took place, I was visiting some friends. Ramazan called my mobile phone and said that he had some urgent business and that we had to meet. He asked me where I was—he called around 5 in the morning. I told him that I would come myself and started to get ready. And when I was already about to leave the house, I saw on the news on television what had happened.

I immediately drove to Guryanov and after everything that I saw there, I decided not to go to meet Ramazan, but to wait a bit. But on September 13, when the second bombing took place in the building on Kashirskoye Highway, and when my photograph was shown on television, I understood that I was being set up. I got in touch with Raul, found out the specifics from him about the other warehouse spaces, then called the police and the emergency services and told them about the buildings at Borisovskie Prudy and Kopotnya. After that, I left Moscow and returned to Karachaevo-Cherkessia. At home I found out from my brother, who was working as a criminal investigator at the time, that there was an intensive search out for me and secret orders from Moscow not to take me alive. From that time until today, I have been forced to remain in hiding.

Now I know that Dyshekov Ramazan officially works for the FSB. At that time, no one could have even suspected him of having any connections with the FSB—he was a secret agent. Chinchikov Raul, who handled business between Ramazan and my firm, was killed shortly after these events took place. His corpse was found in the town of Moskovsky in Karachaevo-Cherkessia. They killed him and tried to burn his body. In this way, the FSB eliminated the main witness in this case.

My relatives and friends are under the harshest pressure from the FSB. They are constantly being interrogated and searched. My sister had to leave the republic after FSB agents took her and her little daughter to a cemetery and threatened to kill the child unless she gave an interview to the press and said that I was capable of doing these things and that I was a mentally unstable person. After that, she feared for her children's lives and had to leave.

There is a photograph of a bearded young man in a black cap on the FSB website, and the FSB presents this photograph as evidence in its favor. I assert that this is a lie. The person in this photograph is not me. A careful comparison of my photograph and the photograph of this man will establish this. In addition, expert testimony has established that this man is not me. And this is the bold-faced lie on which the FSB's whole case against me is based.

Immediately after the bombings my photograph was shown on television and they said on the news that this was the photograph of the man who had rented these warehouse spaces, and that this photograph allegedly came from the copy of a passport that had been left behind in one of the rental offices. But this photograph is identical to the photograph in my actual passport, and as we all know, when a person receives a passport, the passport bureau keeps a copy of the photograph. When the FSB fabricated its case against me, it was no trouble for them to make a copy of the photo and show it on television. There is another significant fact here—the testimony of the person who rented the facilities on Guryanov. When he saw my photograph, he did not recognize me as the person to whom he had rented his facilities. But Dyshekov Ramazan fits the description. I think that if he were shown a photograph of Ramazan, he would recognize him as the person to whom he rented his facilities.

In addition to everything I have said, I have other facts and witnesses that prove that the bombings were prepared and carried out by the Russian state security services. But to this day these people are in considerable danger and for this reason I cannot make these facts fully public. It would be very good if an independent, international investigation of this case were conducted. For my part, I am fully prepared to assist and participate in such an investigation, presenting facts and witnesses. I am certain that only such an investigation can bring to light the real organizers and perpetrators of these bombings.

I have thought a lot about why the security services framed me, a

Karachaevan by nationality, for these bombings. Logically, at that time, they needed to frame Chechens, not Karachaevans. Now this is no longer a secret. The security services were pursuing several aims. They connected these bombings with Chechnya anyway—they were essentially the cause for the war. And second, the FSB was planning and continues to plan a war in Karachaevo-Cherkessia. At the present time, there is a heavy military presence in our republic. A great deal is said about our republic in the media. Before, we were little known as a nation. Now, the whole world knows us, and knows us as dangerous terrorists. In this respect, this FSB has achieved its goal.

Using the media, which they almost entirely control, they regularly report about Karachaevan terrorists. It turns out that not just the Moscow bombings, but practically all terrorist atrocities are committed by Karachaevans. What is needed in order to start a war is an "image of the enemy" and the more frightening this image is, the easier it will be to go to war. Now, if there is a war, everyone will think that Russia is fighting terrorism, although in reality it will be destroying ordinary people. It was for this reason that the security services framed me in these bombings.

And in conclusion I would like to address all the people who want to know the truth about the apartment-house bombings, and in the first place this concerns those who suffered as a result of these bombings. It is imperative that an independent, international investigation be conducted. The government that is now in power in Russia is the government of the FSB. Recall the history of this monstrous organization, how many millions of innocent people became the victims of this organization: now the whole government of Russia is in its hands. What else is there to say when everything is already clear anyway?

ABOUT THE AUTHORS

ALEXANDER LITVINENKO was born in Voronezh in 1962. After graduating from school in 1980, he was drafted into the army and over the next twenty years, he rose through the ranks from private to lieutenant colonel. Beginning in 1988, he served in the counterintelligence agencies of the Soviet KGB, and from 1991, in the Central Staff of the MB-FSK-FSB of Russia, specializing in counter-terrorist activities and the struggle against organized crime. For operations conducted with MUR (Moscow Criminal Investigation Department), he was awarded the title of "MUR Veteran." He saw active military service in many of the so-called "hot spots" of the former USSR and Russia, and in 1997, he was transferred to the most secret department of the Russian KGB, the Department for the Analysis of Criminal Organizations, as senior operational officer and deputy head of the Seventh Section. He is a Candidate Master of Sport in the modern pentathlon. In November 1998, at a press conference in Moscow, he publicly criticized the leadership of the FSB and disclosed a number of illegal orders, which he had been given. In March 1999, he was arrested on trumped-up charges and imprisoned in the FSB prison at Lefortovo in Moscow. He was acquitted in November 1999, but no sooner had the acquittal been read out in court than he was arrested again by the FSB on another trumped-up criminal charge. In 2000, the criminal proceedings against him were dismissed for a second time, and Litvinenko was released after providing written assurances that he would not leave the country. A third criminal case was then instigated against him. After threats were made against his family by the FSB and the investigating officers, he was obliged to leave Russia illegally, which led to yet another, fourth criminal charge being brought against him. He lived with his family in Great Britain, where he was granted political asylum in May

2001. In November 2006 he was poisoned in London by radioactive Polonium-210 and died on November 23, 2006

YURI FELSHTINSKY was born in Moscow in 1956. In 1974, he began studying history at the Moscow State Pedagogical Institute. In 1978, he immigrated to the USA and continued his study of history, first at Brandeis University and later at Rutgers, where he was awarded the degree of Doctor of Philosophy (History). In 1993, he successfully defended his doctoral thesis at the Institute of Russian History of the Russian Academy of Sciences, and became the first citizen of a foreign state to be awarded a doctoral degree in Russia. He has compiled and edited several dozen volumes of archival documents and is the author of the following books: *The Bolsheviks and the Left SRS* (Paris, 1985); *Towards a History of Our Isolation* (London, 1988; Moscow, 1991); *The Failure of World Revolution* (London, 1991; Moscow, 1992); *Big Bosses* (Moscow, 1999).

INDEX

Chubais, Anatoly 38
Chugunov, Gennady 205
Churilov, Oleg 83
CIA xviii, xxix, 218
CIS xxix, 145, 148
Committee of State Security *see* KGB
Commonwealth of Independent States
 see CIS
Communist Party xxi, xxiii–xxv, 4,
 32, 51, 169–70, 189
Communist Youth Organization 4,
 185
Constitutional Court of the Russian
 Federation 214
Cosmic Alternative, bodyguard agency
 23
Credit-Consensus Bank 34
Criminal Procedural Code of the
 Russian Federation 33, 40, 44,
 68, 75, 84, 94, 138, 184,
 214–15, 219, 225
Criminal Investigation Department *see*
 MUR
Croatia xix
Cyprus 192
Czech Republic 200

Dagestan 17, 28, 34, 60, 100–3,
 106–09, 111–12, 114, 117–18,
 121, 134, 143, 146, 161–2, 189,
 209, 217, 245–8, 251, 254,
 270, 280, 286
Dagestani criminal group 34
Dakhkilgov, Timur 134–7, 142
Daniel, Alexander 255
Danilov, investigator 193
Davidovich, Alfonso 104
Dashkovo-Pesochnya office (Ryazan)
 54, 60
Dekkushev, Adam 263, 277–8, 302
Demianenko, Yevgeny 187
Deniev, Adam 217–18, 252
Dinamo subway station (Moscow) 34

District housing management office
 see REU
Djabrailov, Umar 111, 115
Dmitriev, G. F. 225
Dmitriev, L. A. 38, 41
Dokukin, A. A. 38, 41
Dontsov, Vladimir 34
Dudaev, Djokhar 4, 6–7, 9–14, 16,
 18–20, 26–9, 152, 167, 253
Dudaev, Lecha 29
Dudaeva Alla 28
Dulian, cafe owner 201
Duma (State Duma) xix, 12–14, 35,
 37–8, 41–2, 79, 84, 94, 107, 11,
 116, 127, 131, 152–3, 163,
 165–6, 168–70, 179, 197, 202,
 206, 212–13, 215, 228, 230,
 232–4, 242–43, 257, 288
Dyagilev military aerodrom 60, 138
Dyshekov, Ramazan 304–6
Dzasokhov, A. 144

Elders of Zion 149
Electrosvyaz Company 69
Estonia 4
Europe xvi, xxix, 288–9 *see also* West
European Court 195
External Intelligence Service *see* SVR

FAPSI (Federal Agency for Govern-
 ment Communications & Informa-
 tion) xxii, xxix, 31–2, 44, 154,
 205, 227
FBI (Federal Bureau of Investigation
 (USA) xxix, 227
Federal Agency for Government
 Communications & Information
 see FAPSI
Federal Bodyguard Service *see* FSO
Federal Border Service xxii, 17
Federal Counterintelligence Service
 see FSK
Federal News Agency 170

PS

new materials for this edition

UNPUBLISHED INTERVIEW

WITH ALEXANDER LITVINENKO (TAPE EXCERPTS)
BY NICHOLAS LAZAREDES
2003

00:00:26:18 Yes, I've been leaving in London for a bit more than two years now. Of course, it's hard to leave away from my motherland. I miss my home, I miss my friends, but... I want to use this opportunity to thank England, the country that gave refuge to my family and offered us real protection. 00:46:10

00:46:14 Well, emigration is always a difficult thing, especially forced emigration, when you never thought of, never dreamed of leaving your homeland. There are people who live in Russia but want to go to the West – I never had such thoughts, I never wanted that, it just... became a necessity. It was a very hard decision to make both for me and my family. 01:15:14

01:15:18 And I must say that I'm grateful ... to England ... to the British government that made a decision on my case, sorted it out quickly and objectively and granted me political asylum. So the British justice system, the British law-enforcement agencies confirmed that I was a political refugee that I was persecuted in Russia not for criminal reasons... That my motifs were not of a criminal but of political nature. 01:51:00

01:51:04 And of course now... we're getting used to England, so to say... one can say we're putting roots into that soil. My son speaks very pure English now and I'm afraid he's going to forget his Russian. He's turning into an Englishman and I realise that quite well. He is acquiring a mentality of an Englishman. I can see that. He's different... He's different from those children that... that, let's say, grow up in Russia. 02:34:00

02:35:02 It's his... It's the way he sees life. And... My wife also speaks

English quite well. I'm studying English. We're acquiring friends here…
And if, say, I had to go back to Russia right now, if I went back to
Russia… I understand it quite well, that while being in Russia I by now
would have missed London just as I'm missing Moscow now. 03:09:12

03:20:04 Well, my application for asylum… Just a second, may I?…
03:00:25

03:26:10 Marina, Marina, close the door, please, it's too noisy. Please.
Excuse me. 03:31:00

03:35:12 Let's roll it back a bit. I'm sorry. 03:37:00

03:41:04 Well, 1 November 2000 I and my family arrived in London to
the Heathrow airport. Immediately on arrival, I think within an hour, we
addressed the British government and appealed for political asylum. I
was granted political asylum on 3 May 2001. 04:12:00

04:13:00 So, in fact, it took six months. 04:18:00

04:21:08 Well, I was granted political asylum because I was subjected…
because my case was not a criminal, but a political one. I was persecuted
at home because of my political convictions. For the things I said.
04:37:00

05:00:10 Well, I must say that that escape proved to be a very serious trial
for me and my family. … First of all, when I… Before we escaped
Russia… If we consider it stage by stage… First of all, it was very hard
to make a decision, the decision to leave Russia. I understood that if I
leave Russia I'd be leaving it … for a long time. 05:29:21
05:29:30 And I won't be able to come back anytime soon. And I…
thought about it for a long time, so did my wife, before we took that decision. We discussed it. It was a painful, difficult decision. I'd compare it to
suicide. I mean, in fact, it's when a man takes… the question whether to

commit suicide... Well, it was tantamount to suicide. 06:03:21

06:04:00 I understood there'd be no way back. There'd be a new life ahead. And it would be full of things unknown. But I also understood quite well that if I stayed in Russia they wouldn't leave me alone, the Russian secret service, I mean. Because people working in those structures don't know how to forgive. If they start forgiving people, the whole system of secret service would be no more. 06:31:18

06:31:22 I mean, Russian authorities... they don't forgive. Well, this mentality, I'd say, is a Communist mentality. Communists never forgave those who challenged them. And now, unfortunately, that's what perpetuates in Russia, I realised that quire well. 06:56:12

06:56:18 I understood quite well that if I didn't leave Russia, they would never leave me alone, they'd be persecuting me... In the best case I'd be arrested and spend at lest 10 years in prison for nothing. To be left alone I had to recant, to take my statements back. Recant and say, "I'm sorry. I won't do it again" – meaning, "I won't ever challenge the system again." "I won't speak the truth." 07:27:00

07:28:10 And... And that's the best case. In the worst case they'd just murder me ... on my own doorstep, somewhere.

07:38:00 It was quite possible. I was told so. Actually, not a single one of my former superiors cared to dissemble about that. 07:46:18

07:47:00 Well, I can tell you a curious episode. Before we made a decision that I had to leave Russia, naturally it wasn't just my decision, my wife took part as well. I'm telling this to you openly and honestly, so you must understand that it wasn't just my decision. Naturally, I discussed it with those people close to me – my friends and confederates. That, naturally, was Boris Berezovsky and Yuri Felshtinsky (checked). 08:21:10

08:21:14 Well... And, naturally, I didn't wan to leave Russia. And before

I made that decision we tried to make some arrangement with those people at the FSB that were persecuting me… so they might leave me alone or at least refrain from extreme measures. Felshtinsky, Yuri, met my former, the head of my Directorate, General Khokholkov (checked). Khokholkov just said… They talked for quite a long time, a couple of hours I think. 08:53:08

08:53:12 And Yuri asked Khokholkov – I'm sure he'll confirm… Yuri told Khokholkov "You do understand that we're not going to abandon Sasha whatever comes. He's our friend, our comrade and we don't abandon our comrades." From the times… From the times the dissidents were struggling against the Soviet Union these people never abandoned their friends in trouble. That's the reason there's no Soviet Union now and no KGB. 09:24:00

09:24:04 And Yuri told Khokholkov "We're not going to abandon Sasha, we'll keep helping him. Why do you need all this? Leave him alone. He'll get… You dismissed him from the FSB, he'll be getting another job. He's got a wife, a child – let him live in peace," 09:39:00

09:39:20 And Khokholkov said the following… Yuri told me that. He said "Let Berezovsky pay me a figure with six zeroes." That means about… more that a million dollars. It comes to at leas a million dollars. For me it sounded so cynical… If Khokholkov said, "We're not going to leave Litvinenko alone because he challenged the system." – I could have at least understood that. 10:07:00

10:07:04 When Khokholkov… If Khokholkov said, "All right, we'll leave him alone, but he must never defy the system again." – I could have understood that as well. But Khokholkov demanded money, American dollars, mind you. More than a million. And I realised they were bandits. And I realised that in general… I know how influential was Khokholkov. I knew with what kind of people he was associating – Yastrzhembsky, Kokoshin… I mean, Khokholkov could enter any office… including that of Putin. 10:41:21

10:42:00 I understood quite well that the things Khokholkov had been doing he hadn't been doing by himself. He had been doing it all upon consulting with Putin and Patrushev. I realised we were dealing with honest-to-God bandits, who had not a shred of honour or conscience. And simply… You simply cannot treat with those people. And – forget about agreements – I simply wouldn't be able to keep silent. 11:12:00

11:12:04 Because I can… I realised it quite well… It was… That conversation between Felshtinsky and Khokholkov happened in 2000, sometime in March 2000. In March, or perhaps in April… I understood quite well that those people now held power and what they'd be doing with out country. And then I realised I had to escape, really. 11:34:21

11:35:00 Then there came a string of court cases that were breaking the law, that were breaking the constitution… And when the chairman of the Moscow regional military court a lieutenant general answered a question by my lawyer… My lawyer asked him "Why are you breaking the constitution?" And the chairman of the Moscow regional military court, lieutenant general Beznosiuk proclaimed, "Well, you know our system." So he hinted that "We have orders from above, we can't do anything." 12:06:00

12:06:04 And I understood I wouldn't get a fair trial in Russia. That that trial was a fiction. It was just a performance, a comedy of justice – and I had a particular part written for me in that performance. And I had no wish to play that part. And I understood that… that would be just a show-trial. So to save myself, my family, my little kid – I understood I had to run. 12:33:00

12:33:12 Then the threats began… That was when I tried to defend myself at court. I was ready to prove my innocence. I had ironclad proof – like videotapes of interrogations during which… — it was later claimed that I beat suspects into pulp… Though there existed a videotape of an interrogation where that man was questioned by a different person altogether – and nobody laid as much as a finger on him. I have them here in England. 12:57:12

12:57:16 I understood that… Yes, and I was told that if I brought that evidence to court and the court exonerated me – I'd been exonerated twice before that – nobody would be talking to me, they'd just kill my child. That was it. That was said in a very final way and I realised I must escape. And, naturally, we escaped from Russia. That's regarding the time when we lived in Russia. 13:26:00

13:26:04 As for the escape itself… Speaking of the technical side of the problem… The difficulty was that I had no secret/special services backing me. It's one thing if you're working for a secret service or collaborating with a foreign intelligence agency then when you escape the country you have that foreign intelligence service and its agents in place covering you, you get a passport made – or they get you through in a car boot – I had nothing of the sort. I had no secret service backing me up. 13:56:12

13:56:18 The only thing I did have of course, was the money for that escape. Boris Berezovsky helped me, naturally he didn't abandon me – he behaved as a normal human being. And when the question of money cam up Boris said, "Sasha, look. For all practical purposes you saved my life. And it doesn't even matter that you saved my life. What matters that you and me think the same way and we know that with those people in power Russia won't be developing normally. 14:23:04

14:23:08 "It's not only me or you who they'll kill, they'll kill lots of other people. And we must do something that maybe nobody but us can do. We must fight for our ideas, for our convictions and do everything in our power to turn Russia into a normal civilized country. I have the money and I'm going to help you. And say…" 14:46:00

14:46:06 I said… I was feeling uncomfortable; after all we were speaking about money… He said, "You know, — he said, — "if you had the money would you helped me?" I said "Of course, Boris Abramovich." "You see? So I'm going to help you now." But we weren't speaking millions of dollars. It was the kind of money I needed to buy the tickets, to stay at the hotel and... well, to pay for our food. Well... 15:07:00

15:07:05 And you know... I didn't have that kind of money. I just didn't have it. Because I never took bribes, I didn't go into... I didn't go into protection racket milking commercial enterprises like nearly everybody in the law-enforcement agencies did. The FSB too. In Russia. I didn't have the money. I had a pittance... I think... Well, it was a small sum in cash. I think 2.5 or 3 thousand dollars, no more. Where can one go with that kind of money? One one-way ticket and two days at the hotel – that's it, then it runs out. 15:48:02

15:48:06 Well, naturally he helped me with money. He helped me to settle, Boris Berezovsky. He helped me to settle here in England in the beginning, to find my legs. And I'm very grateful to that man. Well... 16:02:21

16:03:00 The most difficult moment of that escape was the time when we were in Turkey... We were followed — now I know beyond doubt that we were followed by the agents of the Russian foreign intelligence service. That was in Ankara. I went to the American Embassy... I was, I was ushered out of there. And I know now that Russia was trying to make Turkey agree to arrest and extradite me. But we still managed to scram out of Turkey and fly to England. 16:37:10

16:37:14 At that moment I had no passport. I had a fake passport of a different state because my own had been stolen during the police search of my house. I had no visa. And we were sitting in a hotel in Istanbul — my wife, a small child who knew something wrong was going on and was very nervous. He asked me "Daddy, where will we be tomorrow?" My wife held out, she is a strong, courageous woman, she held, but she didn't know what would happen to our family tomorrow. 17:10:00

17:10:04 We had a suitcase with our things. We had some money for expenses... I didn't know what would happen to me tomorrow. The only thing I did say to my wife was that under no circumstances I'd allow myself to be taken alive and I would not go to prison again. "Because,- I told her,- I don't want to croak having the stink of prison around me, I'd better die where the air is fresh and the sky is blue. 17:34:21

17:35:00 And... I was looking at my wife, at my child and I was thinking that tomorrow I might be no more. And at that time it was Alik Elfhart (?) who helped me a lot and I'm very grateful to him. He found out, he found out on the net that you don't need a transit visa to go to England — and that's what decided the fate of my family. We managed to get on the last plane, as they say. We got stuck in a traffic jam... and 40 minutes before departure we jumped into that plane — and flew to England. 18:07:21

18:08:00 Sometimes I think God saved me. And when God saves somebody, perhaps He needs it for some reason of His own. 18:16:00

18:35.04 Well. I joined the army... I started working for the army in 1980. I... 18:44:00

18:57:14 I understand. I joined the army in 1980. I started as a private and in 20 years of service I became a lieutenant colonel. I was a vice-director of the most secret Directorate of the Federal Security Service. In principle, I made quite a career in the secret service — at 33 I was a lieutenant colonel, I got that rank ahead of time and actually was one of the youngest lieutenant colonels in the system. 19:25:00

19:27:00 I was transferred to the KGB, to the Committee of the State Security of the USSR in 1988. 1988. I served in the military counterintelligence section. I ended up there because I liked that line of work. It was interesting. I was working with people. There was something mysterious about it. Our papers didn't say that the KGB actually dealt with terrorism. And the job of a counterintelligence officer on an operative installation — and I was servicing the units of the special Dzerzhinsky armoured infantry division — didn't include anything reprehensible. We were exposing people that tried... that stole arms and ammunition or soldiers that intended to escape the unit with their weapons. We did have several such cases — some officers and sergeants were shot. So in fact we were preventing murders. 20:25:00

20:25:12 At the time... and I was involved in field operations since 89, 1989, at that time the 5th, the 6th Article of the Constitution had been already abolished — so that... That's the one on the status of the CPSU. So the KGB no longer worked with ideology. It was the 6th Article, yes, Maria Nikolaevna? Well... it was... an article... Correct me if I'm wrong... An article of the Constitution was cancelled and the KGB practically stopped working with ideology. We didn't charge our agents with finding out who told what joke about whom and who thought what. Our task was to prevent emergency situations, escapes, and, of course, to fight, to limit the activities of the foreign intelligence services. But where would you get foreign agents in an armoured infantry regiment? 21:19:21

21:20:20 Our duties mostly resembled those of a military police though in principle we were a KGB unit. And that unit was a part of the whole KGB system. So... 21:34:00

21:36:16 After the coup of 1991, after the coup failed, I was transferred to the HQ to the unit... to the unit fighting organised crime. That was a unit of the Russian secret service. At that time they created... the Federal Security Agency of the Russian Federation. It reported to Yeltsin. 22:05:21

22:06:00 That's when I started working at the HQ. I was working on the organised-crime-related problems, then I transferred into a counter-terrorism unit. And I served there until 1997. In 1997 I... I and several my colleagues were transferred to the top, most secret unit in the FSB that dealt in — as we later understood as we stared getting our orders — extralegal murder. Our unit received orders from the top officials of our country to liquidate people found disagreeable. 22:49:06

22:49:10 I served in that unit for half a year as a deputy section head... And the fact is we refused to follow the criminal orders of our superiors, actually the unit mutinied, if it needs to be spelt out. Well. 23:09:21

23:10:00 Several sections denounced their superiors to the attorney general's office. For a year an investigation was run on our superiors, then it was illegally closed and we got persecuted in turn. Actually they went after us the first day when we rebelled against our superiors. They started listening to our phone calls and put surveillance on us. Me and my wife were attacked not far from our house. 23:33:21

23:34:00 On several occasions they tried to send me to a mental hospital, to a psychiatrist... Well... It's an old KGB trick, the Fifth Directorate trick... that's the people who maintained the ideology. 23:49:12

23:49:16 When all those things failed, didn't work and persecution grew more severe... When Putin became the FSB Director we were all sacked — on Putin's orders. I was sacked on 10 January 1999. It was his personal signature... Personal... My order of dismissal was signed personally by Putin. 24:15:00

24:16:00 Well... They sacked us, they persecuted us so we made a decision... We realised that we were about to leave the secret service permanently — that they would make a short work of us. So we made a decision, I and five my colleagues made a decision to go to the people, to the parliament and to use the mass media to tell what was happening with the Russian secret service. 24:45:00

24:47:12 And we called a press conference in 1998 where we told everything we knew. Couple of days after that the first criminal charge was brought against me. 24:57:00

24:58:00 As for corruption and criminal activities of the Russian secret service... actually they have historical roots. If you closely read the KGB documentation it becomes clear... that KGB has in fact never been a secret service. Only several small units were involved in counteracting foreign intelligence agencies — i.e. doing what a secret service of a civilised country should be doing. 25:32:00

25:32:04 The main bulk of units and personnel of the KGB, I'd say 70% of all assets and resources that the KGB had at its disposal were busy with maintaining the regime and protecting the communist ideology. In reality it was an appendage, a secret appendage of the Communist Party. 26:00:00

26:00:18 After the Soviet Union... In the Soviet Union, you see, there were two ideologies — the communist one and the criminal one. I mean, the criminal world, it lived by its own laws, and the Communists could do nothing with it. They liquidated the Upright Men (criminal authorities), killed them, shot them, threw them into prisons... but they couldn't do anything. So... In the Soviet Union there were two ideologies — the communist one and the criminal one. 26:31:10

26:31:14 So when in 1991 the Communist Party expired... the communist ideology was superseded by the criminal one. And those people who worked in the KGB for their ideas sake started serving for money's sake. And... since nobody needed the communist ideology any more they made use of the criminal ideology. 27:05:00

27:06:04 It's not an accident, that starting at about 1996 when the FSB command posts became to be filled by people who spent their life fighting the so-called "enemy ideologies", that's the FSB Director, Kovalev Nikolai Dmitrievich, who spent all his life serving in the 5th Directorate units, doing the 5th kinds of jobs, he's the former underling of Bobkov — that's the people who persecuted dissidents. 27:33:00

27:36:00 He was replaced at the post of the FSB Director by Mr. Putin who... though he claims that he served in foreign intelligence — he also all his life… he was recruited as a student by the agents of the 5th KGB Directorate. His first job was within the 5th KGB Directorate. After his posting in Germany he got a job fighting the so-called "enemy ideologies". This man has always served in the 5th Directorate units. The same kind of jobs fell to Mr Patrushev who also all his life run on the 5th D track. In the KGB, I mean. The same story with Mr Cherkesov, the close friend of Putin and his confederate who also served in the 5th D units. 28:16:00

28:16:04 So… all that team… I'll tell you, the only things they knew was how to monitor the mood of the people, how to try to influence what the citizens thought, how to gather gossip, how to gather gossip and fill up files on people — who told what joke about whom… if we're speaking in the everyday life terms. 28:42:00

28:44:00 And… because they were used to… because those people need an ideology and the communist ideology was gone, they adopted a criminal ideology. And it's not an accident that Mr. Putin when speaking on TV or holding press-conferences… we often hear… excuse me, I'm going to quote the President verbatim… I might say something unprintable but I'm repeating after him verbatim "To bump them off in crappers", "to cut off something that will never grow back" — all this comes from a criminal jargon. 29:24:00

29:24:12 And if it might seem to some that he says those things by accident, that it's a slip of a tongue, I'll tell you he doesn't say those things by accident. It's a message to all those people who are part of organised crime groups, it's a message to the corrupt officers in the law-enforcement agencies and our secret service. It's a message to the corrupt officials — that the Russian throne has been taken by the member of their caste, of their social strata. 30:00:12

30:00:16 That they must support him and they must fight to preserve the current Russian regime. And the current Russian regime is criminal, criminal. 30:12:14

30:12:18 And starting from 1996, when I still served in the FSB we started noticing that our colleagues, many of our colleagues appear to spend more than they were supposed to earn, they lived beyond their means. They drove around in expensive imported cars, they spent their holidays at the most expensive resorts, and they had cash… For example I had a colleague that every day carried 10,000 dollars in his pocket. And actually, they didn't even count that money. 30:35:00

30:36:08 Then it got from bad to worse, as they say. You start arresting members of a criminal group — a real criminal group that dealt in murder, protection racket… And as soon as you arrest them you get a visit or a phone call — straight away — from one of your colleagues or your superiors… and you are told that your man must be released because he's on the informant's list of some other unit. That's a cover story. 31:20:08

31:21:00 So they started establishing… the officers started establishing business ties with the leaders of the criminal world. And to legalise those ties, to give them a cover they put those men on the informant's list as our sources. And as soon as you catch him you're told, "You arrested an informant. Let him go." "You arrested an informant. Let him go." 31:43:00

31:43:18 Starting at about 1997 we began catching not just criminals but police and FSB officers… I mean they themselves… they've started committing crimes personally. Let's say we were arresting police officers that were protected by the FSB officers and by the people from the attorney general's office. And we were arresting them not for bribes, not for misuse of authority or exceeding one's commission — we arrested them for such crimes as kidnapping, armed robbery… 32:19:06

32:19:10 I mean, those people formed gangs that robbed, killed and kidnapped people — and our superiors knew what they were. They acted on orders from their superiors who in turn were involved in protection racket, giving "cover" to commercial companies… 32:41:00

32:41:04 After every single such detention or arrest a terrible row would erupt in the Directorate where I was serving, people who took part in those investigations would be hounded and harassed, any work on those cases would be blocked, evidence would be removed... And then it came to direct threats... right up to "How dare you? What right did you have to detain those policemen?" 33:12:04

33:12:08 Let me tell you, right before my dismissal I arrested... It was my investigation... so I participated... I was in command... we arrested a gang made of police officers who dealt in kidnapping, robbery and burglary. They were found guilty. We, I, managed to secure a verdict sentencing them to 9-10 years in prison because we delivered watertight evidence of their criminal activities. But, once again, those who were found guilty were the smallest fry — police sergeants, junior police sergeants... 33:47:08

33:47:12 And when I started reaching for the senior MVD officers, the officers of the Ministry of Internal Affairs, the officers from the very Security Directorate of the Ministry of Internal Affairs, who not only gave cover to that gang but personally took part in the acts of violence... When I found leads to the FSB officers, to generals that had ties to those criminal groups... When we established that that group was not only involved in protection racket and kidnapping but also in illegal arms deals... We found out that those weapons among other destinations went also to the Middle East, naturally, you can well understand where it could have gone... 34:27:12

34:27:16 So we... Who would allow us to follow that thread to the end? The only thing I was told by an officer of the internal security Directorate that I've met was "Sasha, they sell tanks, they sell arms, the sell... I mean, heavy arms, to Africa. Those arms go to the Middle East." 34:55:08

34:56:20 I mean now... To corroborate these words... I saw in the office of my head of Directorate, Khokholkov, that group was linked to Khokholkov... we actually had Khokholkov, the former head of our Directorate, on file as one of the top people in that group... I once saw Boot in his office. There's now an international warrant out for this Boot for illegal arms deals. 35:26:00

35:26:04 That man had ties to Ukrainian criminal groups, that man, according to our records, had ties to the son of Derkach, the former head of SBU (Ukrainian Security Service) and one of the closest associates of Ukrainian President Kuchma. On top of that there were links, there were threads going to the illegal sale of drugs. I mean, the head of our Directorate, Khokholkov, and it was him who ended up in our sights, his connections... He had links, he associated with criminal groups that were running drugs from Afghanistan. 36:05:10

36:05:14 That's Rahi... That's a man called Gafur... he's one of the crime bosses in Uzbekistan, and his associates... in Moscow. That's Salim. That's Mr. Yastrzhembsky and Mr. Kokoshin... All these people are close friends of Khokholkov, and of all those I named. 36:32:00

36:32:04 We established that drugs in huge amounts, tonnes of drugs, including heroin, come from Afghanistan from the General Abdul Rashid Dustum. They go through Russia... it's a transit point, to the St. Petersburg port. From there they go to Spain where they're parcelled up... they go to Spain and from there on to Europe. 36:57:00

36:57:20 Apart from that... Here in the West I met Nikolai Melnichenko, that's the former bodyguard of Kuchma. For two years he managed to tape the conversations in the office of Kuchma, the President of Ukraine. And Nikolai Melnichenko's tapes confirmed that the group we were investigating in Russia for drug dealing, for importing drugs from Afghanistan, the same group imported drugs from Columbia. 37:35:10

37:35:14 I must say that our data cross-matched perfectly. I mean, the evidence we gathered said that in St. Petersburg the drugs went through the St. Petersburg port that was "covered" by the St. Petersburg FSB officers. That criminal group included Patrushev, Cherkesov, ... Ivanov, Smirnov, he's now the head of the St. Petersburg Directorate, and Mr. Putin who is currently President of the Russian Federation. 38:06:00

38:06:04 That's so to speak the highest echelon. On the lower level it was the Tambov organised crime group, who is currently ruled by Kumarin-Barsukov (checked) — he is a major criminal well known in Russian and in St. Petersburg. 38:21:00

38:21:04 Well, Mr. Melnichenko kindly gave me access to his materials, tape-records of his conversation... tape-records of Kuchma's conversations with the head of Ukrainian security service, Mr. Derkach. Derkach reported to Kuchma that... he managed to get evidence from Germany that Putin had connections to the international drug trade, to one of the biggest Columbian drug cartels. 38:52:08

38:52:12 That conversation... he and Kuchma were examining those materials. And... Derkach reported that that the evidence looked very serious. So... That conversation, that tape was authenticated in America. I have the experts' report, it's in English, I can show it to you if you like. I can even make a copy for you. As a gift. I can also copy the tapes themselves. And the expert concludes that the tapes are authentic and the tape had not been subjected to editing or any other... type of counterfeiting or forgery. 39:34:04

39:34:08 So these materials can be used in court as evidence as a part of proof that people currently holding key positions in the Russian Federation are connected to the international drug trade. That the Kremlin offices were taken over by criminals. 39:53:00

40:00:12 So now... Yes... that our generals committed crimes, that FSB was riddled with corruption, that our generals were linked to illegal drug trafficking — I reported all that personally to Putin when he was appointed the FSB Director. That was approximately... I had that meeting with Putin in the middle of 1998, about a week after he'd been appointed the Director of the FSB. He invited me to his office. I came. I reported to him all our findings... about all those crimes; I reported to him all the materials on those facts. 40:44:08

40:44:12 I also presented him with the analytical report on our generals based on the active cases. It was given to me by my comrades, I mean, I compiled it with the help of my comrades including those in the internal security Directorate. I don't want to disclose their names. Here's that report. I managed to get it out to the West. Here it is. Here. 41:07:10

41:07:14 It starts, "Information on the major criminal figure of the Central Asian region Rahimov Gafur Akhmedovich, aka "Gafur". His connections..." And this report... goes on. Here it speaks of... here it lists those, here, those who associate with those men. Here we have Shakro, he's a known Upright Man, "Little Taiwan" Tartahunov Alimjan Tursunovich, born on 1 January 1949, city of Tashkent. Here it says, "lives in Germany", he did live in Germany at the time. Now, you must know, right?, he's been arrested and already extradited, and sent under arrest to the States. 41:53:00

41:53:04 Well... and a number of others. There are people living in America... well.
And here it speaks about... so it goes... this report contains complete information of connections, phone numbers of that criminal group. More. This report mentions Yastrzhembsky. Here, it says, "When Yastrzhembsky was a Russian Ambassador abroad... Gafur stayed, lived at his apartment." Then we were informed that Yastrzhembsky took money from that criminal group and built himself a dacha in the Sokolinaya Gora area — that's not far from Moscow... 42:35:00

42:35:12 Another name mentioned in the report — Alisher. ... Those people have connections in the KGB USSR, with the former KGB officers; now those people work in the FSB and are very highly placed. Here it says that that group has connections with Shamil Tarpishchev, with

Korzhakov Aleksandr Vasilievich, former chief of the protection detail of the President of Russia. 43:08:10

43:08:14 That group is closely connected with Barsukov Mikhail Ivanovich, the former Director of the FSB. And with other... I mean, with many other people at the helm of the Federal Security Service. 43:24:21

43:25:00 This report is not that long but is quite rich in content... It's an extract from our cases, an extract — connections and... the gist of it. The kind of information that is reported to an official of the FSB Director level. 43:42:14

43:43:00 Well then... After that I was sacked and all the people about whom... about who I reported to Putin, including the FSB people, got a promotion. ... And when I had a meeting with my former head of Directorate he told me, "Sasha,"- he said... I said "What's wrong with Putin? I told him all that stuff, why is he doing this?" And he told me, "Sasha, they share the money." Then I understood that Putin... I mean... was directly connected to that criminal group that was involved in all that stuff. 44:19:14

44:19:18 Though he even before showed up in our files as a man who had corrupt connections in the criminal organisations of St. Petersburg. But here I was told directly that the man was connected to that gang, to that group involved in drug dealing. Well, in my book I wrote that within Putin's inner circle I had a trusted source who gave me the same information — that Putin was closely associated with that criminal group involved in drug dealing. When it became known in the FSB that that man has been my source, about two weeks after our last meeting he was killed. And that's despite the fact that at that time he was holding a position of the Economic Advisor to the President. 45:09:21

45:10:10 There was a man called David Dvali who held a post of President's Aide on matters economical, now this position is held by

Illarionov. So he, being Putin's Advisor, at Putin at the time has already been a President, David the last time gave me information on Putin himself. The FSB found us out and two weeks later David was shot. A man who was an Economic Advisor to the President. And silence. They made one announcement on TV and that was it — nobody even tried to investigate that matter... All quiet, as if nothing had happened. 45:50:12

45:50:16 He'd been killed in summer. In summer or in the beginning of autumn. No, he'd been killed in summer, in summer. In summer or in the end of spring 2002. Just a couple of months before I left Russia... he'd been shot. 46:08:00

46:09:00 Well, so I want to tell you that... corruption in the law-enforcement agencies and Russian secret service is not just a case of isolated facts when people are trying to earn some money illegally, it's a system that has its root in the office of the President of the Russian Federation. 46:34:00

46:34:04 And... I know some facts, I have facts at my disposal now when... criminal proceedings have been started against officers of the law-enforcement agencies or secret service — not those who committed or are at the moment committing those crimes, but, to the contrary, against those people who actually refuse to commit crimes when ordered so by their superiors, those people who refuse to trade in drugs, those people who refuse to commit... to participate in protection racket or take bribes. 47:08:04

47:08:08 They first try to run them out of the agencies, and they do run them out of the law-enforcement agencies... And if those people try to resist that criminal system they are sent to prison. At the moment I know that in St. Petersburg there's a major currently in prison because he refused to sell drugs. Well ... Russia is a criminal country. And it all comes from the top. 47:35:14

47:51:08 So here are the results of the expertise, for the tape, I mean.

47:56:08

48:07:12 That's the original. 48:10:00

48:14:20 Let me show you.48:17:00

48:17:04 Yes. You can do it straight away. Switch it on [unclear]. You're going to edit and reshuffle it anyway. So let's shoot it now. 48:24:12

48:25:22 Wait, wait, let's shoot this part before we forget. 48:28:16

49:29:18 All right, let's go. Here we go. 49:35:00

49:36:22 Well... Well... For the first time I heard that somebody in the FSB wanted to kill Berezovsky... I heard about it on 27 December (I'll give you the exact date) 27 December 1997. 50:01:00

50:01:06 Well, on that day we arrested — that was the night of 26 to 27, we arrested a criminal group of police officers that had been involved in kidnapping, armed robbery and burglary. And after we arrested the sergeants — those personally involved in committing those crimes — we got leads to some high-placed MVD officers that were working in the Internal Security Directorate and in the main Organised Crime Directorate. 50:32:00

50:33:00 And we already had those people identified and we were going to pick them up when I got the orders to abort the operation and return to my unit. It was the deputy head of our Directorate, Kamyshnikov (checked). I passed those orders to my subordinates and we aborted the operation — I was on duty and had to follow my orders — and we came back to the Lubyanka. 50:57:16

50:57:20 We came to Kamyshnikov's office — and Kamyshnikov lived on the same floor as the Director of the FSB, in the office next door — so it was the 4th floor, room 413. And the Director of the FSB was in the room

401 — here, if you follow the corridor on the fourth floor here would be the office of the Director and right across it in the room 413, that's where Kamyshnikov sat. Those offices were 10 meters away. 51:22:00

51:23:00 And Kamyshnikov began lecturing us that we were not doing our job, that our unit had been created not to catch criminals but to remove them by using non-standard methods. It was a long conversation. That meeting lasted for 2.5 hours. He was showing us various strategies created by the FBI. "Here, take a look. That's how the FBI works. You see what they do…" Though I've read those strategic plans… I saw that those were secret, top secret documents from within the FBI, I have no idea how he got them… but nowhere did I read that FBI had been killing anybody. "Well, — I said, — they just dig up information, basically we do the same thing." 52:02:21

52:03:00 "Well," he said — he probably showed us those documents to show off. Then he showed us a book by Sudoplatov, that's the former head of the terrorist NKVD Directorate under Stalin. And he said, "That's what you should be doing." So he directly said that what we should have been doing was the kind of work Sudoplatov did. He said, "There are not too many of us — about 80 people in the whole Directorate. That's the total count; those who do operative work are even more scarce. And what we must do is… in general what we must be doing is solving the problems our superiors are facing." 52:40:21

52:41:00 "For example, when Dudaev was liquidated…" he said, "in this way a problem was solved… a problem our leaders had… Our country's leaders had a problem — a living president of Chechnya — he got liquidated and the problem was solved." After that he outlined the main tasks that we had to deal with. The first task was… to get two our officers that the Chechens managed to capture in Ingushetia out of captivity in Chechnya. That was the head of the FSB Ingushetia Directorate Gribov (I think his surname was Gribov) and his deputy, his human resources man, an officer of the human resources section. 53:19:12

53:19:16 For this purpose... he said that our Directorate has an operation planned to kidnap Umar Gebrailov. And we had to kidnap Umar Gebrailov — he was a well-known businessman who later, by the way, even run as a candidate for the post of the President of Russia... We had to kidnap Umar Gebrailov and exchange him... get the money for him... later we found out that Umar was to be killed afterwards... and his corpse was to be left in Chechnya and blamed on some ungovernable Chechen band or Dagestani militia. I have an audiotape, a videotape where my section head says the same. If you wish I can give it to you, you can use it i your film. 53:57:21

53:58:00 Well, and already... Where Gebrailov was concerned work was already going on. They've already found a place where to hide him... and where he'd be killed later... in the Yegorievsk region there were several dachas rented by a unit in our Directorate — there was a private company "Stealth" that was closely working... it was a unit under our "roof", so to speak, in English they call it "undercover". Our Directorate used them to solve some of our problems. So as to, as they say in the secret service, not to show our ears. 54:32:00

54:32:04 That was the first task — I mean, to kidnap Gebrailov, to finish the job and kidnap him. The second task was to pinpoint the apartments where the Chechen terrorists might be hiding in Moscow. And the third task, he said that there were people whom we couldn't touch legally because they had amassed huge amounts of money. And those people prevent... those people hamper Russia's development, those people... interfere with our leadership, they are a torn in our leadership's side. And those people must be eliminated — because it's impossible to put them in prison, they're rich, they have connections everywhere... 55:09:04

55:09:08 Well, and then he came to me and said, "Do you know Berezovsky?" "Well, I do." "Then you have to kill him." I just, I remained silent and pointed at the cabinet's walls because many offices in the Lubyanka were taped. And that surveillance... 55:24:00

55:24:18 No. Why? I pointed at the walls "Well," I meant, "take a look..." I pointed at the ceiling, as they say in our line — there could be equipment there, mikes. He came closer to me, bent just like that, "You must kill Berezovsky. You, personally, must do it." After that it was no joke, it was said in presence of three other officers... After that he said that... 55:48:20

55:54:12 And he... And then he, I mean... It wasn't a joke, it was serious, because he warned us, he said, "If the contents of this conversation become known to anyone else you'll have problems, we won't be talking with you like this."

What if we're arrested, caught red-handed.? Especially when we're to steal Gebrailov — he was guarded by the police officers. So when the head of our section asked what were we going to do with those policemen the head of our Directorate said "Bump the stinks off." That's our criminal jargon. "Bump the stinks off," means, "kill those cops", those policemen. And our section head said, "How can we kill them? Aren't they... I mean, that guy is fine, he's a Chechen, but they're our brother Slavs..." And he said, "They shouldn't guard a Chechen." 57:16:08

We were given a task to kill police officers in the very heart of Moscow. So... 57:25:00

Besides, when one of my men, Major Pontin said, "All right, you're setting us tasks — to kidnap and kill Gebrailov, to kill Berezovsky as well... Before that we were charged with sorting out the situation with Mikhail Ivanovich Trepashkin." (checked) That's the head of the investigative department of the tax police who sued the FSB, our former colleague, we were ordered to kill him as well... 56:29:10

56:29:14 It all has happened in a very brief period of time. And those events were all in preparation... literally in a very short time — one group was working on the murder of Trepashkin, another group was preparing Gebrailov's kidnapping, and the third group was to start preparing for the liquidation of Berezovsky. 56:45:00

56:46:00 So he says, "We're doing all that stuff, killing this guy and that guy… What if we're arrested, caught red-handed…" Especially when we're to steal Gebrailov — he was guarded by the police officers. So when the head of our section asked what were we going to do with those policemen the head of our Directorate said "Bump the stinks off." That's our criminal jargon. "Bump the stinks off," means, "kill those cops", those policemen. And our section head said, "How can we kill them? Aren't they… I mean, that guy is fine, he's a Chechen, but they're our brother Slavs…" And he said, "They shouldn't guard a Chechen." 57:16:08

57:16:12 I mean, in fact we had to… we were given a task to kill police officers in the very heart of Moscow. So… 57:25:00

57:25:04 And so when my subordinate Major Pontin asked, "Well, we start killing those cops or some other people… And what then? If we're arrested, for example… what are we to do?" He answered, "Don't worry. Stay mum. Don't admit it was an order from your superiors. Go to prison, we'll get you out. A year, a year and a half in there and we'll get you out and you'll be all right." 57:48:16

57:48:20 So… Well… it wasn't a joke, it was serious… Actually we had a colleague, Bavdeev Boris, who said, "Then give us a written order." They told him "Who is ever going to give you a written order like that?" There were measures taken… For example, with Gebrailov, his phones were wired, he's been under surveillance for a couple of months, there was work done on his brother Hussein. Well… 58:18:08

58:18:12 Work was done on Trepashkin as well — external surveillance, his pager was wired, we listened to his pager, we established his contacts. I was given his file — they got it out of the archives and gave me his personal file for reference. I mean, it wasn't a joke. It wasn't just a joke. In fact those crimes were planned, measures were taken, units were working in concert… 58:42:16

58:42:20 For example, our unit even had a staff meeting dedicated to Gebrailov's kidnapping. There came the people from the task force who were supposed to organise the kidnapping itself, I mean, the capture of Gebrailov. Then they were supposed to pass him to us and we then had to get him out of Moscow and hide him in a basement. Our section head drove to look over that cellar where we were to hold him, he studied the route... 59:03:21

59:04:00 Well, the people from the task force asked for the money to be paid up front because before that they had stolen some citizen from Chechnya — your lamp is blinking... Well... Before that they had stolen a citizen, I think they had stolen him from Chechnya... and he spent three days handcuffed in a gymnasium, he was handcuffed to the radiator. That's the radiator, they handcuffed him to it and he had to spend three days in the gymnasium... 59:27:12

59:27:16 Then Kamyshnikov picked him up and took him somewhere. Then my subordinate Shcheglov took 150,000 or 160.000 US dollars in a packet to give to some Chechens, to a group of Chechens in Moscow on Kamyshnikov's orders. They called themselves vahhabites. I mean, Kamyshnikov summoned one of my subordinates, Major Shcheglov, gave him a packet — 150,000 or 160.000 dollars — "Go, take that to the Chechens." The ones he's been working with. So I understood it the way that our generals were associating with groups of Chechens involved in kidnapping. 59:58:12

59:58:16 I mean our men kidnapped them and brought them out, those Chechens established contact with the relatives and negotiated a sum. Then the money arrived, it was passed on somehow... and our officers, our generals passed part of that money to those Chechens, those criminals, you see?

**** FREE DVD OFFER *****

If you would like to receive a free copy of
the DVD documentary made of
Blowing up Russia
with the aid of Alexander Litvinenko,
please cut out this page and post it to

Alexander Litvinenko DVD Offer
Gibson Square
47 Lonsdale Square
London N1 1EW
UK

please add your address and postcode
where the DVD should be sent

....
....
....
....
....

This offer is only valid for UK addresses
For all other addresses please go to our
website www.gibsonsquare.com and click through
to the special DVD offer.